Opening up
Hosea

ALUN EBENEZER

Opening up
Hosea

If you are searching for help in appreciating the amazing message of Hosea then look no further. Alun Ebenezer has made a fine job of getting to grips with the contents of the prophecy and he applies it well to our present situations with apt illustrations. There are challenges for the church, the Christian and the unbeliever. I enthusiastically commend this book to you.

Philip H Eveson, former principal and Old Testament tutor at the London Seminary

This commentary captures well the shocking reality of our sinfulness as it is presented in the prophecy of Hosea. We sin against a God who has loved his people passionately and tenderly. Only with such a view of God and of our depravity can we be drawn to worship him truly. How glorious is the Saviour who is presented to us in this book!

Tom Baker, assistant pastor at Tabernacle Baptist Church, Llandrindod Wells and at the Pound Chapel, Llanbister

For many years the surname 'Ebenezer' has been well known to me because of a faithful pastor named Teifi and his wife Bery—now in glory. Although an Englishman, I share their great love of Wales, their concern for India, and their passion for the gospel. It is only in more recent years that I have got to know their son, Alun Ebenezer. To commend his book, *Opening up Hosea:*

The heart of God, is something I do most willingly and enthusiastically. It is instructive and illuminating, convicting and comforting, heart-warming and wholesome. It has been a great blessing to read it and I thank God for it. At times I have been deeply moved.

I have just one big regret—I have had to wait until I am in my 'eighties' to read it! I would love to have had it when I was a new young pastor attempting a series of sermons on Hosea. But better late than never!

Basil Howlett, retired pastor and current elder at Carey Baptist Church, Reading

This little gem really opens up the prophecy of Hosea. The author has so well researched the setting and the text that it will satisfy the mature reader, while keeping the contents accessible to the newest believer and certainly challenging the unbeliever! In reading this, the mind will be enlightened, the heart warmed and the will moved. Alun uses memorable illustrations throughout to press home the truths of Hosea; and having known him for many years, I know he writes of things personally experienced, as a sinner saved by his wonderful Saviour. No ivory tower stuff here; it comes from the heart of God to the author's heart and then to ours—read it!

Andy Christofides, assistant pastor of Heath Evangelical Church, Cardiff (retired pastor of St Mellons Baptist Church, Cardiff)

First published in Great Britain in 2022

British Library Cataloguing in Publication Data
A record for this book is available from the British Library

ISBN: 978-1-84625-731-5

Printed by 4edge Limited

DayOne, Ryelands Road, Leominster, HR6 8NZ
Email: sales@dayone.co.uk
Website: www.dayone.co.uk

To aunty Chris, my first Sunday School
teacher and someone who loves the
book of Hosea as much as me

Contents

	Overview	9
	Background and summary	12
❶	Go and marry a whore	43
❷	What's in a name	59
❸	Talk some sense to your mother	78
❹	God so loved	105
❺	Taken to court	126
❻	On the battlefield	158
❼	Come to God	175
❽	What are you like	204
❾	Israel has forgotten her Maker	227
❿	Do not rejoice, O Israel	255
⓫	Time to seek the Lord	278
⓬	The heart of God	306
⓭	A history and geography lesson	330
⓮	The wages of sin	352
⓯	Come home	373
	Endnotes	395

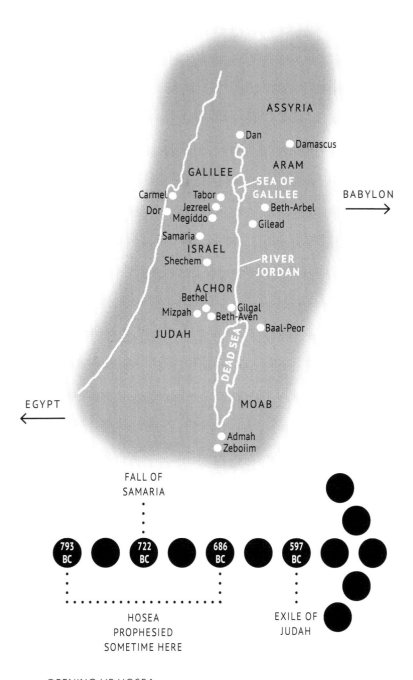

ASSYRIA

Dan
Damascus

GALILEE

ARAM

SEA OF
GALILEE

BABYLON →

Carmel
Tabor
Beth-Arbel
Dor
Jezreel
Megiddo
Gilead

Samaria

ISRAEL

Shechem

RIVER
JORDAN

ACHOR

Bethel

Mizpah
Gilgal
Beth-Aven

JUDAH

Baal-Peor

DEAD SEA

EGYPT ←

MOAB

Admah
Zeboiim

FALL OF
SAMARIA

793
BC

722
BC

686
BC

597
BC

HOSEA
PROPHESIED
SOMETIME HERE

EXILE OF
JUDAH

OPENING UP HOSEA

Overview: The Heart of God

There are many things we can say about the book of Hosea.

It is without doubt a startling book. No other book in the Bible has such shocking language. God tells one of his prophets to marry a whore and to name his children, in effect, 'massacre', 'not loved' and 'not mine'!

The book can be challenging to understand, containing words and phrases which are hard to comprehend, and a style and structure which is difficult to decipher.

Hosea wrote to the people of Israel at a time when there were serious problems in the nation: morally; socially; economically; politically; and spiritually. They were on their last legs and he was sent to warn them of the impending danger just before they were carted off into exile. It can, therefore, be a tough message to read and seem like oracle after oracle of warning after warning about judgement and wrath. It is not hard to see why Hosea has been called the death-bed prophet.

So much more will be said about these things as we go through the book, but what is important to remember is that Hosea is about one thing. Underneath all that was wrong in Israel, the reason they were about to be dragged off into exile—the reason why Hosea had to endure a heart-breaking marriage and a troubled family life—

actually comes down to one thing: Israel's relationship with God was broken.

This is why Hosea is so relevant to us today. With all the problems we face, personally, domestically, nationally and internationally, the cause comes down to one thing: our relationship with God is broken. It is not that we have not got a relationship with God, it is that we do and it is broken. Our hearts are the problem. They are rebellious—we think we know best and do not love God as we should. We love ourselves more.

However, as well as Hosea revealing the state of our hearts, he also reveals to us the heart of God. We may have no interest in God and have turned our backs on Him, but He has not turned His back on us. The fact that we have the book of Hosea to read today is because His heart beats for us. He does not want to give us up! (Hosea 11:8).

> The fact that we have the book of Hosea to read today is because His heart beats for us.

Before we go any further, we also need to say something about Hosea's original audience and who his audience is today. The book was primarily written to Israel but had an important message for Judah too, as well as having huge significance for the other nations. We will find out what Israel and Judah and the other nations were like as we go through the book. But, for now, we need to keep in our minds that today, Israel is like the liberal churches who have 'joined to idols' (Hosea 4:17), turned their back on the God of the Bible, taken the bits out of His Word that cut across our way of life and have sold out in order to keep in favour with the world and a unity with other religions. Judah is like the evangelical churches who need to watch that they do not follow a similar path to a liberal Christianity, which is not a Christianity at all. The nations are the world who, whether they like it or not, must acknowledge that the God of the Bible is in fact the only true and living God—the One we will all have to stand before one day and give an account.

One last thing before we delve into the text. To Hosea, sin was not an abstract doctrine or concept; it was a reality. His home life and broken marriage meant that sin and its effects were very real to him. He was not in some ivory-towered theological seminary pontificating from afar. He speaks to us as sinner to sinner. In the same vein, the author of this book on Hosea is also a sinner and knows only too well its power and guilt. But he also knows and trusts in the God whose heart is revealed to us in this amazing book. The same God who invites us all, in whatever state we are in, to come to him (Hosea 6:1).

Background and summary

Hosea 1:1

The Introduction is by far the longest chapter in this book, but in order for us to have a firm grasp of the prophecy of Hosea, it is important we ask some questions at the outset.

Who?

Who was Hosea?

A MAN

Hosea was a real man. His name means *salvation*. He had a father called Beeri and lived in a particular time in history, during the reigns of 'Uzziah, Jotham, Ahaz, and Hezekiah, kings of Judah, and in the days of Jeroboam the son of Joash, king of Israel' (Hosea 1:1). After the reign of Solomon, the nation of Israel divided into two: Judah in the south and Israel in the north. Hosea was in all likelihood from, and lived in, the North. He certainly prophesied in the North and the reference to 'our king' (Hosea 7:5) reflects the prophet's own origins and loyalties.

Some think he might have been a native of the capital, Samaria, as he would only mention his origins if he did not come from the capital. This is conjecture but would fit with him being a well-educated citizen of Samaria. His book shows he had knowledge of the Torah, Joshua and Judges, which suggest he was thoroughly trained in the Scripture of his day, skilful in his use of language and had a grasp of the political affairs of the nation. All of this would point to him being from the capital.

We know about his wife and children (Hosea 1–3) and that he became a prophet before he got married. In fact, his marriage might have been the first act of his prophetic career (1:2). Given that his prophecy lasted so long (1:1), it implies he became a prophet at quite a young age, in keeping with the custom of his day, possibly when he was about twenty.

He was no doubt a strong character with all that he went through and the way he spoke out.

A PROPHET

But Hosea was more than just a man. He was a prophet; one of the twelve Minor Prophets. They are referred to as such because of the size of the books they left; they were not as long as the Major Prophets (Isaiah, Jeremiah and Ezekiel).

In some ways these prophets were people just like us. According to James 5:17, Elijah was a man 'with a nature like ours', and this is true of Hosea as well, but, in another way, they were very different to us. While all Christians are called to bear witness to the Word of God, the prophets actually spoke the Word of God (Amos 1:1, 3; Jeremiah 1:9). They received a specific and personal call from God (Exodus 3:1–4:17; Isaiah 6; Jeremiah 1:4–19; Ezekiel 1–3; Hosea 1:2; Amos 7:14–15) and stood before the people as men who had stood before God (1 Kings 17:1; 18:15).

'The word of the LORD … came…' (Hosea 1:1a) literally means the Word became actively present to them; that is the Word of God came directly to Hosea and the other prophets and became a personal, living reality to them.

> As we read Hosea, we need to be aware that it is God who is really speaking.

The Old Testament pictures God's decisions being made in a council meeting (1 Kings 22:19, 20) and the prophet being admitted into this 'council' (Jeremiah 23:22; Amos 3:7). The prophets knew the mind of God. Ezekiel 2:2 says, 'As he spoke, the Spirit entered into me and set me on my feet, and I heard him speaking to me'. Therefore, as we read Hosea, we need to be aware that it is God who is really speaking.

But even though the prophecy of Hosea is the inspired Word of God, the Holy Spirit did not suppress the personality of Hosea but raised it to a higher level of activity. It is therefore important to draw attention to Hosea's unique structure and style.

Structure

There is a clear distinction between chapters 1–3 and chapters 4–14 of Hosea. Chapters 1–3 tell the story of Hosea's family: an adulterous wife and a faithful husband. Chapters 4–14 deal with the national situation that reflects Hosea's domestic troubles: an adulterous Israel and a faithful God.

Some commentators break down chapters 4–14 further and think in chapters 4–11 the emphasis is on judgement while chapters 12–14 speak of hope. Others see significance in the number three and therefore divide chapters 4–14 into three sections, mirroring the three children spoken of in chapters 1–3: no knowledge (4:1–6:3), no love (6:4–11:11), no faithfulness (11:12–14:9). The problem with this is these three words appear too often elsewhere in the book.

In reality, other than the distinction between chapters 1–3 and 4–14, there is no discernible structure.

Style

What is clear from the way Hosea writes is that he wants to shake people up and get them to listen. To that end he uses lots of metaphors and similes. He refers to Israel as an unfaithful wife (1:2–9; 3:1–5; 9:1); disappearing morning mist (6:4); hot ovens (7:4–7); a silly dove (7:11); a wild donkey (8:9); a faulty bow (7:16); a sick person (5:13; 6:1; 7:1; 14:4); a flock of birds (7:12; 9:11;

11:11); a trained and stubborn heifer (4:16; 10:11); an olive tree (14:6); a mother in labour as well as an unborn son (13:13); a shrivelled plant (9:16); and chaff blown by the wind (13:3).

The language Hosea uses to describe God is intended to jolt and awaken his jaded audience. God is pictured as a jealous husband (2:2–13); a frustrated shepherd (4:16); a destructive moth or undesired rot (5:12); a ferocious lion (5:14; 11:10; 13:7–8); a trapper (7:12); a forgiving husband (3:1–5); a healing physician (6:1–2); reviving rains (6:3); a loving parent (11:3–4); a protecting lion (11:10–11); a life giving dew (14:5); and a fertile pine tree (14:8).

Hosea constantly wants to keep us on our toes and interested. He soars into flights of poetry (2:2–23) only to revert once more to forceful and logical argument. He uses puns (8:9; 9:16), pithy declarations and illustrations from the agricultural background that his first readers and hearers were familiar with and could relate to.

He can be obscure and makes use of riddles (12:11). In 1:1, Hosea sends a cryptic message by not mentioning the Northern kings apart from Jeroboam. Unlike all the other prophets, Hosea mentions the destruction of the cities of the plain, not by mentioning Sodom and Gomorrah, but Admah and Zeboiim. These cities are not even mentioned in Genesis 19, although linked to Sodom in Genesis 14:2. He says things that seem contradictory. In Hosea 13:14–16, God promises to redeem Israel and then abruptly declares that he will have no compassion on the nation and that their children will be slain and their pregnant mothers ripped open.

All of this is to unsettle his listeners and readers, stretch them and really get them thinking. Hosea wants them to be wise so they can analyse the times and discern the message (14:9).

Behind it all is real emotion and pathos. Throughout the book you can feel his mind turning in endless grief, exhaustless sorrow, and wild cries of anguish, while at the same time the book beats with love and hope, which reaches its climax in Hosea 11:8 when God movingly says, 'How can I give you up, O Ephraim?'

All of this should make us think about how we present our message and how we preach the Lord Jesus Christ to a lost world. We must be committed to preaching as the only means God has promised to bless but we must never preach in a dull, boring way. We have to think about who it is we are preaching to. As Dr Lloyd Jones said, 'We must preach to people where they are, not where we want them to be.'[1] Be relevant and contemporary. Use illustrations and examples people are familiar with and can relate to and apply the message to our generation. We have to get their attention and make them think. But, maybe most importantly, we must preach with feeling and emotion. If the message does not move us, how can it possibly move a world that has no thought for God? Someone said after hearing George Whitfield preach, 'I don't believe in God but if I did, I would believe in Mr Whitfield's God.'[2]

When?

Hosea prophesied at a particular time in history. Verse 1 says, '… *in the days of* …' and that particular time was during the reigns of '*Uzziah, Jotham, Ahaz, and Hezekiah, kings of Judah, and in the days of Jeroboam the son of Joash, king of Israel*' (1:1).

Uzziah reigned from 792 to 740 BC; Jotham reigned from 750 to 740 BC; Ahaz from 740 to 716 BC; and Hezekiah from 716/15 to 686 BC (but he probably reigned alongside his father from about 729 BC). Jeroboam reigned from 793 to 753 BC. We can deduce therefore that Hosea prophesied sometime after 793 BC to sometime before 686 BC.

However, there is no explicit statement about the start and finish dates of Hosea's ministry. We can only rely on clues to work out when he may have started and ended.

His initial message recorded in Chapter 1:2–5 implies that the dynasty of Jehu was still ruling in Israel and this agrees with the mention of Jeroboam II in 1:1. The first three chapters should therefore clearly be dated in

Jeroboam's reign. The Jehu dynasty fell in 745 BC with the murder of Zechariah by the usurper Shallum and this was predicted as a future event in 1:4.

As to the end, perhaps the mention of Shalman in Hosea 10:14 is Shalmaneser V (727–722 BC), in whose reign Samaria fell. Also, the description in 12:1 fits well with the diplomatic intrigues of the troubled reign of Hoshea (732–723 BC). The fact Hosea prophesied during Hezekiah's reign is significant because that means he lived to see the fall of Samaria (722 BC). However, he does not mention the fall of Samaria in 722 BC specifically. This may well be what brought his ministry to an end.

It could be assumed from the mention of Hezekiah in 1:1 that Hosea must have been alive after Hezekiah's ascension in 715 BC. While we have no direct evidence, it is not unreasonable therefore to assume he ended his days in Hezekiah's Jerusalem and that his book was preserved there. As we have already noted, it could have been that the prophet escaped to Judah and it was there that he wrote up his memoirs. If all that is the case, assuming Hosea started his ministry late in Jeroboam's reign—a few years before his death, no later than about 755 BC— and ended fairly early in Hezekiah's reign, Hosea's career went from about 760 to 710 BC, roughly 50 years.

However, evidence exists for a co-regency between Hezekiah and his father beginning in 729 BC and on that basis, some think that Hosea's ministry ended in the early part of Hezekiah's reign (when he was junior partner with his father) and before the fall of Samaria. If that is the case, Hosea could have begun his ministry some point before Jeroboam's death in 753 BC and ended sometime during Hezekiah's co-regency with his father from 729 BC; so, his ministry was nearer 25–30 years.

We cannot be exact about when Hosea prophesied but know it was around this time. What is important is that, while all these names may mean nothing to us today and these dates are thousands of years ago, they are no less real. If this world was to carry on for thousands more years, in the same way as we look back on the countries and kings named here, so will people of the future look back on the names of presidents and kings of our day. Hosea concerns real times and real people.

Where?

A DIVIDED KINGDOM

Judah ... Israel (1:1)

God called one man, Abraham, out of all the nations and people of the earth. He promised Abraham that he would make him a great nation, give his descendants a land and that, through him, all the world would be blessed; that is from Abraham's line, the Saviour of all the world would be born (Genesis 12:1–3).

Abraham had a son called Isaac, Isaac had a son called Jacob and then Jacob had twelve sons who became the twelve tribes of Israel. They spent four hundred years in slavery in Egypt before God heard their cry, had compassion on them and delivered them through a man called Moses. Moses led the people through the Red Sea and then they wandered in the wilderness of Sinai for forty years before finally entering the land of Canaan—the land promised to Abraham—under the leadership of Joshua.

After conquering the land, God put judges to rule over them, but the people asked God for a king to be like other nations. This was a rejection of God as their king, but God gave them what they asked for. First came Saul; then David; then Solomon. David was Israel's best king; he was a man after God's own heart. Under the rule of David and Solomon, Israel really prospered. Solomon was succeeded by his son, Rehoboam, but under his reign the nation of Israel split into two. Rehoboam remained king of the southern part of Israel, known as Judah, which comprised of two tribes. The other ten tribes formed the Northern Kingdom, known as Israel. Their first king was called Jeroboam I.

Jeroboam had idols of golden calves placed in sanctuaries at Bethel and Dan and a priesthood appointed in their service, in order that people might be diverted from the Temple at Jerusalem and from its services and festivals. Initially the calves were intended merely as a representation of Jehovah, but they subsequently became associated with the worship of

Baal. After King Ahab's marriage with Jezebel, Baalism was introduced into Israel and Ahab built a temple for Baal at Samaria—although he still counted himself a follower of Jehovah. Jehu later rooted out Baalism from Israel, but still retained the golden calves; eventually people reverted to the worship of Baal.

THE NORTHERN KINGDOM

Hosea prophesied mainly in the North (Israel) about two centuries after the division of the two kingdoms. We know this because the places he refers to were all in the North—Jezreel, Gilgal, Bethel, Mizpah, Tabor, Shittim, Gibeah, Ramah, Gilead, Shechem, Samaria, Baal-Peor, Beth-Arbel. The only exception is Achor (2:15) which lay on the border between Judah and Benjamin (Joshua 15:7) and so was technically within the area of the Southern Kingdom. Hosea refers to Ephraim, the largest tribe in the North, thirty-seven times; Israel forty-four times; and Judah only fifteen times.

> Hosea prophesied mainly in the North (Israel) about two centuries after the division of the two kingdoms.

Even so, while he devoted himself to his mission and duty to the North, Hosea is aware of affairs in the South. At times he criticized the South as much as the North (5:5, 12), but he hoped for better things for the South and prayed they would not follow the lead of their northern neighbours (4:15). Hosea saw the South (Judah) as the rightful heirs of David's throne and looked for salvation and re-unification (3:5).

LONG LIVE THE KING

Hosea began his prophecy in the North during the reign of Jeroboam II. Hosea 1:1 says, '... in the days of Jeroboam the son of Joash, king of Israel'.

Jeroboam II was a capable ruler and had a long reign. He came to power when Syria and Assyria, Israel's two enemies to the north, were weakened by internal conflicts and threats from without. The absence of external aggression and the consequent relief from paying tribute to foreign powers left Israel free to enjoy the surplus generated by its agricultural fertility (2:5; 12:8; Amos 3:15; 5:11). They also received tribute paid to it by neighbouring peoples and profited from the international trade routes that crossed its territory. Under his rule, Israel's economy boomed and they were prosperous.

Israel also enlarged its borders under Jeroboam. After the death of Ben-Hadad II of Syria, Jeroboam extended the domain of Israel as far north as the city of Damascus itself (2 Kings 14:25–26). His territory stretched from Central Aram (Syria) to the Dead Sea. Amos 6:13 alludes to two victories won under his reign.

He also enjoyed good relations with Judah, who were

likewise experiencing a time of prosperity and security under Uzziah.

However, a two-tier class system developed: the lower class suffered increasingly under oppression and poverty while the upper class enjoyed power and excess.

Moreover, while he was successful in so many ways, Jeroboam 'did what was evil in the sight of the LORD. He did not depart from all the sins of Jeroboam the son of Nebat, which he made Israel to sin' (2 Kings 14:24). He was an example of the ungodly who prosper in the world and increase in riches (Psalm 73:12).

The best of times and the worst of times

Hosea prophesied during the best of times and the worst of times. In many ways, under the kingships of Uzziah and Jeroboam II, Israel and Judah enjoyed a golden age, but, at the time of Hosea's prophecy, their long reigns were coming to an end.

POLITICALLY

Israel's old enemy, the Arameans (Syrians), were in a weakened position, while the rising power of Assyria was still at this point preoccupied with its eastern and northern borders. So, Israel did not feel any significant external pressure during this period. This gave a false sense of security from military prestige (5:5) and national defences (8:14).

There was also a growing abuse of power and privilege.

There was widespread corruption among the leaders of the nation (Hosea 4:1–2; 5:1–2; 6:6, 9; 7:1, 6–7).

ECONOMICALLY

Hosea's prophecy began during a period of expansion and prosperity but this economic progress made them self-confident and proud.

SOCIALLY

The social structure in Israel at the time of Hosea encouraged power, greed, self-indulgence, corruption of justice, luxurious living among the upper classes, and the decay of social unity. There was a big gap between rich and poor.

RELIGIOUS

As far as the religious state of the land, it was all about Baal (2:8, 17; 11:2). Israel was an agricultural society and the productivity of the land, flocks and herds was of the utmost importance. As Baalism was a fertility cult, the Israelites were drawn to worship Baal. Baal was thought to be the son of Dagon and was considered the most important deity in the Canaanite pantheon. He was the god of rain and storm and the source of all the blessings of nature. The fertility of the land, flocks, herds and even the family was allegedly a benefit conferred by him. He gave lightning, fire and rain and grain, oil and wine. He could revive the dead, heal the sick and grant the blessing of offspring. What could be more relevant to the life of any Canaanite farmer anxious over his wheat crop and cattle shed? When Baal was in top form the world was pregnant with life. That is why the first fruits were a tribute to be paid to him.

In Canaanite theology, the fertility of the land depended upon the sexual relationship between Baal and his consort. The revival of nature was due to sexual intercourse between Baal and his partner, Ashtoreth or Ashtart. But his adherents didn't sit back and let Baal do it. Canaanites practised sacred prostitution as part of their worship. So, there were cult prostitutes. The man would fulfil Baal's role and the woman, Ashtart's. The idea was that this would encourage the divine couple to do their thing and thus the rain, grain, wine and oil would flow again.

It is easy to see why all of this made Baalism quite an attractive religion to the Israelite. Baalism appealed to sensuality. Sexual rites were built into the liturgy. What did it matter if one's marriage was rotten, one's wife uninteresting, one's life generally dull? This religion was the answer to all of that.

Altogether, the worship of Baal demanded incense (Jeremiah 7:9), animal and human sacrifice (Jeremiah 19:5), bowing and kissing, sacred cakes, grossly licentious practices and sacred prostitution (Hosea 4:1–3). Their worship also incorporated idolatrous images (8:5; 13:2; 14:8), sacred pillars (10:1–2) and the consulting of spirits (4:12). The people practised idolatrous worship on hilltops (4:13) and there were alternative centres of worship at Bethel and Gilgal (9:15; 10:15).

Morally

Morality was at an all-time low. Every commandment of God was broken habitually. Deceit to God produced faithlessness to man. There was lying, adultery, murder, excess, armed robbery, oppression, false

> Morality was at an all-time low. Every commandment of God was broken habitually.

dealing, perversion of justice, crushing of the poor and drunkenness (Hosea 7:7). They were greedy and self-indulgent and turned their backs on God.

The priests were no better. They loved and shared in the sins of the people. Corruption had spread throughout the land.

The king is dead

After Jeroboam II's death, the situation in the North began to unravel. His reign was the Indian summer of Israel. Dark days were ahead. After stability under Jeroboam II, Israel entered a time of political chaos. Almost every king of Israel after him died by assassination at the hands of his successor or military coups. In the next thirty years Israel had six kings.

To add to Israel's internal weakness was the rise of

a resurgent and increasingly aggressive Assyria under Tiglath-Pileser III (745–727 BC) and his successors, Shalmaneser V (727–722 BC) and Sargon (722–705 BC). To the Assyrians, Syria and Israel (Palestine) were desirable because of their indigenous resources (timber of Lebanon) and also the trade routes which traversed the area. On top of that was the prize that lay beyond: Egypt. Eventually, in 722 BC, Assyria overwhelmed and destroyed the Northern Kingdom of Israel. The run up to this defeat provides the historical background to Hosea's prophecy. There were three stages to the Assyrians taking control. Firstly, Israel was allowed to retain its traditional ruler and nominal independence but had to contribute substantial sums to the coffers of the Assyrian Empire. Secondly, Assyria imposed a regime change with a new indigenous ruler and a diminished realm. Thirdly, Assyria had total domination in which the territory of Israel was reduced to a province of the Assyrian Empire under an Assyrian governor.

While all this was going on, some of the kings of Israel favoured an alliance with Egypt, others with Assyria. But none of them favoured or turned to Yahweh!

Pretenders to the throne

It is significant that Hosea mentions only Jeroboam and neglects to mention the other six kings of Israel who reigned in a period of about thirty years, during his lifetime. It would seem that this was because he regarded Jeroboam II as the last legitimate king of Israel. The others were assassins and had no right to the title, "king". This is clear in his assessment of the monarchy in Hosea 7:7. It is as if he cannot bring himself to mention the others and passes over them in silence.

But, while Hosea does not mention them, to give a flavour of the state of things, we will.

ZECHERIAH

Jeroboam was succeeded by his son, Zecheriah, who was murdered within six months and replaced by Shallum. His end marked the end of the Jehu dynasty that had lasted about ninety years (2 Kings 9–10). Zecheriah 'did what was evil in the sight of the LORD' (2 Kings 15:9).

SHALLUM

He reigned for a month before being assassinated by the brutal Menahem (2 Kings 15:14).

MENAHEM

Menahem clung to power for ten years but was then killed and succeeded by Pekahiah. He continued in the religion which typified the North (2 Kings 15:18). In 740s BC, Assyria started to rise against Israel. In 738 BC, Tiglath-Pileser took Hamath. Rezin of Syria and Menahem of Israel tried to stave off further aggression by paying tribute (2 Kings 15:19–20). This marked the first stage in the Assyrians extending control over an area. Menahem did that which was evil in the sight of the Lord (2 Kings 15:18).

Pekahiah

Menahem was succeeded by his son Pekahiah in 742 BC. He ruled for two years before being killed by his military commander, Pekah, who took the throne in a military coup. Pekahiah did that which was evil (2 Kings 15:24).

Pekah

Again, Pekah, like the others, 'did what was evil in the sight of the Lord' (2 Kings 15:28), but there was perhaps a bit more about him than the other *pretenders* (2 Chronicles 28:6). Even before he was king, it would appear Pekah had maintained a regime in Gilead, east of the river Jordan, which had rivalled that of Menahem in Samaria. This harmonises Scripture and explains the figure of twenty years given for his reign in 2 Kings 15:27. Over the land as a whole he reigned for only eight years. It may well be that, as well as the strength of Assyrian aggression, it was the constant threat of Pekah that induced Menahem in the 740s to submit to Assyria and to pay the emperor 'a thousand talents of silver, that his hand might be with him to strengthen the kingdom in his hand' (2 Kings 15:19 NKJV). It would seem that on Menahem's death, Pekah entered into some arrangement with Pekahiah, becoming his second in command. But the alliance did not last and soon Pekah assassinated Pekahiah and seized the throne of

Samaria making himself king of Israel (2 Kings 15:23–25). He pursued anti-Assyrian policies. Pekah formed an alliance with Rezin of Syria to try to escape the authority of Assyria. For this they wanted the help of Judah, but Ahaz, king of Judah, refused. So, Israel and Syria joined together to fight against Judah and force Ahaz to join their anti-Assyrian coalition. This war is called the Syro-Ephramite War (2 Kings 16:1–9; 2 Chronicles 28:5–7; Isaiah 7:1–8:22; Micah 7:7–20). Ahaz responded to this threat by calling on the help of Tiglath-Pileser III. The Assyrian king defeated the Syrians and destroyed their capital, Damascus, in 732 BC and, in 733 BC, Israel was brought totally under Assyrian vassalage with the annexation of Gilead, Galilee and Naphtali (2 Kings 15:29). This represented the third stage of domination in which a territory was reduced to a province of the Assyrian Empire under an Assyrian governor. All Galilee and the plain of Jezreel became the province of Megiddo; the coastal plain south of Carmel became the province of Dor; and Transjordan became the province of Gilead. Many of the population, particularly the upper classes, were deported. The kingdom of Israel was reduced to an area of about one third of its former size, becoming just an enclave centred on Samaria and including the surrounding hill country of Ephraim.

Hoshea

At same time in Samaria, Pekah was assassinated by

Hoshea, who Tiglath-Pileser was pleased to appoint king because he was pro-Assyrian. Hoshea and Israel were regarded as their vassal again on payment of substantial tribute (2 Kings 15:30). The Northern Kingdom stuttered on for a decade with its status at the second stage in Assyrian domination of the area: regime change with a new indigenous ruler and a diminished realm. For a while Hoshea paid tribute to Shalmaneser V (727–722 BC), Tiglath-Pileser's son and successor (2 Kings 17:3). But Hoshea's loyalty was fragile. Hoshea engaged in political intrigue to secure Egyptian help (compare with Hosea 12:1) and withheld his annual tribute from Assyria. Shalmaneser V, after Hoshea was imprisoned, besieged Samaria for three years before taking it (2 Kings 17:5; 18:9–10). The remainder of the land was then also subjected to the third and final stage of Assyrian conquest. It no longer had a native ruler. Its inhabitants were deported to Mesopotamia (2 Kings 17:6) and peoples of other nationalities were settled in the territory (2 Kings 17:24), which had now become the Assyrian province of Samaria. In 722 BC, within thirty years of the death of Jeroboam II, the kingdom of Israel ceased to exist and it was the end of the ten Northern tribes.

A prophet without honour?

It is never easy or popular to speak against the outlook of your day. When Hosea started, his message ran contrary to the mood of the time. His words were met with ridicule, resentment or just ignored. But Hosea's concern was to relay God's evaluation of those trends and events; what God thought was all that mattered.

While Hosea was in the minority, he was not completely isolated. Amos prophesied in the North around the same time. It is also worth remembering that a century before, Elijah had felt completely isolated until the Lord showed him there were still 7000 who had not bowed to the pressure of Baal worship (1 Kings 19:18). These would have been Northerners. Moreover, there must have been some who were sympathetic to Hosea's message. His hearers must have included faithful Israelites who preserved the bare wordings of his oracles. But it is reasonable to assume that, on the whole, Hosea was unpopular in the North and had no credence in the South until Southerners, after the fall, recognized his words to have been predictively true.

Bringing it home

Hosea prophesied in a place thousands of miles from where most of us, reading this book, live—during the reign of kings with funny sounding names, aeons and aeons ago. The whole thing could not seem more distant or more far removed from us.

Yet, on the other hand, the situation in Hosea's day could not be more similar to ours. In the West we are economically prosperous. So many of us want for nothing. We live in comfortable houses, have the latest gadgets, wear the latest fashion, eat good food and enjoy nice holidays. But there are others in our society who have nothing and live in deprivation. Even many, who seem to have so much, spend what they cannot really afford.

In Britain, we are living during times where we are not sure of our country's role in the world. Who knows what the future of Britain and the European Union is and what will become of America? The times we live in are uncertain. Leaders, who one day seem so powerful, are stripped of their power the next. They are also dangerous times. Almost every few weeks there seems to be a terror attack of some kind.

As for the religious and moral state of our times, people can believe whatever they want as long as it does not harm anyone else. Everything is centred on us and our rights and what makes us feel happy. Certain agendas are pushed and there is no thought for God. What the Bible says is irrelevant and is actually becoming offensive to people. To believe the Bible today is completely out of step with the modern world view, thinking and behaviour.

If Hosea was to come to Britain or America today,

he would find so many things different to ancient Israel. He would not have a clue what a car is, let alone an aeroplane. He would be amazed by the televisions, computers and technology. He would know nothing about the premier league, or social media. But, after a few weeks with us, reading our newspapers, watching our televisions, listening to our conversations, coming to work with us, spending time in our homes, he would look at ancient Israel and us and conclude, 'You lot are just like that lot.'

Hosea was written a long time ago but his message is as relevant to twenty-first century Western civilisation as it was to ancient Israel.

What?

So, what is the message of Hosea?

A SHOCKING MESSAGE

Hosea is not an easy book. Hosea was sent to minister to a spiritually hardened people who had turned their back on God. It begins with a prophet receiving a command to marry an adulterous woman, who is nothing short of a prostitute, and promptly describes the births of his three children—each of whom is given a bizarre but significant name. The prophecy consists of one narrative of Hosea's own marriage (1–3) that reflects God's own relationship with Israel (4–14).

HOSEA AND THE REST OF THE BIBLE

Hosea's message was in line with the rest of God's Word. He makes constant allusions to the Torah, the first five books of the Bible. In fact, Genesis and Exodus dominate Hosea: Hosea 1:10 (compare with Genesis 22:17); Hosea 2:18 (compare with Genesis 1:20–25); Hosea 4:3 (compare with Genesis 1:20–25); Hosea 6:7 (compare with Genesis 3:6); Hosea 6:9 (compare with Genesis 34:1–31); Hosea 9:6 (compare with Genesis 47:29); Hosea 9:14 (compare with Genesis 49:25); Hosea 11:8 (compare with Genesis 14:2 and chapter 19); Hosea 12:2–5 (compare with Genesis 25:19–35:15 {story of Jacob}); Hosea 12:12–13 (compare with Genesis 29:1–31:16); Hosea 13:15 (compare with Genesis 41:2, 18); and the sin of Adam (Hosea 6:7).

There are allusions to Exodus in Hosea 7:13; 8:4–6; 9:10; 10:9, 10; 11:1–4; 12:9–10; 13:4–6 and Hosea 4:2 refers to the Ten Commandments.

Hosea's main metaphor of Israel, as an adulterous wife, is founded upon the Pentateuchal depiction of apostasy as whoredom (Exodus 34:11–16; Leviticus 17:7; 20:4–6; Deuteronomy 31:16; Judges 2:16, 17).

As well as the first books of the Bible, Hosea shows awareness of other books of the Bible. Hosea 9:9 looks back to the bizarre history of Judges 19–21. Hosea 9:15; 13:10–11 refers to the early monarchy and Hosea 1:4–5 recalls events in 2 Kings 9:14–37.

COVENANT RELATIONSHIP

God made the world, perfect and beautiful. God placed humanity in His world to be His people; to know and enjoy Him; to love Him and be loved by Him; to be His people and for Him to be their God. But we rejected God and were unfaithful to Him. As a result, the world was cursed and humanity came under God's judgement. We made a mess of our relationship with God and our relationships with one another. But God planned to create a renewed world with renewed people. With this renewed people—the people He set his love upon—He made a covenant.

Hosea's message is rooted in the covenant. We need to understand the Sinai covenant to understand Hosea. He only mentions it three times (2:18; 6:7; 8:1) but, while it is not always picked up by our English translations, Hosea uses 'Yahweh' or 'LORD'—the covenant name of God—throughout the book. A relational God is clearly important to Hosea.

The covenant demanded exclusive loyalty. The terms of the covenant were not optional. Israel had entered into a covenant with God and Hosea's task was simply to warn them that Yahweh intended to enforce the terms of His covenant. There were blessings and curses attached to the covenant.

The covenant was like a promise made in a marriage. Breaking the covenant therefore was like infidelity.

Hosea says that this is what Israel was guilty of when they broke the first two commandments (Hosea 3:1 compare with Exod. 20:3 and Hosea 8:5–6 compare with Exod. 20:4). Hosea's use of the terms *whoredom* and *adultery* emphasize the abhorrent nature of Israel's betrayal and the pain they caused the Lord. There are numerous references throughout the book to infidelity (1:2; 2:5, 8, 13; 4:1, 10, 12; 5:4, 7; 7:10, 13, 15–16; 9:7, 17; 10:3; 11:2, 7, 12; 13:6, 9).

Israel was unfaithful to Yahweh in the way they went after Baal worship; something they had been well warned against before entering the land (Lev. 18:24–30; Deut. 7:1–5).

We cannot underestimate the heartbreak and pain this caused Almighty God. Israel breaking the commandments was not so much of them *breaking the rules* but *breaking God's heart.* This is why Hosea was told to marry an adulterous woman who would break his heart over and over again. So that he would preach with pathos and drive home to his listeners the love of God like no other, he had to, in some small way, enter into the deep personal sorrow, feelings and heartbreak of the God of Israel. But this was no weak love of a *doormat* of a husband. Through his own experience, Hosea could impress upon the people the gravity of their misconduct and to plead with them to return in repentance, otherwise God would act against them in judgement.

But God will not give up on them. The, *I will care for them,* in Hosea 14:8, is a pledge of a love that will work through lengthy and painful discipline to achieve the spiritual change which is required to restore harmonious relationships and usher in an age of eternal satisfaction (1:10–11; 2:23; 14:3–8). Yahweh did not treat them like they treated Him. He refused to abandon those who had abandoned Him (Hosea 11:8). He was going to keep the covenant.

EXILE

The exile is also a huge theme in the book of Hosea. He warns the people of Israel that the Assyrians would come and carry them off into exile. As a political entity, the Northern Kingdom was wiped from the map. Hosea reveals that he is aware of a similar destiny awaiting Judah (12:2; 6:4; 5:5, 14; 6:10–11), even though Judah, for a while, experienced divine relief (1:7). But it was not really Assyria behind the exile; it was God. Because of their sin and unfaithfulness to Him, there would be a period of isolation and deprivation during which Israel would

> It was not really Assyria behind the exile; it was God.

be convinced to abandon her infatuation with pagan worship and return in fidelity to the Lord (3:4–5).

RETURN

Hosea uses the words 'Turn', 'Return' or 'Repent' twenty-two times throughout his prophecy.

Although judgement is justly inflicted on the errant people, God will not allow their disobedience to nullify His promises. He will summon them and they will return to Him (11:10–11). To some degree this was fulfilled when the exiles returned to Judah after their Babylonian exile (1 Chronicles 9:3). These were not just from the South (Judah) but from the North (Israel) as well. When the time for restoration came, remnants from the South and North would both be involved in it (1:11).

There are different facets to the fulfilment of this *returning to Him*. The return to the land was fulfilled in ethnic Israel (1:10–11; 11:10–11). Romans 11:17–21 would also seem to suggest an influx of Jews coming to trust in the Lord Jesus Christ as Messiah before the end. But the real fulfilment is found in the real seed of Abraham. The true Israel are people from every tribe and nation, Jews and Gentiles, who have true faith in the Lord Jesus.

God told Abraham that He would make him a great nation (Genesis 12:2) but this nation would eventually consist of many nations (Genesis 17:4; Ephesians 2:12; John 10:16). He would have more children than the sand on the seashore (Genesis 22:17). These children, Abraham's true seed, would be those who put their faith in the same promise as Abraham believed. Abraham is the father of all of them that believe (Romans 4:11; compare with Genesis 17:2–7; Galatians 3:8, 16). According to Galatians 3:29 (NKJV), 'If you are Christ's, then you are Abrahams's seed, and heirs according to the promise.'

God will keep His promise to save all those who return to Him, and those who do are the true Israel.

It is shockingly in line with the rest of the Bible, covenant, exile and return. These are the main messages of Hosea and through them we get a glimpse of the heart of God.

Kings of Israel	Kings of Judah
Jehu 841–814 BC	Uzziah 792–740 BC
Jehoahaz 814–798 BC	Jotham 750–740 BC
Jehoash 798–782 BC	Ahaz 740–716 BC
Jeroboam ii 793–753 BC	Hezekiah 716/5–686 BC
Hoshea 732–724 BC	

Kings of the Assyrian Empire
Tiglath Pileser III 745–727 BC,
Shalmaneser V 727–722 BC,
Sargon 722–705 BC

For further study ▶

FOR FURTHER STUDY.

1. In what ways was Hosea dedicated to God through his challenging ministry?

2. Why had the worship of God been neglected?

TO THINK ABOUT AND DISCUSS

1. How does the state of the United Kingdom compare to the time of Hosea's prophecy with the worship of false gods?

2. How do we respond and answer someone who says they don't need God?

1 Go and marry a whore

Hosea 1:2, 3a

The words found in Hosea 1:2 must be some of the most startling, striking and shocking words in the entire Bible. 'Go, take to yourself a wife of whoredom and have children of whoredom, for the land commits great whoredom by forsaking the Lord.' Holy God commands one of His prophets to marry a whore! He was to marry a woman who he knew was immoral and would continue to be immoral even after he married her.

There is some debate over whether she was a promiscuous woman or a prostitute. While the book in other places seems to give the impression that she was a prostitute, it must be stressed that Hosea is more interested in conveying her behaviour and character rather than her profession. This was a woman who voluntarily had sex with other men. Repeatedly! She was notorious for her behaviour. According to Calvin[1], this woman was, 'a common harlot who prostituted herself, not once, nor twice, nor to a few men, but to all'.

To be commanded to marry such a woman must have been a shattering demand. The woman God tells His prophet to marry is quite simply a filthy whore. The language is jarring, graphic, unrefined—intentionally so. According to Mackay[2]:

> It is an ugly, abrasive accusing term which should not be narrowed or toned down. It is God's 'sit up and take notice' kind of a way of getting his message across.

It really did happen

Some think that God commanding His prophet to marry a whore is so shocking that it cannot be true. Understandably, they find it hard to reconcile that a God of infinite holiness and purity who cannot look at wrong (Habakkuk 1:13); who commands us to avoid sexual immorality and all impurity (Ephesians 5:3); who repeatedly condemns adultery (2 Samuel 11:1–5; Proverbs 2:16–19) and severely punishes it (Lev. 20:10; Deut. 22:23–24); who will judge the sexually immoral and adulterous (Hebrews 13:4), tells one of His prophets to marry a whore. How can the same God who forbade His priests to marry a prostitute (Lev 21:7, 14), demean His prophet by requiring that he does? They conclude, therefore, that it must be parabolic, allegorical or a vision.

But there is no hint of that in the text, which is nothing other than a straightforward account of what actually happened. John Calvin[3] says there is no reason why it cannot be a vision, but surely, we cannot conclude then that it is a vision because it does not deny this. We would not use this method to interpret other parts of the Bible.

However startling the picture is—however difficult it is for us to grasp and get our heads around—it is true; this actually happened. Gomer was a real woman who had a real father called Diblaim (1:3). The content does not indicate in the slightest that Gomer and her children are anything other than historical figures.

Whatever else we will learn from this account, it shows we cannot put God in a box. Isaiah says, 'For as the heavens are higher than the earth, so are my ways higher than your ways and my thoughts than your thoughts' (Isaiah 55:9). None of us can think we have got our theology and our understanding of God all sewn up. 'His greatness is unsearchable' (Psalm 145:3). Who can know his mind? (Romans 11:33). He is huge! We can only begin to grasp the edges of His ways (Job 26:14) and must bow in humility and awe. How can we begin to understand Christ becoming sin for us (2 Corinthians 5:21), the doctrine of the Trinity, God's sovereignty and man's responsibility? As Augustine said of all our doctrines and dogmas, they are just 'fences around the mystery'.[4] And, at the beginning of Hosea, we are confronted again with a God who is 'past finding out' (Romans 11:33 NKJV).

It also teaches us that God may ask us to do difficult things. But if He does, He will give us the strength to carry them out and they will be for our good; they will do us more good than if we did not go through them (2 Corinthians 4:8–9, 16–18).

Furthermore, it teaches that the very thing we think might disqualify us from usefulness to God, may be the very thing that makes us most useful. One would think that having married an immoral woman and then having the marriage collapse because of his wife's gross infidelity would be enough to disqualify anyone from claiming the role of God's spokesman. But the opposite is true. The tragedies of Hosea's personal life are the foundation of his ministry and the very credentials for serving as God's spokesman.

> The tragedies of Hosea's personal life are the foundation of his ministry and the very credentials for serving as God's spokesman.

God and Israel

The reason God wants Hosea to marry a whore is given in Hosea 1:2: '... for the land commits great whoredom by forsaking the LORD'. Through Hosea's marriage to Gomer, God wants to colourfully and dramatically illustrate his relationship with Israel. Hosea has entered into exactly the same kind of marriage that God is in with Israel. He wants Hosea to experience the same kind of heartbreak He feels and impress this upon the Israelites.

THE SPECIAL RELATIONSHIP

God's relationship with Israel was like a husband and wife. God chose Israel out of all the other nations. He delivered them from slavery in Egypt (Exodus 14) and established the covenant with them. In the desert He looked after them, met all their needs, guided and protected them (Psalm 78:13–16). He brought them into Canaan, a land so fertile it was 'flowing with milk and honey' (Exodus 3:8). Today we would say, 'rich with oil'.

THE UNFAITHFUL WIFE

But they had forgotten Him! They were engrossed in their prosperity and progress and they acted like He didn't exist. The way Israel was treating God was the same way the unfaithful Gomer was treating Hosea. Hosea could not trust Gomer. She would have flirted with every man in the room. She would have dressed and acted seductively. He could not turn his back on her for a minute. Can you imagine how angry and hurt Hosea would have felt? It would not be normal if he was not jealous. This is the way Israel's behaviour made Yahweh feel.

But it is not just Gomer and it is not just Israel. God

has been kind to us. We have all benefitted from His common grace, which is the undeserving favour God shows everyone. We have food to eat, clothes to wear, jobs, houses, friends, family. And yet the only time many of us think about or turn to God is when things go wrong. We rarely thank Him. The better things are in our lives, the less we think of Him. The good things God gives us end up occupying us and diverting our attention away from God. We close Him out.

I remember when I had just become a deputy headteacher and attended a conference for deputy headteachers and headteachers in a classy hotel in Usk, South Wales. I was young and did not know anyone and everyone else seemed to know each other. They stood in circles chatting and laughing, drinking their drinks, and however hard I tried I could not really get in. They closed the circle on me, not intentionally, but they did not know me and I was ignored. This is how we treat God. Other things are more important and we do not even notice Him. We close the circle on Him.

There are so many things that take up our attention and that we prefer to God. We love our sin more than God and even things which are in and of themselves good become gods to us and take the place of God. We love the rest of our lives more than God.

According to Thomas Guthrie,

If you find yourself loving any pleasure better than your

prayers, any book better than your Bible, any house better than the house of God, any table better than the Lord's table, any person better than Christ and any indulgence better than the hope of Heaven, take alarm.[5]

THE AMAZING HUSBAND

A man does not normally take back a woman who has behaved the way Gomer did. But God is not like us.

You may view God as a hard, callous, cold Sovereign. A God who has planned everything and we are just pawns—an angry, 'out to get you' ogre. Or you may view Him as a big, old, soft grandfather who will forgive and love you no matter what.

Hosea tells us what God is really like. He is not an unfeeling God. He is a passionate God. He feels. He is angry. He is hurt. He is jealous (Deuteronomy 32:21). He is heartbroken. He is committed. And all of this because He loves us. Israel, like Gomer, was an awful wife, but God is an amazing husband!

For better or worse, God was bound to Israel, who were a wilful and wayward people (Deuteronomy 9:6). Despite them being worthless and unlovely, He loves His people and will not give up on them. He is determined to forgive and to make the relationship right.

But forgiveness is never easy. According to C.S. Lewis, 'Everyone likes the idea of forgiveness until they've got something to forgive.' [6] The offended have been hurt badly and that hurt has to be dealt with.

In leaving the glory of Heaven, being born in a manger, becoming a man and dying on a cross, God showed the lengths He was willing to go to put things right. To forgive us cost God everything. His love is amazing. He 'so loved the world' (John 3:16).

> In leaving the glory of Heaven, being born in a manger, becoming a man and dying on a cross, God showed the lengths He was willing to go to put things right.

When my son was small, I used to ask him, 'How much do you love me?' At the time we lived in Cardiff and my parents lived in Ebbw Vale, about thirty miles away, and he would say to me: 'Dad, I love you all the way to Ebbw Vale!' But then he started watching *The Koala Brothers*, a children's TV show set in the Australian Outback, and he would say to me: 'Dad, I love you all the way to Australia!' He then progressed to watching *Lunar Jim* and would say, 'Dad, I love you all the way to the moon!'

If you were to ask God, 'How much do you love me?', He would take you to an animal's feeding trough in which a baby is lying. But this is no ordinary baby. He is fully human but at the same time fully God. In the words of the carol, this is 'our God contracted to a span, incomprehensibly made man' (Charles Wesley, 1757–1834). He left heaven, where He had been adored by the angels, where He had been worshipped from eternity. He subsequently grew up in Nazareth, a rough, northern town in Israel. God says, 'That's how much I love you.'

But that is not all. He then takes you to a garden called Gethsemane, and you see a man in turmoil. He is facing death on a cross and is swallowed up in sorrow, overwhelmed to the point of collapsing and dying (Matthew 26:38). He feels trapped and hemmed in on every side with the horrible feeling of not being able to get out. His soul is in such agony that He does not know what to do with Himself. He does not know how He is going to get through what He is about to go through. He is agitated. As He prays, He falls on his face (Matthew 26:39). The Son of God is literally throwing himself to the ground (Mark 14:35). He is dreading what He is about to face so much so that His sweat turns to blood. Luke, who was a doctor, actually notes that there were great drops of blood falling to the ground (Luke 22:44). Not only is He sweating and bleeding, the Creator of the universe is also crying out with strong tears (Hebrews 5:7). He is arrested by a mob of 300 men with torches and lanterns and put on trial. And God says, 'That's how much I love you.'

But there is more still, because God says, 'I love you all the way to Golgotha.' It means, 'the place of a skull'

(Matthew 27:33), and there you see a cross on a hill outside Jerusalem. The figure on the cross is so marred that He does not even look like a human being. There is a crown of thorns on His head, He is naked and has been beaten and spat at and nails have been driven into His hands and His feet. It grows dark and He cries out in the darkness, 'My God, my God, why have you forsaken me?' (Matthew 27:46). And God says to us, 'Because that is how much I love you.' Bethlehem, Gethsemane, Golgotha.

An Indian philosopher, in explaining the difference between Islam and Christianity, said that Allah was too majestic to lie in a dirty manger and had too much dignity to hang on a shameful cross.[7] But the Bible says, 'Look in that manger, go to that garden, survey that cross and behold your God!' And here, through Hosea's marriage to Gomer, God says to Israel, 'Behold your husband!'

All of this should really make us think about how we treat God. It would make a huge difference to how we live our lives. We think so little of our sin. But sin is against the person of God. It hurts Him. No husband would be happy if their wife said to them that they loved them but loved other men more; she still wanted to live in the same house, spend some time with them, particularly at Christmas and Easter, even cook, clean and iron for them but most of the time she would rather be with other men. However, this is just how we treat God and He will not stand for it. According to Davis:

> Now that is the problem of having the God of the Bible as our God. To have a God who loves his people is to have a jealous God. And to have a jealous God is to have an intolerant God.[8]

We must repent and as the hymn writer says:

The dearest idol I have known

What ere that idol be,

Help me to tear it from thy throne

And worship only thee.

(William Cowper, 1731–1800)

Mother Israel

Hosea does not just talk about a husband and wife. Hosea 1:2 says, '… a wife of whoredom and … children of whoredom.' There are children involved too which we will consider in more detail in the next chapter. But, if we are to understand the prophecy of Hosea properly, it is important to establish exactly who the 'wife of whoredom' is and who the 'children of whoredom' are.

The 'wife of whoredom' is mother Israel, the establishment, the institution of Israel—everything Israel stands for. 'The land' in verse 2 refers not so much to individuals but to the culture, institutions and ethics that filled the land: the shrines, sacrifices, official teachings, priests, kings, ruling class—what gives the people their identity.

This establishment had turned their back on God. It was like He did not exist. It was all about them, and they went after anything and everything that they thought would bring them happiness and success. This is why they went after the gods of Canaan. Israel was an agricultural society and these Canaan deities were largely patrons of fertility. To get the best results out of farming they needed to enlist their help. Yahweh, they thought, was out of His depth.

The 'wife of whoredom' had abandoned her husband. She had embraced new lovers who had enticed her — ones that she thought were able to protect her and make her life better.

The children

The institution of Israel is the adulterous wife and mother. The children are therefore individual Israelites. Hosea's three children bore the disgrace of their mother's behaviour. They were more than just Hosea's children; they were signs for the Israelite people. They bore the stigma of immorality.

In the same way, the children of Israel bore the disgrace of mother Israel. The children were the common people—farmers who want good crops. These children had followed their mother, gone along with her. However, the people were themselves promiscuous and were in that sense just like their mother. The culture and social values of the nation of Israel had worked itself out in the lives of individual Israelites. They were the *promiscuous children* of a *promiscuous woman*.

They needed to see the damage their mother was doing to them and return to their father. But mother Israel could not see it and neither could her children. They could not repent or even see the need to. It is only when God strips mother Israel, this 'wife of whoredom', of all she had that they would see what was what and return to husband and father.

> It is only when God strips mother Israel of all she had that they would see what was what and return to husband and father.

Us

So how does this relate to us today?

As a general rule, we can apply the prophets preaching to Judah, to the true church of the Lord Jesus Christ today; the prophets preaching to Israel, to the apostate, though professing church; and we can apply their preaching to the nations, to the unbelieving world around us.

This means that Israel is the liberal church today. They are not bound to the Bible as the Word of God but do whatever they need to, by taking things out or adding things into the Bible, to fit in with the society we are in and how people want to live. Israel chased after other nations and went after other gods in their pursuit of happiness, prosperity and success. In the same way, the liberal church thinks that they need to follow society and those in positions of power, including the media, to succeed. They seem afraid to stand upon the Word of God and speak out against the sins of society.

But I imagine there are many people reading this book who attend Bible believing churches. So, what of us? Are we okay with nothing to worry about? We too need to watch and take heed. Liberal, apostate churches do not turn into liberal, apostate churches overnight. It happens over time. We need to ensure that our churches are faithful to God. We must judge everything that is taught and takes place in our churches against the Word of God, the Bible. We are to be discerning and careful that heresy (false teaching) does not come into our churches. We must also ensure that we do not try to change what the Bible says to justify the way we want to live.

Moreover, there are many sound, correct churches around today but they have no real love for Jesus Christ. It is as if they have dried up and gone cold. The love they once had has been lost. Above all else, as the book of Hosea will show, God wants us to love Him and do all the other things we do because we love Him.

But how can we know we love Him? Well, do we delight

in reading the Bible? Do we spend time in prayer? Do we love other Christians? Do we have a burden that so many of our friends, family, classmates, college friends and work colleagues are on their way to a lost eternity? Do we keep His commandments because we want to please Him? These are all signs that we love Him.

If you did love Him like this but you no longer do, remember what it used to be like. To build on the analogy of husband and wife in Hosea, imagine a husband and wife who used to be so much in love but now their marriage has gone stale. They do not spend much time together because they are so busy and everything else has taken over. They are tired and do not make much effort with one another. To rekindle their love, they go back to where they first met; they make and spend time together and fall in love again. If we have lost our love for Christ, then we have to do something similar. We are to 'survey the wondrous cross on which the Prince of glory died' (Isaac Watts, 1674–1748). Meditate—that is, think deeply—on His love, His grace and His mercy.

And in our attempt to reach out to a fallen, messed-up world, we are winsome and kind and loving, but we must never compromise or become like them to win them. We are to be distinct. Not like an adulterous, unfaithful whore, but faithful to our God.

For further study ▶

FOR FURTHER STUDY.

1. Are we too comfortable in our present situation?
2. How real is our commitment to God?

TO THINK ABOUT AND DISCUSS.

1. Do we really listen to what God asks us to do, or are we afraid of what it might entail?
2. Do we find it easy or difficult to forgive those who have hurt us?

2 What's in a name?

Hosea 1:3b 2:1

We associate names with people; they carry connotations. Hosea had three children with three incredible names. The names were significant and carried meaning.

Names are important. When our son was born, deciding on a name was really difficult. My wife and I are both teachers and over the years have taught thousands of children. When we were going through names, it was almost impossible because names reminded us of children that we had taught! There were certain names that were absolute no-goes because of a bad experience with a child of that name.

As well as incredible names, there were also other question marks over these children. 'She conceived and bore him a son' (v. 3) suggests the first child was Hosea's. The other two children are introduced in a more ambiguous way. Verse 6 says, 'She conceived again and bore a daughter' and verse 8 says, '... she conceived and *bore a son'*. Hosea is not mentioned, raising the question that maybe they were not his children.

So, in Hosea 1:3b–2:1, we are confronted with three children, born to an immoral woman, possibly with question marks over who their father is, and Hosea is told to give them names that have meaning and significance; names to try to shake Israel out of their infidelity.

Three names

JEZREEL (1:4, 5)

Hosea is told to call the first child, who was a boy, *Jezreel*. Jezreel had become a byword for bloodshed. It would be like calling a boy today, *Twin Towers* or *Auschwitz*.

Jezreel was the place where Jehu had massacred the family of Ahab. After the nation of Israel divided, Jeroboam I became the first king of the Northern Kingdom of Israel. He established idolatrous worship in Israel. The five kings that came to power after Jeroboam—Nadab, Baasha, Elah, Zimri, Tibni—did nothing to stop the idolatry and came to power through bloodshed and a succession of coups.

Then, following five years of civil war, Omri became king in 880 BC and established a dynasty. His dynasty was cruel and wicked.

Omri's son, Ahab, followed him and one of Ahab's palaces was in Jezreel. It was there he was desperate to get his hands on a local vineyard that belonged to a man called Naboth. Naboth did not want to sell Ahab his vineyard, so Ahab's wife had Naboth falsely accused and murdered and took his vineyard anyway. This act became the epitome of the abuse of power in Israel's history (1 Kings 21). Ahab's wife was Jezebel, whose name is synonymous with idolatry and spiritual adultery. Together, they effectively made Baal worship the state religion in the Northern Kingdom. This move towards Baal worship was opposed by the prophets Elijah and Elisha. Ahab was succeeded by his children Ahaziah and Joram.

But God raised up an army officer called Jehu to bring down the house of Omri. Jehu took power through bloodshed and slaughtered the leading figures in Ahab's family at their palace in Jezreel. He then had the severed heads of all seventy of Omri's grandchildren brought to Jezreel.

So Jezreel became synonymous with bloodshed and massacre (2 Kings 9–10). And Hosea is told to call his first son by that name!

There is some debate over the phrase, 'I will avenge the bloodshed of Jezreel upon the house of Jehu' (v. 4, NKJV). Some maintain that bloodshed will come upon the house of Jehu because, even though Jehu did what God commanded, he did it with such excessive cruelty. The difficulty with this view is the Bible does not say that. In fact, in 2 Kings 10:30, the way Jehu carried out the task so thoroughly is commended by God.

The problem was that, although initially Jehu opposed Baal worship (2 Kings 10:18–28), he turned out to be just as bad (2 Kings 10:29–31). The bloodshed of Ahab was therefore in vain. It did not lead to Israel being purged of idolatry. Jehu removed Baal worship but replaced it with other forms of idolatry. And, in time, Baal worship was back on an even bigger scale. Outwardly, Jehu did as he was ordered but, inwardly, he did it for his own glory. His self-confessed passion for the Lord was not genuine nor was it sustained. Jehu was succeeded by son, grandson and great grandson—Jehoahaz, Jehoash and Jeroboam II—so that all four generations of Jehu's family ruled over Israel, but this family were little better than Omri and Ahab.

> Outwardly, Jehu did as he was ordered but, inwardly, he did it for his own glory.

This is why God brought 'the bloodshed of Jezreel upon the house of Jehu' (1:4). Under Jehu, sin was still rampant in the nation, so God vowed to bring retribution four generations later. We now know that the dynasty ended when Shallum assassinated Zechariah, the last king of Jehu's dynasty. The Greek translation of 2 Kings 15:10 is correct when it says Shallum killed Zechariah at Ibleam, a town located in a southern part of the valley of Jezreel. The dynasty ended as it had begun with the assassination of the ruling house in the valley of Jezreel.

The judgement was not just going to fall on Jehu, but in a little while judgement was going to fall on Israel as a whole. God says, 'I will put an end to the kingdom of the house of Israel' (v.4). God will 'break the bow of Israel in the Valley of Jezreel' (v.5). A bow was a symbol of military strength (Genesis 49:24; 1 Samuel 2:4; 2 Samuel 1:18; 2 Kings 13:15–16; Psalm 7:12; Ezekiel 39:3). However, it is not the bow of Israel's enemies that God will break, but the bow of Israel itself. It is as though God is going to send Israel out to fight with no bullets in their guns. They are heading for disaster, which Israel brought on themselves. Deuteronomy 8:19 says, 'If you forget the LORD your God and go after other gods and serve them and worship them, I solemnly warn you today that you shall surely perish.'

For us today this teaches us two important lessons:

It teaches us that God is sovereign. The kingdoms of this world are all in God's hand and under His control. Nations rise and fall at His command. What He orders comes to pass. The Psalmist says that when the nations roar and the people plot and plan; when the kings of the earth take their stand and the rulers take counsel together against the Lord, 'He who sits in the heaven laughs' (Psalm 2:4). When clever people today say there is no God and mock Him or marginalise Him and treat

Him as an irrelevance, God laughs at them in disbelief. It may not seem like it today, but if we could fast forward the film reels of history, we would see at the end of time God is God, and the Lord Jesus Christ is victorious and all His enemies are under His feet.

Just like Jezreel, there is a day of judgement coming. Hosea 1:11 says, 'They shall go up from the land, for great shall be the day of Jezreel.' This describes the day when history will come to an end and God will judge everyone who has ever lived. On that day God will divide the world into two: those who have trusted him and those who have not—and those who have not will be sent to hell.

While we may, even as Bible-believing Christians, try to sanitise hell and cover it up as some kind of embarrassing family secret, hell is as real and terrifying today as it has always been. As you sit reading this book wherever you may be, there are people who once walked this earth and lived and breathed like you, but now find themselves in torment in hell.

Jezreel was a warning to Israel and is a warning to us; there is a far worse judgement to come.

Lo-Ruhamah (1:6, 7)

The second child was a daughter and, as we have already noted, we cannot be sure Hosea was the father. Hosea was told to call her, *Lo-Ruhamah*, which means 'not loved' or 'no mercy'. Can you imagine Hosea taking her to the park and her running off from him and he has to call out to her, 'Not loved, come here!'

God's dealings with Israel had always been tempered with mercy. Even though they were a stubborn, disobedient people (Exodus 32:9; Acts 7:51), He had loved them, shown them compassion and been patient and longsuffering with them. But the way they lived and treated God showed they did not want Him or love Him, so He was now going to give them what they wanted. He was about to reject and abandon them to all the troubles of the world; He would no longer have mercy on the house of Israel.

In the same way that people probably murmured about whether Lo-Ruhamah was really Hosea's child, people would ask, are these really God's people? *Abandoned. No mercy. Unloved.*

Maybe you have convinced yourself that God will always be merciful to you. Perhaps you say to yourself, 'Don't worry, He will always forgive me.' But you cannot presume upon the mercy of God. One day, the day of grace will be over.

It is a sobering thought. One day it will be too late. You will call to Him and He will not hear you. That day might be tomorrow. Only today is the day of salvation (2 Corinthians 6:2).

There was an article in *The Times*[1] about the

thirty-three Chilean miners who spent sixty-nine days afraid beneath the Chilean desert, certain they were going to die. With them was a Christian minister who read the Bible to them and prayed with them every day. The men prayed and believe God heard their prayers, as all thirty-three of the men were rescued. The title of the article was, 'When a man screams to God then he will answer their prayer'. However, a time will come when the day of salvation and grace will be over—when a man can scream and shout and beg and plead and do whatever he wants, but God will not hear his prayer. Mercy is over, judgement has come. 'Depart from me' (Matthew 7:23). But today those lips still say, 'Come to me' (Matthew 11:28). He will still receive whoever comes to Him. Today there is still mercy with Him. Pray, call out to him; 'scream' to him, while you can.

Lo-Ammi (1:8, 9)

Verse 8 says when Gomer had weaned Lo-Ruhamah, she conceived and bore a son. Weaning could take up to three years; there was certainly a year in between each child. It could be that Gomer was faithful for this time. There was definitely plenty of time for Gomer to change her ways in between each child. Similarly, God keeps giving time for Israel to repent and turn back to God. God is merciful and gracious, slow to anger

(Exodus 34:6). He repeatedly gives us warnings and time to repent. (2 Peter 3:9).

The third child was called *Lo-Ammi* which means, 'Not my people'. Again, can you imagine Hosea picking him up from school and calling out to him, 'Not my boy'!

God is dramatically saying to Israel, 'you are not my people and I am not your God'. This would have stunned Israel. God had always said, 'You shall be my people and I will be your God' (Ezekiel 36:28; compare with Exodus 6.7; Leviticus 26:12; Jeremiah 24:7; 30:22; 31:33; 32:38; Revelation 21:3, 4). This was like the song or theme tune of the Old Testament. But not anymore. Couples very often have a special song. When you were younger and you really liked someone, you would make a compilation tape of your favourite songs and give it to them. It was a tape of songs that meant something to you both. 'You are my people and I am your God' was the special song between God and Israel; the theme running through the Old Testament *compilation tape*. But now it is as though God breaks the tape or CD and throws it out!

> 'You are my people and I am your God' was the special song between God and Israel.

God is going to leave them to their own devices with a superpower bearing down on them. A few years later, the Assyrian army would come crashing in on them and wipe them out. All that would remain were a few people, mixed with other nations, half remembered, following a syncretistic version of their religion—which by the New Testament era were the bitter enemies of the Jews, the loathed and hated Samaritans.

Today it would seem that we live in a day and age where the liberal church has rebelled against God and ignored Him to the point at which He has handed them over and said, 'Not my people'. He has left them to it. It was damning that, in Princess Diana's funeral in 1997, the most watched programme ever on TV, the Archbishop of Canterbury mentioned the name of the Lord Jesus only once in the whole service. And that was in the benediction at the end!

God says to such churches, 'You are not my people.'

Two contradictions

Ruhamah (2:1)

All of this is very bleak and hopeless. But these verses also show us that God's ways and thoughts are higher than ours (Isaiah 55:8–9).

Hosea 1:6 says, 'For I will no more have mercy on the house of Israel, and I shall completely forgive them'. This appears to make no sense. On the one hand it says He will show no mercy and on the other hand it says He will completely forgive.

Some of the English translations try to get around this seeming contradiction. The ESV translates it as 'I will no more have mercy on the house of Israel, to forgive them at all,' whereas according to the NIV, 'For I will no longer show love to Israel, that I should forgive them at all.'

However, even though it is jolting, it is important to retain the original. The answer lies in where *Lo-Ruhammah* ('no mercy') and *Ruhammah* ('you have received mercy', 2:1) met. God is angry and has to punish sin. But at the same time God is love and pardons sin. At the cross His anger and His love met. The Lord Jesus Christ suffered the full wrath of God so that all those who trust in Him do not have to. Christ experienced God's judgement without mercy so that we can experience God's mercy without judgement.

What all this means is this: because of Israel's continual rebellion and sin, God will show them no mercy and send them into exile. His mercy will run out; 'no mercy'. But God will keep his hand on those who trust him. He says in Hosea 1:7, 'But I will have mercy on the house of Judah'. When the Assyrians had devastated Israel, they turned their attention to Judah but their plans were wrecked, not in a military battle but when 'the LORD sent an angel, who annihilated all the fighting men and the leaders and officers in the camp of the Assyrian king' (2 Chronicles 32:21, NIV). God kept Judah safe. Even when Judah was sent into exile in Babylon in 586 BC, after seventy years in captivity Cyrus allowed captured expatriates to return to their nation. God will always keep a remnant. In Israel at this time there would have been some who trusted in God. Hosea for one.

This is true today. God's wrath may be upon certain nations and peoples because they have turned their back on Him and He may well hand them over to their sin and to judgement. But He will always have His church, however small, fragile, persecuted or marginalised it may seem. Until He comes again, He will continue to build His church and the gates of hell will not prevail against it (Matthew 16:18).

> God will always have His church, however small, fragile, persecuted or marginalised it may seem.

On the final day, God will pour out His wrath on the whole world. Because of their sin and rebellion God will have mercy upon the world no more. He will send sinners to hell. Yet for those who trust Him—the true Israel, the remnant—they will be safe and go to be with Him in heaven. On that awesome day, when many will be shown 'no mercy', Christ will say to those who are trusting Him, 'you have received mercy'. For some a day of no mercy; for others a day of mercy.

Ammi (2:1)

After declaring in Hosea 1:8,9 that the Israelites were no longer His people and God was no longer their God, according to Hosea 1:10–2:1, God's people will be as numerous as the sand of the sea. It is echoing the promise God made to Abraham (Genesis 13:16; 15:5; 22:17).

Again, this seems laughable. In 2 Kings 15:19–20, at the time of Hosea, God's people are puny, especially compared to the Assyrian might. But even though Hosea's generation might be wiped out, as we have seen, a remnant will remain and from this remnant God will restore his people.

By the time of the birth of the Lord Jesus this remnant was very small. But, after the Lord Jesus died and rose again, He commissioned His apostles to go out into the world and preach the gospel, first in Jerusalem, then Judea, then Samaria and then to the uttermost parts of the earth (Acts 1:8), because true Israel are not just Jews but Gentiles too, made up of people from every tribe and tongue and nation (Revelation 7:9).

So here we are today in Britain, America, China, Australia, Europe, and the gospel has reached and spread to us. Across the world today and passing through the corridors of time have been millions and millions and millions of 'children of the living God' (1:10).

NEW COVENANT

This all looks forward to a renewal of the covenant; what theologians call the New Covenant. The refrain 'you are my people and I am your God' that has echoed down Israel's history will be re-released.

The New Covenant and the Old Covenant are the same covenant, just dispensed in different ways. The New Covenant is superior. The Old Covenant was ministered through servants—Abraham, Moses, priests—whereas the New Covenant is ministered through God's Son. In the Old Covenant the gospel was partly revealed, whereas in the New Covenant it is clearly revealed. The Old Covenant was mainly centred on one nation; in the New Covenant it is spread across the whole world. The Old Covenant was largely material—land, temple, kings, priesthood; the New Covenant is entirely spiritual. In the Old Covenant the Spirit did work in the lives of people but now He has been poured out (Acts 2:17). The Old Covenant was like a child whereas the New Covenant is like an adult: mature, capable of understanding better and able to enjoy the relationship more.

Hosea and the other prophets, as with Abraham, saw the New Covenant 'from afar' (Hebrews 11:13); they spoke better than they knew. Jeremiah, in particular, looked forward to the time of the New Covenant when people would love God with their hearts (Jeremiah 31:31–34).

The Lord Jesus, who ministered the New Covenant, came and said it is all about the heart. It is not what is on the outside—not about the rules. It is about whether you love God in the first place and then about loving others as much as you love yourself (Luke 10:27). It is keeping the commandments out of love for God that matters. True Christianity is not a religion but a relationship—a relationship with the living God. People like you and me can actually know God. We can have a real sense of fellowship with God; a deep consciousness of His love for us (John 17:26). We can know the Lord Jesus as a person, just as well as we get to know people well (spouse, family, friends, colleagues, neighbours). Jesus actually said, 'Behold I stand at the door and knock. If anyone hears my voice and opens the door, I will come in to him and eat with him, and he with me' (Revelation 3:20).

Hosea 1:10 looks forward to a time when we will be 'Children of the living God' (1:10). The expression, 'living God', speaks of life. Verse 11 says that Israel and Judah will be reunited and 'appoint one head'. From the line of David, a king will reign over a united nation. This captures the spirit of the redeemed people. They are united and follow this king, the Lord Jesus Christ, not because they have to but because they want to. They do it out of love.

This 'wanting to' is the main thrust of Hosea's prophecy and shows us the heart of God.

Unity

The New Covenant looks forward to a time when divisions are repaired. The 'children of Judah and children of Israel ... gathered together' (1:11). The division of the kingdom is perverse to Hosea. He looks ahead to a day when God's people will be united.

Today, the church is sadly characterised by splits and divisions. But imagine a day when we will all be united. We will be with all God's people from throughout history—the Old Testament, New Testament, church history, present and future. You may be in a small church now and find it hard. You may enjoy going to large Christian conferences to meet up with thousands of other Christians. They are your favourite times of the year to be surrounded by so many other believers. Well, in heaven, there will be millions and millions of Christians. It will be a great multitude which no one can number, of all nations, tribes, peoples and tongues (Revelation 7:9). And we will all be united (Psalm 133:1, 3; John 17:21)—no falling out or churches splitting. As the hymn writer, Charles Wesley (1749–1834) says,

Names and sects and parties fall,

Thou, O Christ, art all in all.

Even so, unity can only be with those who hold to these truths as they are in God's Word. It is evangelical not ecumenical unity we must strive for. According to Edwards[2]:

One of the sad marks of the church in its normal life is that it is often found uniting with those from whom we should separate, and separating from those with who we should unite

One day

THE DAY OF JEZREEL

As well as the day of Jezreel being a day of judgement, the word *Jezreel* actually means 'God plants'. It is no longer synonymous with bloodshed. This could be a metaphor for the grave and resurrection. From the debris of the exile, the remnant will come forth and from the remnant, the Messiah will be born. Life will spring up from the land.

Today, judgement has not yet come. It is still a day of salvation. Through the Lord Jesus Christ's death and resurrection, there is hope. People who were dead in trespasses and sins can have life (Ephesians 2:1–5). God still plants and, like a plant, or even a tiny mustard seed (Matthew 13:31), the church is growing; there are still people being converted. God is still doing a work in people's lives.

But it is something only He can do. People cannot become Christians unless the Holy Spirit does a work in their heart; His work is essential. Without the Holy Spirit we would have no interest in God. We would never put our faith in Jesus Christ or believe the gospel.

This should encourage and

> People cannot become Christians unless the Holy Spirit does a work in their heart; His work is essential.

motivate us to pray for God to do a work in our day and age. Jezreel is also a prayer to God. 'May God sow'. It is a prayer for productivity of the land. We need to pray earnestly that God will plant life in many people's hearts.

Revival came to Charlotte Chapel in Edinburgh in 1905 and, two years later, the church was still in the full experience of it. Joseph Kemp, describing the part prayer played in the revival, said, 'If ever you should be asked of the secret of this church's great spiritual prosperity, you can tell them of the prayer meetings.'[3]

We may live in dark days but we should cry out once again, 'May God sow', that God would bring life to individuals, churches and to our land.

One day!

FOR FURTHER STUDY.

1. What importance do we put on the meaning of names today?
2. How important is prayer for Hosea and for us?

TO THINK ABOUT AND DISCUSS.

1. Does it amaze us when we consider the depth of God's love?
2. Always remember to pray for our lost family members and friends.

3 Talk some sense to your mother

Hosea 2:2–23

Hosea's marriage to Gomer is a picture of God's relationship with His people. This is not just a picture of a dysfunctional Middle Eastern family that lived nearly 3000 years ago; this is a picture of our relationship with God. We have done to God what Gomer did to Hosea and, in the same way Hosea is pleading for his wife to return home and for his children to reject their mother's behaviour, God pleads with individual Israelites to return to Him.

The scene at the beginning of Hosea chapter 2 is of Hosea asking his children to talk some sense to their mother. He is desperate that Gomer sees the error of her ways and turns from them. He is calling on his children to reject, disapprove and set themselves apart from their mother's behaviour. He does not want them to suffer the same fate as her. In 2:2 he says, 'Plead with your mother, plead'. Hosea is begging them.

On a domestic level this is a tragic picture. A heartbroken husband at home with three children, while his wife has abandoned them to go off with her lover. A dad wanting the children, when they next see their mum, to try to talk sense to her and ask her to come home so they can be a family again. He is pleading with them to see the error of her ways so that they do not go down the same self-destructing path.

Maybe your view of God is that He is cold and unfeeling. Nothing could be further from the truth. The God of the Bible pleads with people to turn to Him. He implores us not to go after and be enticed by the world, but instead to make a stand for Him in the world and plead with people to come to Him. He wants us to stand out for Him in our communities and be salt and light (Matthew 5:13–16)—to talk some sense to society and, with the help of the Holy Spirit, show them their sin and point them to the Lord Jesus Christ. The apostle Paul says, 'Therefore, we are ambassadors for Christ, God making his appeal through us. We implore you on behalf of Christ, be reconciled to God' (2 Corinthians 5:20).

It would have been very hard for the children to reject their mother's behaviour. Whatever she was doing, she was still their mum. Growing up, I thought my mother was perfect. To have to disapprove of her would have been a huge ask. I cannot imagine a child would go against their mother self-righteously or judgementally. They would have done it lovingly. But they still needed to speak out and talk sense, for their mum's sake! In the same way, Christians need to speak out against society—lovingly, sensitively but clearly. We must go into school, university, work and live like a Christian, faithful to Jesus Christ. It is difficult because in this modern world God, His law, the Bible, and the need for a Saviour can all seem a bit out of date. People have convinced themselves that hell cannot be real and that the judgement is too far-fetched. The culture of the day has well and truly seduced people.

> Christians need to speak out against society—lovingly, sensitively but clearly.

Hosea begs us to see what is going on, see the destructive path this culture is taking us down and 'talk some sense to it'. Stand up and stand out. As Davis[1] puts it, we have 'been sucking up the bland milk of tolerance from the breasts of an anaemic culture for too long'.

A wife behaving badly

If Hosea is pictured as a pleading husband in chapter 2, the picture of Gomer is of a wife behaving badly.

Selfish

She is very selfish. She says, 'I will go' (Hosea 2:5). It

is Gomer who is chasing her lovers to satisfy her own wants rather than them pursuing her—those she loves rather than those who love her. She is determined, bent on going after them.

Hosea 2:2 says, 'For she is not my wife and I am not her husband,' although it could be translated: 'She is behaving as though she is not my wife.'

Imagine the terrible shock the first night that Hosea came home to find the children crying, unfed and wondering where their mother had gone. As Gomer enjoyed herself in the company of her lovers, she did not think or care much for her children or husband. All that mattered was how she felt.

Gomer's behaviour is true of us today. All of us by nature are selfish. There are sins we just have to commit and do not think about how they will affect us or others. Her behaviour also pictures what our *mother culture* has done to us today. It is a self-centred approach where it is all about our rights and a sense of entitlement; we should be allowed to do whatever makes us happy. But this determination to do what we think is right, ignoring God and pleasing ourselves, has got us in a mess.

Rob Liddle, in his article entitled, 'The Kids aren't all right: we think we are protecting them but we are harming them'[2] said:

A recent Unicef report discovered that British children were the least happy in the Western world. Rates of depression and anxiety among children have reportedly increased by 70% in the last 25 years and the number turning up in A&E wards reporting psychiatric conditions has doubled since 2009. In a 2016 survey for Parent Zone, 91% of teachers reported seeing more mental illness among their charges. A year later it was reported that suicides among teenagers had reached a 14-year high. Whatever way you look at it, we are not bringing up our children terribly well. Something is wrong—perhaps many things are …

Ungrateful

As well as being selfish, she is taking Hosea for granted and not showing any gratitude for all that he does for her. In Hosea 2:5, 8, the image is of Hosea taking groceries down to the house, giving them to the lover who pretended they were from him. Her lover could not look after her, so Hosea waited around to make sure she gets them. All the time Gomer did not know it was Hosea who had provided.

God provided for Israel every year. They had grain, new wine, oil, silver and gold. At harvest, Israel was supposed to acknowledge that all the bounty of the land came from God (Leviticus 23:10–20; Deuteronomy 26:10–11). They had plenty but year after year they kept attributing it to Baal. In fact, they used the gifts God had given them to worship Baal.

Again, this is true of us today. God has given us gifts but we think our success and possessions are all down to us. We use these gifts to please ourselves. God has given men and women brilliant intellects but they use those intellects to go about disproving God. He has given people the ability to play sport at the highest level but they play sport on the Lord's Day. Nations have become successful and powerful only to use that success and power to pass laws that cut across the Word of God.

This ingratitude and selfishness are the worst thing about our sin. We do not think about God. We act like He does not exist.

FLIRTING

Gomer was also a flirt (Hosea 2:2, 13). The women of Israel wore sacred jewellery to go to the Baal shrines. There they would have ritual sex. They thought this was necessary to ensure healthy breeding of the flocks and herds. Gomer is, therefore, wearing the jewellery and make-up of a prostitute. The reference to 'adulterous look from her face' (2:2 NIV), is really talking about her personality, whereas the reference to the breast is drawing attention to a particularly sexual part of her body. She wants to make it clear that she is available. She is going out to seduce and entice men.

In the same way that Gomer's flirting and going-off with other men would have caused embarrassment and shame on Hosea, our behaviour brings shame on God. We are meant to live for His glory and yet, by the way we live, we drag His name in the dust. We make a fool of Him in the eyes of the world. They think He cannot be much of a God if they treat Him like that.

Gomer cheapened herself and would have lost any respect she had with other people. The church today is so desperate to be accepted and be cool and trendy that we have sold out. We have no convictions. Imagine a lady saying, 'My husband is great. He is so laid back and relaxed, he lets me go out and do whatever I want with whoever I want to. It's just like I am single except I've got him to fall back on.' You would think, 'What kind of husband is that? She can't love him very much or respect him and he can't think much of her.' And yet, as Christians, we can sometimes give this impression to the world, that we are just like them, only we believe in Jesus. We go around behaving exactly like they do. We try to make church and our lifestyles as much like the world as possible. But, surely, they must look on and conclude, 'Why would I want this God if He is no better or different to what I have now?' Dr Martyn Lloyd Jones said that the church was at its best when it was totally different to the world.[3] We are called to be radically different. God is holy and we are called to be holy— separate, faithful and different.

Dysfunctional Family

The result of Gomer's behaviour is that her family are completely dysfunctional. Home life has broken down. Hosea 2:4 (NIV) says, 'I will not show my love to her children because they are the children of adultery.'

The children are not loved. It is noteworthy that Hosea refers to them as 'her' children. Here are children whose mother is not really looking after them, setting them a terrible example to follow and who do not know their father.

Today we live in a day and age where many are illegitimate to the claims of being God's children. We live in a culture that has given birth to children who do not know God. What many believe to be Christianity has little or no resemblance to Biblical Christianity. There are churches that are not standing on the Word of God, are diluting their message and just telling people what they want to hear. Even some evangelical churches are trying to let people get way with as much as possible; be as worldly as possible; are not legalistic about the Lord's Day; and find ways around difficult parts of the Bible. As a result, a generation is rising up who are *unconverted believers*.

> Today we live in a day and age where many are illegitimate to the claims of being God's children.

The product is a dysfunctional family, an ineffective church and a broken society.

As a nation we have tried to run society our way, that fits around us and does not cut across our way of life. We think we know better than God. But when you look out on the world today and then look at what God says, do you have a better idea about how the family should work? Do you have a better idea about how society should be framed? Do you have a better idea of how to find fulfilment and hope and significance? Imagine if we all lived out the Ten Commandments. Those 173 simple words. Society would function as it should.

JUSTIFY HER ACTIONS

The problem was that Israel really thought there was nothing wrong with the way they were living. Outwardly they were keeping all the festivals. They were carrying out the outward duties of faith without realising that God had rejected them. They saw nothing wrong with attending the feast of the Baals (v. 13) and then attending her own yearly festivals of new moons, Sabbath days and all the other appointed feasts (v. 11).

Today, there are people who go to church on a Sunday because it is the thing to do, or they will go at Christmas and Easter, and then think they have done their bit for God. They sing the carols, take communion and enjoy the 'feeling', and then continue to live just as they like.

On top of this, there is a push towards joining with other faiths and religions. The ecumenical movement is all about centring on the things that unite us: 'Let's not focus on the things that divide us.' But they end up dumbing things down so that they believe nothing that is distinctively Christian, resulting in a fake Christ who affirms everything and demands nothing.

While it is easy and convenient to do this, and however much we try to justify it, the church, and then society, is not pleasing to the only true and living God.

Learn the hard way

DO NOT PRESUME

We cannot presume upon God. Hosea 2:2 says, 'For she is not my wife and I am not her husband.' She is not behaving like Hosea's wife so neither can she rely on the fact that Hosea is still her husband. It is as though the informal divorce proceedings have begun, but before he files for divorce, he wants her to change her ways so he can stop all of this. He just wants them to be a family but it cannot carry on the way it is.

Today we too presume upon the patience of God. We think that we can behave as we want and have our fun because somehow, He will always forgive us; He will always be merciful. But it cannot carry on. One day His patience will end and His mercy will run out. God says that His Spirit will not always strive with man (Genesis 6:3).

We cannot assume we are Christians. The only way we can be sure we are in the light is if we are walking in the light (1 John 1:7). There are lots of churches with great architecture, liturgy, impressive music, well connected people in attendance, supported by the good and the great, years of history and tradition, but unless they are faithful to the Word of God then they are not really churches at all. They cannot presume they are God's children and have no claim on Him.

God is not to be mocked

Hosea 2:3 says, 'Lest I strip her naked and make her as in the day she was born and make her like a wilderness, and make her like a parched land, and kill her with thirst.' While 2:9 warns, 'I will take back my grain in its time, and my wine in its season and I will take away my wool and my flax, which were to cover her nakedness', and in verse 13 God threatens to 'punish her for the feast days of the Baals'.

The reference to Baals is either different deities who all carry the name Baal or one deity that is honoured in various shrines throughout the land. These verses appear to be saying that Hosea's patience ran out and he ended up throwing Gomer out of the house naked. What we know is that, after the birth of Lo-Ammi, she departed. It is also clear from verse 9 that Gomer was deprived of things. Hosea is not some weak, doormat of a husband. Gomer will be humiliated. Today you can imagine a husband cutting up his unfaithful wife's credit cards. She cannot carry on the way she is and keep spending his money.

God will turn His back on Israel in the same way she has turned her back on Him. He will not stand back and be mocked while she flirts with other nations and gods. Israel will lose everything. The land will be emptied. They will be deprived of the necessities—food and clothing.

GRASS IS NOT GREENER

Israel needed to see that the grass is not greener on the other side. Verse 12 (NIV) says, 'I will ruin her vines and her fig trees, which she said were her pay from her lovers; I will make them a thicket, and wild animals will devour them.'

And there would be no one to help her. In verse 6 and 7a, the picture is of thorns used as hedgerow to keep wild animals out of a garden. Today we would use barbed wire or even electric fences. Their path is blocked and even if it was not, there are too few people left to stop wild animals taking whatever crops remain. The loss of vineyards and fig trees would be catastrophic. Grains could be replanted and bear fruit in a single year but these could not.

It would seem that, at first, when Gomer went off with her lovers, they took care of her. They gave her nice things and spoilt her. The grass certainly seemed greener. But they soon grew tired of her and, once they got what they wanted, they left her and they were unable, or could not be bothered to look after her—so that by the end she was eating from the trash. She had sunk lower and lower and ended up living rough in the poorest part of the city.

This dramatically showed Israel that her attempts to get what she wants from foreign nations will come to nothing. Nations would help Israel, or be seen to befriend her, until they got what they wanted. Then they would abandon her, or worse, destroy her. Assyria would storm in and ransack the country. Israel would be taken off into exile, where they would be enslaved and blocked from going home. There would be too few of them in Israel to stop the Assyrians plundering the land.

Here we have a picture of sin for what it really is. William Gurnell[4] says, 'Faith ... looks behind the curtain of sense, and sees sin before ... it be dressed for the stage,' while Joel Beeke[5] says, 'Faith sees the ugliness and hellishness of sin without its camouflage.' In an interview with Michael Parkinson in the 1970s, Orson Welles said:

> I believe that I have looked back too optimistically on Hollywood ... because I realised how many great people that town has destroyed since its earliest beginnings; how almost everybody of merit was destroyed or diminished ... and I suddenly thought to myself, why do I look so affectionately on that town? It was because it was funny ... and everything that we're nostalgic about ... but really it was a brutal place ... and the story of that town is a dirty one, and its record is bad.[6]

Sin will ruin you and nothing the world has to offer will really fulfil you. In the book of Ecclesiastes, the preacher took the here and the now and what was available, to see if he could work it all out and find peace. Wisdom left him frustrated and restless; work made him tired and angry; leisure caused him pain; stuff just made him sick and sad. He lived the American dream before there was an America and said it was a dead-end street.

SHAME

In front of the lovers that she was unfaithful to Hosea with, Gomer would be put to shame. In verse 10, the image is of stripping the woman—public disgrace. In the same way, God will shame Israel in front of the nations. In fact, He will use those nations to bring Israel down. They will be tools in God's hand and no one will be able to stop God from doing this. Israel is about to be carted off into exile and stripped of all her wealth and humiliated.

Guilt and shame paralyse us. Psychologists say that the biggest problem they deal with is guilt. So many of us live our lives worried we may get found out. Every one of us has got guilty secrets. Some of them are so shameful. Lyrics from an Avett Brothers song talk about shame, boatloads of shame and it being the same, day after day, being desperate for someone to make it stop, lift it off, take it off. These are words under which most of us live. To live in this world is to experience shame— boatloads of shame. You may be quietly hoping and thinking that you have got away with it. But you have not. God has seen everything and you will one day suffer all the shame your sin deserves. Everything you have done has been recorded in heaven and one day it will all come to light.

The wooing of God

THE AMAZINGNESS OF GRACE

Verse 14 (NIV) begins with the word 'Therefore', which should introduce the logical consequence of what Hosea had just stated—that God should abandon His wife as she had abandoned Him. But strikingly, God says, 'Therefore I am now going to allure her.' Once again this is disconcerting. Instead of abandoning her,

God promises a new and tender courtship. He speaks tenderly to her. God shows amazing grace, undeserved kindness.

WILDERNESS

Verse 14 and 15 goes on to say:

> I will lead her into the desert and speak tenderly to her. There I will give her back her vineyards and will make the Valley of Achor a door of hope. There she will sing as in the days of her youth as in the day she came up out of Egypt. (NIV)

The *Valley of Achor* literally means the 'valley of trouble'. It was near Jericho where Achan and his family were judged (Joshua 7:24). When the people of Israel had conquered Jericho in the first wave of their invasion of the Promised Land, Achan had taken the spoil of Jericho that the people had been told by God they were not to take. For this, they lost the next battle at Ai. After an investigation, the sin of Achan was discovered and consequently his family were stoned in the Valley of Achor, which took its name for this incident (Joshua 7:26).

The reference here, though, is saying that the Valley of Achor will be a door of hope. Israel is about to go into exile, a 'valley of trouble', as part of God's judgement, but this trouble will become a 'door of hope'. Hope would spring out of this period of judgement. For this to be possible God is going to take her back into the wilderness so that He may win back her love.

For most, the wilderness is something to avoid. The Israelites would rather have died in Egypt than suffer in the wilderness (Exodus 14:12). The wilderness is a hard place (Jeremiah 2:6), a place of drought and deep darkness; a land where no one lives and no one passes through. The wilderness is not just a place of deprivation and desolation but a place of punishment.

But the wilderness is also a place where a person is forced to rely on God. There are no distractions or comforts there. Everything is stripped bare. To survive in the wilderness, you must rely completely on God's grace. God provided food for Israel (Exodus 16:11–16) and their clothes did not wear out (Deuteronomy 29:5). In the wilderness Elijah was sustained by ravens (1 Kings 17:4–6); it was a place of sanctuary for David when he was being pursued by his enemies (1 Samuel 23:14). John the Baptist was in the wilderness (Matthew 3:1); the Lord Jesus was driven by the Holy Spirit into the wilderness (Matthew 4:1–11); Paul spent time there before his ministry (Galatians 1:17). Jacob wrestled with God in the wilderness (Genesis 32:24–31); Moses met with God at the Burning Bush in the wilderness (Exodus 3); and in the wilderness Elijah had his greatest encounter with the Word of God (1 Kings 19:10–18). In

Hosea 2:14 God promises to come to his people in the wilderness.

The wilderness, therefore, becomes a place of renewal and innocence (Jeremiah 2:2; 31:2; Ezekiel 20:10–38). This is why the Psalmist longs for the security of the wilderness (Psalm 55:6–8). It is a place of testing and repentance.

> Sometimes God brings us to an end of ourselves. He strips everything away, removes all our human props so we are closed in with Him.

Sometimes God brings us to an end of ourselves. He strips everything away, removes all our human props so we are closed in with Him. All we can do is seek His face.

A CHANGE OF HEART

In anticipation of the promise of Hosea 2:16, the unfaithful wife will seek her husband (2:7b). This is reminiscent of the parable of the Prodigal Son. After leaving home and going into the far country, where for a while he had the time of his life, the son's money runs out, his friends desert him and he ends up in the pigsty. It is here that he comes to his senses and remembers how much better it was in his father's house.

We need the Holy Spirit to do a work in our hearts, to change us and give us new desires so that we will see our sin for what it is and long for holiness. Pray that God would bring you to this state.

Renew marriage vows

FALL IN LOVE AGAIN

In verse 2 of chapter 2, God says of Israel, 'I am not her husband'. In verse 16 this is reversed. He says, 'In that day, declares the LORD, you will call me "My Husband".' Because of Israel's sin, God hands them over to Assyria. He sends them into exile. It is as if He is no longer her husband. But He always keeps a remnant. And from this remnant the Saviour of all the world will come bringing salvation to millions who will be able to call God, 'My Husband'.

The marriage between God and Israel is not a marriage of convenience or a loveless marriage. Verse 16 of chapter 2 (NIV) says, 'You will no longer call me "my master."' God is no longer master but husband.

You can be in a contract or agreement with someone with no love. People sign a contract when they work somewhere. They agree to arrive at a certain time and leave at a certain time, carry out certain duties and behave in a certain way. The company they work for agree to pay them a certain amount of money and to ensure certain working conditions. All of this can happen with no love on either part. But this is not the picture here. The relationship between God and His people is a relationship of love. Verses 19 and 20 (NIV) say, 'I will betroth you to me forever; I will betroth you in righteousness and justice, in love and compassion. I will betroth you in faithfulness, and you will acknowledge the Lord.' A better translation than 'acknowledge' is 'know'. 'You will know the Lord.' The goal of God's wooing is that the marriage vows are renewed and that Israel really 'know' Him and love Him again. Tozer[7] says, 'A loving personality dominates the Bible ... men can know God with at least the same degree of intimacy as they know any other person or thing that comes within the field of their experience.'

The hymn writer, Charles Wesley (1707–88), says, 'For closer communion I pine'. Our prayer should be that we would fall back in love with the things of God—that the Holy Spirit would make the things that we read in the Bible come alive and real.

Is that not the whole reason we open our Bibles? That you may find Christ and then get to know Him better and better and better; to fall in love with the God of the Bible. The ones who find God are those who diligently seek Him (Hebrews 11:6), who seek Him with all of their hearts (Jeremiah 29:13). He wants to know that you are serious about Him. We should make this our goal as we read our Bible and listen to preaching, that our eyes would be opened to the fact that this is almighty God speaking to us and we would see Him in all His love, glory, beauty and majesty. He would then become precious to us (1 Peter 2:7, KJV).

HAPPY AND SECURE

This relationship will be characterised by faithfulness, righteousness, justice, love and compassion. Peace will come. Imagine a family that has been in turmoil. Parents always arguing, children getting upset; doors slamming, people storming out, crying, screaming and shouting—tension. Then, the mother leaves and no one really knows where she is. The father is heartbroken and the children rebel. It is awful. But now the parents are in love again. The home is stable. It is calm and safe and happy.

For this to happen, all idolatry, love of other gods and going after other things must be removed. Verse 17 says, 'I will remove the names of the Baals from her mouth and they shall be remembered by name no more.' My Baal actually means 'my Lord', so one could call Yahweh, 'my Baal'. Since the name was also the name of a Canaanite deity, the devotees of Baal could make use of this overlap to smuggle their cult into Yahweh's worship. But here, Hosea looks forward to a time when Baalism

> Hosea looks forward to a time when Baalism will be completely removed.

will be completely removed. God's people will be in an exclusive relationship with Him.

This is a great picture of what the church will be like one day. When the kingdom of God will fully come. This kingdom has been set up in the hearts of Christians today. They begin to experience happiness, peace and security. But they will not fully enjoy it until this world ends and Christ returns and there is a new heaven and a new earth—a reconstructed cosmos. A place where God will dwell with His people and all sin will be removed.

A taster of what this will be like occurs in times of revival. During such times, God becomes very real and His presence is felt. The church is revived and many people are converted. Even the wider community is affected; there is a fear and respect for God. Would it not be great if this was to happen in our day? That once again people would turn to God and know real happiness and security.

Looked after

God will look after Israel. In contrast to 2:9, a good harvest is promised. Everything would be reversed, if only Israel will turn back to God and be faithful to Him. Verse 21 and 22 says:

> 'In that day I will respond,' declares the LORD. 'I will respond to the skies and they will respond to the earth

and the earth will respond to the grain, the new wine and the olive oil.' (NIV)

Wine and oil speak of celebration and wealth. God will abundantly supply all her needs. It will not just be the basics of food and shelter. These verses in Hosea are saying that He will move the whole universe to bring it about. This is true for Christians today. God will supply all our needs according to His riches in glory (Philippians 4:19). The whole universe is in His hands; all the resources of heaven are His (Psalm 50:10–12). God does not just control history, He drives it. 'The earth is the LORD's and the fullness thereof, the world and those who dwell therein' (Psalm 24:1).

One day God will take us to heaven with Him. Over 2000 years ago, the Lord Jesus went to a cross to 'prepare a place for us that where he is there we would be also' (John 14:3). It will be paradise. But until then. in this world, God will look after us. He will provide for us and will work all things for the good of those who trust him (Romans 8:28) and for those who suffer in this life, He is using it for a greater weight of glory (2 Corinthians 4:17).

According to Boller[8], during the time Sam Rayburn was the 43rd Speaker of the United States House of Representatives, the teenage daughter of a reporter he knew died suddenly. The next morning, the reporter heard a rapping on his apartment door, opened it and found Rayburn standing there. Rayburn said, 'I just came by to see what I could do to help.' The reporter, stuttering and trying to recover his surprise, indicated that there was not anything the speaker could do—they were making all the arrangements. Rayburn inquired, 'Well have you all had your coffee this morning?' The reporter confessed that they had not had time to do that yet. 'Well, I can at least make the coffee this morning,' Rayburn said. Rayburn went in and made his way to the kitchen in search of coffee. While Rayburn was busy with coffee making, the reporter remembered that Rayburn usually had a stated weekly appointment on this particular morning. So, he half-inquired, 'Mr Speaker, I thought you were supposed to be having breakfast at the White House this morning.' 'Well I was,' admitted Rayburn, 'but I called the President and told him I had a friend who was in trouble and I couldn't come.'

God has a world to run. He has a moon, a sun, stars and planets to uphold. He has seas to control, nations to oversee but his priority is His church, especially in their need. He will look after them. That is why Peter urges us to 'cast all our care upon him because he cares for us' (1 Peter 5:7, KJV).

New home living happily ever after

They will set up a new home together. Once more the threat of 2:2 is reversed. Hosea now looks forward to the restoration of the creation order (v. 18). It is a picture of what it will be like when Christ comes again.

At the beginning of Revelation 20, John sees a new heaven and a new earth for the first heaven and the first earth had passed away. This is the new home that God has set up for His people to live with him (21:3). Christians will enjoy God's company forever. It will be a place of breath-taking beauty. It is not just human beings that are under the sentence of death but the whole of creation (Genesis 3:17–19; Romans 8:20–21). The way things are today is not the way they are supposed to be. The entire creation groans and suffers, waiting for all things to be made new. One day this tormented, distressed, afflicted earth will be wrapped up and there will be a new heaven and a new earth. There will be peace between nations and peace with animals. According to Isaiah 11:6–7, 'The wolf shall dwell with the lamb, and the leopard shall lie down with the young goat, and the calf and the lion and the fattened calf together.'

In this new home, God and His people are going to live happily ever after (Hosea 2:21–23).

Right now, we live in a bad world. It is a world full of evil, pain and sadness. Marriages and families break up; addiction takes hold of people; pornography dominates the internet; paedophilia, rape, murder, lies, deceit, theft, terrorism, greed are all around us. People get ill, depressed, suffer pain and heartache;

we have issues with ourselves and issues with other people; family problems, financial worries, failure; natural disasters leave countries and peoples devastated. We all know something of these in one way or another because we live in a fallen world. As a result of the fall, fear entered the world (Gen. 3:10). Blame entered the world (Gen. 3:11–13). Pain entered the world (Gen. 3:16). Relationships break down (Gen. 3:16), shame is felt (Gen. 3:7). Just making it through life is a chore (Gen. 3:17).

But, one day, there will be no more sin, no sorrow, no pain, no night, no death (Revelation 21:4, 27; 22:5). Every tear will be wiped away (Rev. 21:4).

In John 21:9–12, we have one of the most wonderful scenes in the Bible, a little foretaste of heaven. A cooked breakfast around a charcoal fire at daybreak on the Sea of Galilee, cooked by the Son of God. Beautiful setting, great food (Revelation 19:6–9) with friends, in the company of the Son of God—forever.

For further study ▶

FOR FURTHER STUDY.

1. How challenging is the statement, 'Ingratitude and selfishness are the worst thing about our sin. We do not think about God.'

2. Do we understand how much our sin hurts God?

TO THINK ABOUT AND DISCUSS.

1. Does the forgiveness of God fill us with joy?

2. Have we ever felt so bad that we have doubted God's forgiveness?

4 God so loved

Hosea 3

According to Boice[1], Hosea chapter 3 is the greatest chapter in the Bible. That is quite a statement, but it is hard to disagree when you consider what it teaches us about the heart and character of God: His love for unlovable men and women, boys and girls, like me and you.

God does not give up on us

It demonstrates that God does not give up on us. In 3:1, Hosea tells us, 'And the LORD said to me, "Go again, love a woman who is loved by another man and is an adulteress, even as the LORD loves the children of Israel."'

Some argue that Gomer and the woman of chapter 3 are two different women. They argue that the Hebrew text of 3:1 only calls her 'a woman' and not 'your wife'. However, I do not think there can be much doubt that this woman is Gomer. The context clearly implies that Gomer is meant. The only immoral woman we know anything about in the book is Gomer and it seems a bit odd that another immoral woman is introduced. Furthermore, the message of Hosea does not really make sense if it is another woman.

It is also important to note that chapter 3 is not the same story as chapter 1 told from a different perspective, as some maintain—the one account being in the first person and the other in the third person. The word 'again' implies continuity. Rather, God is telling Hosea to go and love the same woman again. His wife, Gomer, who has disgraced herself and broken his heart, is the woman he must go and love again.

So why is she not named? Why is she referred to just as an adulteress? Because, through her adulterous behaviour, Gomer had forfeited her identity and her right to Hosea's love. She did not act like or bear any resemblance to Hosea's wife. One would never have thought Gomer was a married woman. She was a serial adulteress who now found herself a slave in the slave market with no rights.

When Adam and Eve fell, all of humanity fell with them. Adam and Eve, as our representatives, broke God's command. They rebelled. Now every boy and girl, man and woman are born in sin and rebellion against God. We are a fallen race. If God was to treat us fairly, He would send us straight to hell. We have no rights. No claim on God.

Like Gomer, our sin has enslaved us (Hebrews 2:15; Col. 1:13). We think we do what we want and no one tells us what to do, but the reality is we are in bondage to sin and to Satan and slaves to our sinful lusts. In the ancient world, there were three ways in which a person could become a slave: born into slavery; fall into slavery through conquest; become a slave through debt. The Bible speaks of sin in these three ways. We are born into sin. Human's original state was sinless but since the fall sin has a hold on us. Our nature is sinful and corrupt (Psalm 51:5; Ecclesiastes 7:20; Jeremiah 17:9; Romans 3:10; 1 John 1:10). We are captivated by sin, slaves to our lusts. And our sin has put us in such a debt with God that we cannot pay it back.

> Our sin has put us in such a debt with God that we cannot pay it back.

You may find that offensive but think about what you are like when you are on your own: what you naturally do left to your own devices; how angry, nasty and jealous you get; how gossipy you can be; how dirty your mind is; how shameful some of the things you have done are (or would have done given half the chance and could have got away with it!). Think about your internet history. Think about your language, your pride, how you look down on others. Think about how lazy you are. But none of this is the worst thing about our sin. Even though sin has messed and tangled up our lives and the lives of others, the real horror and heart of sin is that it is against God.

However, God did not give up on us. He says to His Son, 'Go'. 'Put on human flesh, become a man, go into that fallen, sinful, dirty, messed up world and save sinners.'

In 1964, Kitty Genovese was murdered in Kew Gardens in New York.[2] It was witnessed by thirty-eight people who saw the killer come into the park and carry out the attack. They shouted from the windows for him to stop and even though he did leave the park, he came back and killed her. When the police asked the witnesses why they did not come down to help the lady when they saw the danger she was in, they said that they did not want to get involved. But Jesus Christ, when he saw the mess that we had made of our lives and the danger we were in, did not just shout down from heaven, He came down, right down. He rolled his sleeves up, put on human flesh, became one of us, went to a cross and took on Himself all our sin.

Look at the state of her!

In chapter 2, Gomer has left the family home and by chapter 3, Hosea's marriage to her is over. There is nothing good to say about Gomer, and Hosea is well within his rights to have kicked her out. Friends and those looking on would tell him he would be a fool to take her back—better off without her. The state she is in at the beginning of chapter 3 is shameful. By now, who knows how many men she has slept with or the degradation she has plunged into?

The 'other man' in 3:1 is what we would regard today as a *partner* or *boyfriend*. From the text it would appear she has gone off with another man who now does not want her. Gomer's new lover turned out to be as useless and heartless as herself and she was soon his drudge and virtual prisoner. We are not told the exact details but it would seem that she is in debt and has been working as a prostitute for an owner. It is clear that she is still committing adultery and making a fool of Hosea, her children and herself. The fact Hosea had to buy her back indicates she had probably fallen into poverty and had finally been forced to give herself over to slavery to survive. But she is now in such a state that her master or owner wants to sell her on!

At this point Hosea is told, 'Go again, love a woman who is loved by another man and is an adulteress' (3:1). So, Hosea makes his way to the slave market.

Slaves were sold naked and we can only imagine Hosea making his way among the slaves looking for Gomer—scarcely able to recognise her with her sunken eyes and ravaged body. Gomer was sold at a discount; she was not just shop soiled or second hand, she was a disgusting left over that nobody wanted.

This image demonstrates that sin is powerful and destructive. If you do not kill sin, sin will kill you. It ruins and destroys lives and traps and ensnares you. People think they can control it but the reality is that sin takes hold of a person and controls them. When Gomer had fun with her lovers, she did not plan on ending up naked and washed up in a slave market.

> If you do not kill sin, sin will kill you. It ruins and destroys lives and traps and ensnares you.

Sin destroys lives and causes much suffering. It troubles your conscience and wracks you with guilt. It leaves you feeling dirty.

Gomer was damaged goods. Her sinful, unfaithful life had tangled her up and trapped her. She was a complete mess, dirty and pathetic—no good to anyone. That is apart from Hosea, who tells us, 'So I bought her' (3:2).

Cost him everything!

And it cost Hosea everything to buy Gomer back. The going rate for a slave was about thirty shekels (Exodus 21:32). It is clear that Hosea did not have thirty shekels, so had to make up the rest of the amount with barley (Hosea 3:2). Even though barley is an important crop, it was less valuable than wheat. A *homer* is a dry measure used for grain, perhaps about 48 gallons (220 litres). A *lethech* is about half a *homer.*

Buying Gomer back was costly. It would have been difficult for him to make the complex deal. He had to scrape it together and use all the resources he had. It would have been shameful and humiliating to put together everything he had to make up the value. The prophet would be held in contempt by some, bringing upon himself this disgrace.

But this again is a picture of what it cost God to redeem his people. He had clearly said to them that they should have no other gods before Him (Exodus 20:3), but they kept turning to other gods. It was an almost impossible task for God to put aside all the wrong and hurt He had suffered. But He had set His heart on them (Deuteronomy 7:7–8; 10:15). His heart beat with love but His justice cried out to be satisfied.

All the sins of His people had to be punished in full. The only way He could do it was by becoming them, taking on all their guilt and punishing Himself in the person of His Son. 'For our sake he made him to be sin who knew no sin ...' (2 Corinthians 5:21). He became Gomer!

Through His death we have been freed from bondage to the guilt of sin and from its ruling power in our lives (Rom 6:11, 14). By redeeming us, Jesus has delivered us from the power of sin and paid the price for our forgiveness (Matt. 20:28; Mark 10:45; 1 Peter 1:18–19; Heb. 9:12; Rom. 3:23–26; Eph. 1:7; Col. 1:14), paying the ransom for our sin to God, whose holiness and justice had been offended. The debt we owe has been paid in full. Christ has finished paying it off so we can be free. He paid a 'ransom for many' (Mark 10:45). His death liberates us from all the ravages of the fall.

All of this was costly. Forgiveness with God is free, but it is not cheap! When God created the world, He spoke and this great universe came into being. But to save fallen men and women, boys and girls, He had to come down from heaven; be born of a virgin; grow up as a boy on those rough back streets of Nazareth; be misunderstood; betrayed by one of his closest friends; arrested at night by a large mob of about 300 people with swords and clubs, lanterns and torches; abandoned by all His other friends; and go through a series of mock trials. He was beaten by a battalion of up to 600 men, spat at, laughed at and had a crown of thorns squeezed on His brow. His body was probably so torn and lacerated that you could see His inner organs and He would have been beaten until his kidneys were visible. Jesus was just a bleeding mess of torn flesh. So much so, He was unable to carry His cross through the busy Jerusalem streets and eventually collapsed from exhaustion. At the site of crucifixion, soldiers laid Jesus on the cross and nailed Him to it. They would have then lifted the cross up and dropped it into a prepared socket. Every bone in His body would have jolted and His nerves would have shivered with the excruciating pain. He was then essentially forced to inflict upon Himself a very slow death by suffocation. To make matters even worse, as His longing for oxygen became unbearable, His back, which had been torn repeatedly by previous floggings, would scrape against the wooden cross with each breath He took. By now He was so disfigured He was beyond human likeness (Isaiah 52:14); people were astonished and appalled at Him. He looked like a thing of horror—like a lump of flesh, unclear whether it was an animal or human. People hid their faces from Him (Isaiah 53:3). He was crushed (to pieces), wounded and pierced (Isaiah 53:5).

But, worse than all of this, He took upon himself the wrath of a sin-hating, holy God. When they hammered Jesus onto that cross, He was taking the hammering our sins deserve. On the cross He was saying to God in effect, 'Don't punish them for their unfaithfulness and sin; don't be angry with them; take it all out on me!' As the Son of God is being sacrificed in the place of millions of sinners, under so much stress, He is abandoned by God and screams out, 'My God, my God, why have you forsaken me?' (Matthew 27:46). On the cross for three hours, Jesus was forsaken by God. There is no sadder word than 'forsaken'. Think of a widow coming home from the funeral of her husband, or a child whose parents have been killed in a car accident. If a child is in trouble, need or pain, they call out 'Dad, Dad'. But imagine Dad does not come. Forsaken, abandoned, alone! But not even these compare with being forsaken by God in your hour of need (see John 16:32). On the cross Jesus faced the weight of the guilt of millions of sins, faced the anger and wrath of God and went through hell alone. Satan whispered in his ear, 'Despair and die. God has abandoned you!'

He who spoke and a universe came into being; He who put the planets in their place; He who built every mountain and rolled out every sea; He of whom the disciples said, 'even the wind and the sea obey him' (Mark 4:41); He who was from the beginning God, subjected Himself to this!

To rescue Gomer, Hosea had to scrape together everything he had. It cost him everything. To save us, it cost God everything. No wonder, in her hymn, Katherine Agnes May Kelly (1869–1942) says,

Oh make me understand it

help me to take it in

what it meant to Thee, the Holy One,

To bear away my sin.

Perhaps the state of Gomer in that slave market is how you feel about yourself. Maybe you are a Christian but have fallen into sin. You feel that you cannot be too committed because of your failings. You have badly let the Saviour down. You still love Him but cannot believe that He still loves you—or if He does, you can never be close to Him.

But Hosea chapter 3 shows that He so wants you to be reconciled to Him. However, you must tell Him everything; look into your heart, leave no place out of bounds to Him. It will be painful but it is the only way to be fully restored and have intimate communion with the Saviour. Examine your heart (Lam. 3:40). Confess and repent of any known sin (1 John 1:8–9). He wants to draw near to you.

> Examine your heart. Confess and repent of any known sin.

He does not want anything between you and Him. He wants you to serve Him fully. He says to you, 'Return to me, and I will return to you' (Malachi 3:7).

Whatever you have done, if you come to Him in repentance and faith, He will save you. There is a verse in the Bible that really troubles people. It is in Mark 3:28–29 (NIV) and says,

> I tell you the truth, all the sins and blasphemies of men will be forgiven them. But whoever blasphemes against the Holy Spirit will never be forgiven; he is guilty of an eternal sin.

But, if we look at the verse closely, it is actually a really encouraging verse. It says, 'All the sins and blasphemies of men will be forgiven them.' Everything you have done, (everything!) can be forgiven. Except one thing. And that one thing is to refuse to repent and believe on the Lord Jesus Christ. That, and that alone, is unforgiveable.

On the side of a plumber's van in Coventry it said, 'No hole too dark, too dirty or too deep that we can't reach.' Hosea 3 shows that there is no heart too dark, too dirty or too deep that God's love cannot reach.

It is hard to imagine standing face to face with the Lord Jesus Christ knowing that, before the sun, the moon and stars were put in their place, He loved me; that 2000 years ago on that little hill outside the city of Jerusalem He died for me; that He has seen everything I have done, the big sins, the grand mistakes that have disfigured my life, knows everything I have thought and heard everything I have said and yet still came to sin's slave market to seek and to save me. When I see Him face to face, all I will be able to say is, 'I can't believe you loved me and gave yourself for me!' John Newton, when losing his memory, said he remembered two things: 'That I am a great sinner and that Christ is great Saviour.'[3]

Fit to be called his wife

However, if Hosea was going to take Gomer back, she needed to be fit to be his wife. Verses 3 and 4 says:

And I said to her, "You must dwell as mine for many days. You shall not play the whore, or belong to another man; so will I also be to you." For the children of Israel shall dwell many days without king or prince, without sacrifice or pillar, without ephod or household gods.

To understand the meaning of these verses some words and phrases need to be explained.

'Many days' is a reference to an extended but limited period—not forever but a set time. It is a time of restoration to bring Gomer to repentance and renewed love for Hosea.

'You must dwell' means that Gomer must sit still. She will not be engaged in all the activity she has been. Hosea says, 'you will dwell as mine'. She will be Hosea's and Hosea will be hers. Gomer will now abstain from prostitution and sexual immorality.

'Pillar' or standing stone refers to a memorial pillar such as was found in early times (Genesis 28:18, 22; 31:13; Exodus 24:4). However, these pillars increasingly became identified as an aspect of pagan worship and banned from use in Israel (Hosea 10:1; Exodus 23:24; 34:13; Leviticus 26:1; Deuteronomy 7:5; 12:3; 16:22). They were part and parcel of the mixed-up syncretistic worship of the North.

'Ephod' and Teraphim refer to various aspects of the cult. Originally the ephod was part of the high priest's attire (Exodus 28:1–35; 39:1–26), a sleeveless tunic worn over his other garments. It was made of costly and colourful materials—gold, blue, purple, scarlet, fine linen. Attached to the ephod was a breastplate in which twelve precious stones (representing Israel's twelve tribes) were set in four rows. There was a pocket or pouch in the breastplate which contained the Urim and the Thummim (Exodus 28:30)—objects used to discover Yahweh's will on particular matters (see Numbers 27:21). Since the breastplate was attached to the ephod, requesting the priest's ephod meant to ask for Yahweh's direction by Urim and Thummim (see 1 Samuel 23:9–12; 30:7–8). But the Ephod was misused and was a garment associated with illegitimate worship (Judges 8:27; 17:5; 18:14–20) which more probably is intended here. Teraphim are generally understood as household gods (Gen 31:19, 34; 1 Sam 19:13, 16). Both refer to the debased worship practices of Israel.

Israel will go into exile. They will have no king or prince and live in a land under a foreign ruler. They will not be able to offer sacrifices but, during this time, they will abstain from idolatry. They will return to God. They will come in fear, reverence and respect—no longer taking Him for granted. Not treating Him shabbily but knowing that He is God: 'It is he that has made us, and we are his' (Psalm 100:3).

The reference to 'David their king' (3:5) is looking forward to David's greater King, the Lord Jesus. The King that all kings in the Old Testament pointed to and found their fulfilment in. None of Israel's kings were perfect—nowhere near it. Some were terrible and even the best of them fell short. But they pointed forward to the real King, the Son of God.

So, what does all this mean for us?

The exile is a picture of our exile from God after the Fall. Sin separated us from God. But through the death of the Lord Jesus Christ, we have been reconciled to God. On the cross, when Christ cried out 'It is finished' (John 19:30), all the wrong and grievance was put right between us and God, and we can be accepted by Him. But we still have to live in this fallen world. Sin remains. In our hearts there is a new government but there is still the opposition. We are not at home with God in heaven yet.

Like the Israelites living in a foreign land, as Christians this world is a foreign land to us; in the same way Gomer had to learn to be Hosea's wife again and go through a period of cleansing, God is working in Christians in this world, making them more like Him, conforming them to the image of His Son (Romans 8:29). This process is called sanctification.

This process does not save us or make us right with God. We are justified—made right with God—through the atoning death of the Lord Jesus Christ and trusting completely in His finished work. But Christ died to sanctify us no less than to justify us (John 17:19; Ephesians 5:25–26; Titus 2:14; 1 Peter 2:24; Colossians 1:22). He died to make us good.

Sanctification is an inseparable consequence of

our regeneration and conversion. We are still in this world but our actions, although imperfect, and cannot justify, are pleasing in the sight of God (Hebrews 13:16; Colossians 3:20). When we are converted, we are changed. Conversion brings newness: new life; new direction; new inclination; new affections. The old has gone and the new has come. The Holy Spirit gives us a new awareness of sin, a new interest in the Word of God, a new passion for holiness, a new desire for prayer, and a new sense of the majesty of God. We still sin but now we want to be holy. We now want God to be our King, and we gladly submit to His kingly rule.

Sanctified people are the happiest people on earth as a general rule. 'Great peace have those that love your law' (Psalm 119:165). 'My yoke is easy and my burden is light' (Matthew 11:30).

Like Gomer, for 'many days' on this earth we must 'dwell', sit still, not engage in the sins of this world, put our sins to death and seek God. We will never attain sinless perfection in this life but one day we will be with Him and be like Him—perfect (1 John 3:2). Today, as we read this book, Gomer lives. She is alive in another world with God. This dirty, sex-crazed, messed-up, sin-ravaged slave is now perfect, pure, clean and spotless.

> Sanctified people are the happiest people on earth as a general rule.

Rev Vernon Higham, pastor of the Heath Evangelical

Church in Cardiff, on more than one occasion referred to a lady who attended the Heath in the 1980s. She had lived a particularly dirty life but had started attending the Heath Church, realized her sinfulness and trusted the Lord Jesus Christ to save her. She would go back where she was staying with many other women who would taunt her, that someone like her should never be going to church and that she could never be forgiven with her past. She felt hopeless and unclean. But she told Mr Higham that one night, and after a particularly bad evening, it was like the Lord Jesus Christ Himself drew near to her and said, 'In my sight you are a chaste virgin.'

Go!

In chapter 3 verse 1, Hosea is charged to 'Go'. He is commanded to go and bring this dirty, messed-up, ruined, unfaithful, dirty woman home to be his wife again.

We are also commanded to 'Go'. Go and tell sinful men and women, boys and girls, who are hurtling full throttle to hell, that Jesus Christ receives sinners.

In Matthew 28:19, before the Lord Jesus ascended back to heaven, He told the apostles to make disciples, and to do that they had to 'Go'. He did not say 'Wait here and I will send people to you who you can preach to.' He said 'Go'. Maybe, today, the reason so many of our churches are empty is because we are waiting there patiently for people to turn up and listen to us preach.

The message we give is 'You come and get it', but that is not the way. We need to 'go and give it'.

We do that in our workplace by inviting people to church and witnessing by the way we live and what we say. Going to where people are and preaching to them, whether it be in the open air or by joining clubs and societies, getting to know and love people—going to wherever people are and talking to them about our Saviour. Winsomely, urgently and clearly.

We cannot sit in our churches and bemoan the state of the nation, complaining about young people today, how bad our politicians are and so on. We need to go out and declare to them that there is a God, a judgement, a heaven and a hell. We need to tell them that they are sinners, but Jesus Christ died to be their Saviour. We need to urge them, implore them and plead with them to repent of their sin and trust Him.

We must love people. If we have not got a burden for the lost, then we need to ask God to give us one. Evangelism pulsates through God and our pulse rate needs to be the same. When Christ saw the multitude, He had compassion on them (Matthew 9:36), and we need to have the same love for people.

Importantly, we need to get the gospel into all nations (Matthew 28:19), for 'God so loved the world' (John 3:16). At times we can be guilty in the West of thinking that Christianity is for white middle-class Westerners.

But we forget that it actually started in a Middle Eastern country and moved out and out and out. And we need to keep moving it out!

A missionary spoke at a South Wales Church a few years ago. He told us about his parents who were among the first missionaries to go to Indonesia. As these Indonesians were told about the cross and resurrection, hundreds and hundreds of them were saved. One of the chiefs of the tribes asked the missionaries, 'How long ago did Jesus die? Last week, last month, last year?' When the missionaries said He died 2000 years ago, the people could not believe it and asked them why it had taken them so long to come and tell them!

According to Woolsey[4]: 'With horror, Duncan Campbell saw thousands from the Highlands and Islands of Scotland drifting to their doom, and heard a voice calling, "Go to them, go to them."'

If the resurrection is true; if we believe that Jesus did really die and rose again, then we should be telling others. If there is a heaven to gain and a hell to avoid; if unnumbered souls are dying and pass into the night, it should move us to tell as many people as we can. We should therefore say with Paul, 'as much as in me is' (Romans 1:15, KJV). 'I'll give it all I've got.'

We need to pray for a love for the lost—a passion to see people saved. Preachers, evangelists, all Christians must keep going to them. Hosea is told, 'Go again'. Keep going back with the great message that whoever comes to Jesus Christ will never be turned away.

Raisin cakes, really?

Verse 1 of chapter 3 says something quite peculiar. '... The LORD loves the children of Israel though they turn to other gods and love cakes of raisins.'

The Israelites turned their back on God because of raisin cakes! These cakes were offerings to pagan gods. They played a part in the promiscuous, ecstatic and wild celebrations of the fertility cult.

Hosea's tone is sarcastic. They will actually give up God for raisin cakes!

What will you give up God for? What is the thing that prevents you giving your life to God?

Is there is a particular sin you really struggle with, or a way of life, or a relationship, that you just cannot give up? Sex, popularity, power, possessions?

But, as the Lord Jesus Christ said, 'What will it profit a man if he gains the whole world and forfeits his soul? Or what shall a man give in return for his soul?' (Matthew 16.26). The bottom line is this: is whatever you are clinging to, worth going to hell for?

Don't go to hell for raisin cakes!

FOR FURTHER STUDY

1. Think how much it cost Almighty God to give His Son for us.
2. What in our lives need to change?

TO THINK ABOUT AND DISCUSS.

1. Do we understand the pain Christ went through for us?
2. Is anything or anyone more important to you than God?

5 Taken to court

Hosea 4:1–5:7

Hosea's message was of critical importance for the Israelites; they really needed to take it to heart and act upon it. But they were a hostile and unreceptive audience. They were not interested and did not want to hear what Hosea had to say, so he had to really grapple with the problem of getting them to listen.

The fragmented and disjointed style that we are confronted with in Hosea 4 is probably intended. It seems to suit the chaotic situation it addresses.

He, therefore, uses vivid and startling metaphors and employs symbolic actions which are shocking—jumping from one to the other in his determination to grab their attention.

In chapters 1–3, Hosea has taken us to his wedding; to the maternity ward; the home; the wilderness; and the slave market. In Chapter 4:1–5:7, we find ourselves in court.

Up until now the prophet has used the broadest brush strokes in describing what God thinks of Israel. Now, in chapter 4, he comes to the detail and the main focus in 4:1–5:7 is on the religious decline of the Northern Kingdom.

Time

Hosea is a literary masterpiece. Under the inspiration of the Holy Spirit, the prophet has thought carefully about how and what he says and his prophecy is sophisticated and nuanced. But it comes to us *en masse*. What he says does not readily divide into discrete prophecies that can be pinned to particular dates and times. No doubt Hosea preached the material found in this book on numerous occasions.

But while we do not really know when the events occurred that Hosea is referring to, there are some clues. Chapters 1–3 would seem to have taken place in the closing years of Jeroboam's reign, before the nation descended into internal squabbling and strife, and before it had to face mounting pressure from Assyria (probably 755–745 BC). Assyria is first mentioned in 5:13, and so 5:8–14:9 must be dated after 745 BC. It seems reasonable to detect a general chronological order, with later chapters increasingly reflecting the turbulent conditions of the 730s BC, and then the confusion and plotting of Hoshea's reign.

It is probable therefore that the material in 4:1 to 5:7 derives from the same period as chapters 1–3, before Assyrian aggression came to dominate the nation's affairs. While Jeroboam's reign was the second golden era in Israel's history, it was not free from problems. The desire for self-advancement drowned out concern for the less advantaged in the land. Such decay in social attitudes and justice stemmed from the religious decline of the nation.

There is a link between chapter 4 and chapter 2 as the word, 'controversy', in 4:1 is related to the word, 'plead', in 2:2. In chapter 2, Hosea was calling on his three children to denounce their mother's behaviour with the intention of getting individual Israelites to reject Israel and its culture. Here in chapter 4, the case God pleaded in chapter 2 is now brought to the law court.

Case for the prosecution (4:1–3)

The opening verse of chapter 4 is like a formal prosecution. The picture is of one party to an agreement giving notice to the other party of a grievance against their conduct, seeking to convince them that they are in the wrong and urging them to take action to put the situation right. God made a covenant with Israel. But Israel has broken the covenant. God is therefore giving notice to Israel of His grievance and urging her to sort it out. Hosea wants Israel to acknowledge that

God's complaints are valid and that His case against her is strong. The charges God brings against Israel are summarised in verse 1: 'There is no faithfulness or steadfast love, and no knowledge of God in the land.'

Even though we are in the law court, the marriage analogy could also still be in the background. The husband is saying in effect, 'My wife doesn't know me, doesn't love me, isn't faithful to me.'

No faithfulness or steadfast love (v. 1)

Part of God's case against Israel is that there is no faithfulness or integrity. Integrity is a life that follows principle rather than convenience. It is knowing the truth and living by it. Someone with integrity is faithful, reliable, and constant in his actions. However, the

> Integrity is a life that follows principle rather than convenience.

Children of Israel are living a lie. They say one thing but are doing something different; they cannot be trusted. There is no moral integrity.

As well as no faithfulness, there is no steadfast love. If people are no longer faithful, then they will do whatever makes them happy or feels good; loyalty goes out of the window. A person's own happiness will be put above the wellbeing of others. People will be out for themselves and become cruel and self-centred, resulting in a lack of compassion with no one going above and beyond.

All of this manifests itself in the sins listed in chapter 4:2: 'There is swearing, lying, murder, stealing, and committing adultery; they break all bounds and bloodshed follows bloodshed.'

This is an allusion to the 3rd, 9th, 6th, 8th and 7th commandments—the social crimes of the Ten Commandments. It is the social manifestation of abandoning God.

Hosea says that lying, swearing, murder, stealing and adultery 'break all bounds', like a river overflowing its banks. Once the people abandon God and everyone does what they think is right, in effect, *all hell is let loose!*

Violence and recrimination dominate Israel. There is chaos in the land. Evil is widespread in the community. No sooner has one incident occurred than another happens. The country seems out of control. The more they sin, the less of a big deal it becomes. Sin leads to more sin—as long as they can get what they want and cover their tracks.

This is illustrated for us in the Old Testament in the life of King David. He was at home in his palace when all his men had gone to war (2 Samuel 11). From the roof of his palace, he spots a beautiful woman bathing and thinks to himself, 'I have got to have her'. Her husband is away at war and they end up having sex. However, she becomes pregnant and now their illicit affair is in danger of becoming found out. To cover up the mess he is in, David arranges for her husband, Uriah, to come home from battle to spend the night with her and to make it look like he is the father. But, being a good soldier, he will not go to bed with his wife while he is meant to be on duty and so the plan did not work. Desperate to cover his tracks, David then arranges for Uriah to fight on the front line of the battle and to be abandoned, resulting in his death. What started as an afternoon of fun, ended up with lies, betrayal and murder. Sin is not what it appears. It is destructive. It gives momentary pleasure but destroys people's lives. Sin always leads to more sin.

Returning to the marriage analogy, Hosea impresses upon the people that marriage is more than just a legal agreement. For a marriage to work it requires steadfast love—a commitment to the spirit of the marriage relationship. This was lacking in Israel's relationship to God. They did not love Him, were not faithful to Him and the effects were clear for all to see in society. If husband and wife are not living in harmony, it affects the family and the home. The more a country or people turn their back on God, the more evil things become. We should never be surprised by the extent or depths of sin.

We will soon turn our backs on Him if we no longer love Him as we should. The way you prove and show that, is by keeping His commandments. Love for God is not just emotions; it is action. It is living a consistently faithful life. The Lord Jesus said, 'if you love me, you will keep my commandments' (John 14:15).

No knowledge of God (v. 1)

As well as no steadfast love, there was no knowledge of God. There are two types of knowledge: knowing about and actually knowing. You can know about someone without knowing them. Growing up, I knew all about my sporting heroes, players who played rugby for Wales and football for Tottenham. I could tell you all about them but I did not know them personally. In mind here, is both these kinds of knowledge. The Israelites did not really know about Yahweh and certainly did not know Him.

> There are two types of knowledge: knowing about and actually knowing.

Yahwehism had been mixed in with Baalism, so that the people were ignorant. Their view of God was not right; neither did they have a personal relationship with God. They did not know Him. They were robbed of understanding and sound judgement. This was evident in the way they thought about God, thought about themselves, worshipped God and lived their lives.

Verses 11–14 are framed by initial and concluding proverbial sayings which point to the mindless behaviour of those who act in this fashion. Their understanding has been taken away by 'whoredom, wine and new wine' (4:11), '... and a people without understanding shall come to ruin' (4:14).

This lack of understanding and knowledge of God means that their behaviour really was mindless (v. 12). They made idols out of wood: these were wooden pillars erected to represent the goddess Asherah at the Canaanite sacred sites (compare with Jeremiah 3:9). The walking staff was something that was whirled around, thrown down and the direction it fell could be taken as a divine sign to inform them how to proceed (Ezekiel 21:21). Without the knowledge of God, the people worshipped sacred trees (4:13), engaged in ritual prostitution (4:14) and asked a piece of wood for advice! They think a stick can tell them the future (4:12, New Living Translation).

This lack of knowledge is also evident in the descriptions Hosea gives us on how they worshipped God. Verses 11, 13, 14 and 18 provide insights into the Baal worship Israel was engaged in. It was conducted on elevated sites. Originally these sites were close to mountain tops where the worshippers believed they were nearer to the gods (Isaiah 57:7). Later 'high places' could just be artificially heightened sites in more accessible locations. Many sacred sites were surrounded by groves of trees. The oak and the terebinth and poplar provided relief from the scorching heat and sun. In Psalm 36:7 and 121:5, shade expresses the spiritual protection afforded by being close to God, but here the shade has merely secured physical relief from the glare of the sun.

The Baal cult also involved ritual prostitution, in which worshippers acted out the fertility sought from the gods with shrine prostitutes. The religion owed much of its appeal to the belief that one's crops could be magically made fertile through a sacrifice and sex act at the sanctuary.

The new wine mentioned generally refers to fresh wine or even newly pressed grape juice, unlike wine that has fermented for a long time (Proverbs 3:10; Isaiah 65:8). Yahweh provided this new wine for His people but they mistakenly attributed this to the Baals (Hosea 2:8-9, 22). In all likelihood such wine was consumed as part of the harvest festivals at which Baal was honoured. There, those who participated in the Canaanite cult, engaged in two major activities: to sacrifice and to burn incense (2:13).

The whole thing was a cocktail of sexual and alcoholic indulgence. Under the influence of drink, they indulged in all kinds of sexual promiscuity and orgies. Daughters and daughters-in-law became ensnared in the practices of Baal worship and lost their purity. Married women committed adultery, undermining the sanctity of their marriage vows. Men had sex with cult prostitutes as part of sacrifices and claimed women in the name of the goddess. Even though the women committed adultery and acted like prostitutes, they were exonerated more than the men because it was the men who had led women into this; husbands had encouraged their wives to take part.

You can see in some ways how Baal worship was very pleasant. It had an aesthetic attractiveness which would appeal to the senses. The sacred area was cool, the burning incense would give off a pleasing fragrance, and there would be meat to eat from some of the sacrifices.

Moreover, this was not just taking place at Baal shrines. It would seem such practices had invaded sites where it was ostensibly Yahweh who was worshipped. The Israelites tried to combine the best bits of Baalism with the best bits of Yahwehism. So, Israel committed adultery literally and metaphorically.

These verses underline that how we worship is important. It is not just about our feelings and what makes us feel good or *spiritual* or *tingly*. Right doctrine is fundamentally important in worship. We need to know who it is we are approaching and what is pleasing and acceptable to God. Our worship has to be Biblical. Many churches today have introduced things into the way they worship which make the worshipper feel good but are not glorifying to God. Some even try to copy how the world does things and introduce that into church. Our worship is all about what people want and what will attract them.

Furthermore, what we do on a Sunday needs to be consistent with what we do through the rest of the week. Our lives must be living sacrifices to Him. (Romans 12:1). Our lives must back up the words we say and sing.

But it is clear that we are all made to worship. If we do not worship God, then we will end up worshipping other things—anything. According to G.K Chesterton, 'When we cease to worship God, we do not worship nothing, we worship anything.'[1] We may not bow down to idols made of wood or stone today but we do bow down to idols: careers, houses, family, friends, image, our bodies, knowledge, fame, popularity, money, sport, sex, entertainment and leisure. In a nutshell, we worship ourselves. Whatever makes us feel good or we think will satisfy us and make us happy.

Once we start worshipping ourselves and we do not think about or consider God, we lose our ability to see clearly the reality of Him, His provision for us and His demands on our lives. Once the faculties have become dulled in this way, we are open to all kinds of debased conduct.

In the dock

THE PRIESTS (4:4–9)

Like people, like priest

After presenting the case for the prosecution, God puts the priests in the dock. This no doubt came as a surprise.

The priests probably thought, because they were priests, they were somehow immune from God's judgement. The people also undoubtedly looked up to them and found this unexpected. Yet it is to these men He says, '... let no one contend, and let none accuse, for with you is my contention, O priest' (4:4). He is saying in effect, 'You priests, don't start blaming the people or bringing charges against them; don't for a minute think you are not included. In fact, you priests are the worst!' It is '... like people, like priest ...' (v. 9).

In verse 5, Hosea mentions prophets as well. Together the priests and the prophets represent the religious leadership. The issue with these prophets was that they were not really the spokespeople of God. Rather they were prophets who spoke lies (Isaiah 9:15).

There is no special treatment for the priests. In fact, the reality is that their position makes them more culpable. While God's case is against the people of Israel, Hosea does not want the reader to regard the people as primarily responsible for this situation. It is the religious leaders.

The way the people think and act is evidence against the priests. The NIV translates verse 4 as, 'Your people are like those who bring charges against a priest'. The way the people are behaving is testimony to the fact that the priests are a disgrace to their high calling. The people do not want to be challenged about the way they are living and the priests do not want to be unpopular. But the priests and prophets are not ultimately answerable to the people but to God. Today, there are preachers who have congregations with just a handful of people, while others have a congregation of hundreds but, in reality, they all have a congregation of one—God!

Poor teaching

But what exactly was the problem with the priests?

First and foremost, they should have taught the people about God. Their primary function was to teach. Failure to teach people right is a grievous offence (Matthew 18:6; James 3:1). People perish because of ignorance of God and His Word (Hosea 4:6).

The responsibility of these priests was to teach the people about God. Failure to do this had an impact on the whole nation. Verse 6 says, '... I will also forget your children'. The priesthood was hereditary so this could mean your children will not become priests. But really, *children* here mean *all those who have been misled by the priests*. If we disown God's teaching, He will disown us and our children, the next generation. Therefore, nothing is more wicked than for someone to claim to speak for God but make a virtue out of the toleration of unbiblical teachings and ideas in the name of love and unity (2 Thessalonians 3:14; 1 Timothy 4:1–5; Titus 3:9–11).

Today we are all priests (1 Peter 2:9). In the Old

Testament, the people could only approach God through the high priest once a year (Hebrews 9:7). But today, we all have access to God through the Lord Jesus Christ. We are a kingdom of priests and a holy nation (Exodus 19:6; Isaiah 61:6). With this, we have a huge responsibility. In the way we live and by taking opportunities to speak to people, we should point them to the one and only Saviour.

Our responsibility is to rebuke one another and lead our brothers and sisters away from sin (Gal 6:1–3). We must tell the truth, even though people do not want to hear it (2 Timothy 4:3–4). In the 1980s, *Fleetwood Mac* sung a song which said, 'Tell me lies, tell me sweet little lies.' In other words, tell me what I want to hear. My wife and I went to the cinema once to watch Oceans 11. I whispered to her halfway through the film, 'Who's the best looking? Me, Brad Pitt or George Clooney?' She whispered back, 'I don't know, but you're definitely third!' I kind of knew, but wished she had told me what I wanted to hear.

> Our responsibility is to rebuke one another and lead our brothers and sisters away from sin.

The truth can be difficult to hear and even harder to live by, but deep down you know it is true. It is foolish to suppress it and deliberately reject it (Romans 1:18–32). Better to believe the truth than listen to and live a lie but end up in hell.

Bad motives

The vast majority of people who were in the priesthood had become priests out of bad motives. During times of prosperity in Jeroboam's reign, more people entered the priesthood. There was a status and privilege to the priesthood. The increase in the numbers of priests was seen as a sign of spiritual vitality but verse 7 says, 'The more they increased, the more they sinned against me.'

Verse 8 says, 'They feed on the sin of my people; they are greedy for their iniquity.' The word *sins* can also be translated *sin offerings*. In mind Hosea has the wickedness of the whole sacrificial system which had lost its original intent. Instead of a means of confession and grace, it had become a means of permissiveness for the people and gluttony for the priests. The priests were divinely entitled to eat portions of many sacrifices (Leviticus 24:9) and they became greedy for the people's sin offerings (Lev. 6:26). These offerings were made whenever Israel gathered to worship. The more sacrifices the better, so the priests would not do or say anything to correct the moral situation in the land. Furthermore, the wickedness of the laity increased the power of the religious professionals because it gave the leaders a means of manipulation.

The priest of Bethel, Amaziah, gives us an insight into the state of the priesthood just before this time (Amos 7:10–17). He served at a shrine founded and maintained by the kings of Israel. He was an establishment figure who was career minded and committed to preserving the status quo. He had no regard for the truth. But God was about to bring priests like this into disgrace. People would recognise them for the frauds they were.

Before the Reformation, Roman Catholic priests played on the fear and superstition of poorly instructed people to get them to do what they wanted. Even today, parts of the so-called church tell people to live as they want, so long as they do not hurt other people. 'Please yourself, no one is perfect; who is anyone else to tell you how to live?' They do not want to offend people, so they say, 'Do what you like, we will get God to fit in with you'. They just want to protect their position, influence and status. Some churches are in danger of going down a path that will do pretty much whatever it takes to keep people happy and attending. And it is not just the church. Today there are industries that feed on people's sins and addictions. Drugs, alcohol and sex are big business.

THE LEADERSHIP (5:1–2)

So far, the brunt of the attack has been on the priests but, as well as the priests being in the dock, Israel's leaders are too. God rounds on them because they have willingly been led by the priests (5:1–2). Hosea uses the words, 'Hear', 'pay attention', 'give ear', to emphasize the importance of concentrating on the message he wants to get across to them.

Three groups within Israel's leadership are highlighted in 5:1–2. The priests, already mentioned, are one group. They considered themselves as worshipping the Lord but they had readily adopted innovations drawn from Canaanite practice. This compromised priesthood was founded by Jeroboam I (1 Kings 12:31). The second group within the leadership were royalty, 'house of the king'. The third group was the' house of Israel'. This was the middle and upper classes. The ones who thought of themselves, and actually were, the backbone of the country. Not the political or the religious elite but neither the impoverished peasants or landless labourers.

> While the commoners were responsible for their apostasy, the leaders had shown them the way.

Together, these three groups had control of the institution, Israel. This leadership took the people into the decadence of the fertility cult, with the result that the worship of Yahweh was hollow and without repentance. While the commoners were responsible for their apostasy, the leaders had shown them the way.

An example of what was happening was at Mizpah and Tabor. While there were lots of towns called Mizpah, the one mentioned here is probably the most important one—the Mizpah in Benjamin located some ten kilometres north of Jerusalem. Like Gilgal and Bethel, Mizpah was one of the principal cities on Samuel's itinerary (1 Samuel 7). It was an important city for the tribes before the monarchy and it probably contained a sanctuary.

Tabor was a mountain much further in the North, some twenty kilometres southwest of the Sea of Galilee. It was the scene of the victory of Deborah and Barak. It rose above the Jezreel valley but was now infamous. Tabor was probably the location of a 'high place', a cult shrine to the fertility gods.

To get caught up with what was done there, was to wander into a trap. These kind of sites were sacred to the people and sponsored by the leadership. They were traps that induced the ordinary people into apostasy. Through these sites, the leaders wooed hundreds of frequenters away from the true faith.

But what they had done to others would happen to them. God says to them, 'And I [am] a fetter to them all' (Hosea 5:2, YLT). The traps, nets and pits they had used to ensnare would, in the end, trap them. Through their policies, they had led people deeply into sin, 'deep into slaughter', but now they would face judgement. 'Fetters' implies captivity, which indeed was the fate of Israel.

In mind here is not necessarily the exile. It could refer to hardship that would involve God in withdrawing their previous prosperity and causing drought and famine (compare with 2:9; 4:3). The word *discipline* brings hope, not final punishment. What God really wants is for them to return and acknowledge Him (5:4).

Witnesses

Israel is in the dock. The case for the prosecution has been brought against them. Now the witnesses are called for.

GOD

The first witness is God. God has seen all that is going on. He says that Israel is not hidden from Him (Hosea 5:3). He has mother Israel in mind—the culture and institution. By mentioning the leading tribe Ephraim, it is not the specific tribe but the cultural leaders that Hosea is particularly focused on. They had led the people into paganism and immorality. Ever since Jeroboam I had installed calf idols in Bethel and Dan, the institutions of Israel had been guiding the people into apostasy and immorality resulting in them becoming defiled or corrupted. God had noticed it all and it was loathsome to Him. Above all they had turned to prostitution. Hosea's central accusation was that God's people were serving other gods like an adulterous wife (1:2; 5:7).

Israel may no longer know or care about God, but God knows all about them. God's knowing is never cold.

He cares and it matters to Him. Despite their sin and rebellion, He still persists; He will not give up on them. Isaiah 57:18 says, *'I have seen his ways, but I will heal him.'*

OUR OWN WITNESS

The next witness brought to the stand is Israel herself. According to verse 5, 'The pride of Israel testifies to his face; Israel and Ephraim shall stumble in his guilt; Judah also shall stumble with them.'

Israel is arrogant in court. The political, social and religious leaders are in focus. They were self-sufficient and self-assertive and thought they had the right to rule; they threw off all allegiance to God and reliance upon him for their wellbeing.

But pride always goes before a fall and they are saddled with guilt. The court of public opinion testifies to Israel's face. The nation is about to fall and everyone will be able to see why and who and what it was down to. Israel says to herself, 'Look at the laws you've passed, look where it has all led to.' While the people seemed to enjoy it while it lasted, they now can see it for what it is, the damage it has done, and the danger they are in. And it is all their own fault. They testify against themselves.

The same spirit was in Judah. It is as if Hosea says, 'By the way, Judah is going the same way as Israel.'

CREATION

The third witness is creation. In Hosea 4:3, we have a

personification of the land. Everything is affected. The entire population, including wildlife, withers and pines away and the land is suffering drought. Animals, birds, fish are all disappearing. The whole of creation (earth, sky, sea) is suffering the wrath of God. Creation testifies that something is wrong.

When Adam fell in the Garden of Eden (Genesis 3), the whole creation was cursed (Romans 8:20–22). Romans 8:22 says, 'For we know that the whole creation has been groaning together in the pains of childbirth until now.' The fact the world we live in is no longer perfect, is down to what we call *The Fall*. The Fall is the cause of all the problems in the world today—has been from the beginning and will be right up to the end. Not only did humankind fall but the whole of creation is now under a curse. This explains the natural disasters that occur and cause such devastation. Earth produces thorns and thistles. All of creation fell so that creation itself now eagerly awaits freedom from its decay (Romans 8:20-25).

The judgement

The witnesses prove that the case against Israel is just. As with all court cases, if found guilty the judge makes a judgement.

There is a judgement

The first thing to say is that there is a judgement (4:5, 9, 14). God says to the Israelites, '*I will destroy your mother'* (4:5). As we know, mother is a metaphor for the institutional Israel. Destroying 'your mother', refers to the overthrow of the power and prerogatives of the religious leadership.

The orgies and drinking are about to come to an end. 'Stumble' in verse 5 is not a minor loss of balance but a major, fatal disaster which befalls those who abandon the way of God. It will be day and night a constant disaster. Israel is warned that they are about to go into exile and we know that the exile did happen. If you had been around in Israel 722 BC, sadness would have sunk into your spirit as you would have seen the exiles being dragged off to Assyria and wall-less ruins smoking in Israel.

An even sadder and terrifying day will one day come, when all who have sinned against God and refused to repent and trust in the Lord Jesus Christ, will be thrown into hell by an angry God.

Given over

Before this final judgement, God will give them over to their sin. Verse 7 says, 'I will change their glory into shame.' They will become a disgrace.

Romans chapter 1 is like a commentary on what is happening in Israel at the time of Hosea. The people have 'exchanged the glory of the immortal God for images resembling mortal man and birds and animals and creeping things' (Romans 1:23). They do not worship God anymore.

They have 'exchanged the truth about God for a lie' (Romans 1:25). They do not trust God anymore. As a result, God gives them over to sinful desires, shameful lusts and a depraved mind (Romans 1:24, 26, 28). The outcome of exchanging the truth of God for a lie, is that they end up worshipping and serving created things rather than the creator (Rom. 1:25). If we continue to sin, God gives individuals and nations over to their sin. We become hardened to God and think that wrong is right and right is wrong.

NEW GENERATION

Because they had been given over, there was now a generation that did not know about the things of God (Hosea 5:7). The apostasy of Israelite culture has given rise to a generation that could more accurately be called children of Baal than children of Yahweh. They had no knowledge of God. They did not know Him. They were now children of foreign gods.

This is true of the day and age we live in. There is a generation now who know nothing about true Biblical Christianity. We live in a pluralistic, liberal society. There are lots of religions and each is given equal credence. We are led to believe that none of them are right but none of them are wrong. Whatever you want to believe is permissible as long as you are not too extreme and what you believe does not impinge on others. Everyone seems to have an opinion on everything, especially God. Rather than someone to be feared, God is a topic for discussion and debate.

All this would be well and good if it was not for the fact that one day we have to stand before the only true and living God—the one who said that there is no other God beside him (Isaiah 45:5). When we stand before

> Rather than someone to be feared, God is a topic for discussion and debate.

Him, heaven and hell will be at stake and the only name under heaven given among men whereby we must and can be saved (Acts 4:12) said, 'I am the way, the truth and the life. No one comes to the Father except through me' (John 14:6).

No satisfaction

As well as having to stand at the judgement, the result of the way Israel were living would be worse for them in this life too. Instead of society being happier and safer, there will be no satisfaction. Hosea 4:10 says, 'They shall eat, but not be satisfied; they shall play the whore, but not multiply, because they have forsaken the Lord to cherish...' This could be translated, 'For the Lord they have abandoned to keep' or 'abandoned keeping faith with Yahweh'.

The Israelites had sexual intercourse with the sacred prostitutes to secure the fertility of the land. The priests thought that fulfilling the sacred rites would ensure that they would become more prosperous—their wives would bear children, their livestock would calve, and they would enjoy the life of plenty. But God tells them they will 'play the whore but not multiply' (4:10). Only Yahweh could give fertility and prosperity. Baal was impotent. Their idols could not provide for them. They would be shamed and the downturn in their national circumstances, and the defeat and slaughter and capture they will experience, would mean they would be unable to increase in number (compare with Hosea 9:11–14, 16).

They put all their hope in food, sex, wealth and religion but none of it would satisfy. All of it would leave them feeling discontented.

GOD WALKS AWAY

But worst of all, God walks away. According to 5:6: 'With their flocks and herds they shall go to seek the LORD, but they will not find him; he has withdrawn from them'.

These are chilling words. God withdraws from them. God is going. God is a jealous God and will not share His glory with another (Isaiah 42:8). He was married to Israel and demanded faithfulness. It was a religious age so there was plenty of ritual and ceremony. But their religion was full of hypocrisy. Israel was treating Yahweh like Baal, another god to placate through sacrifice and offering.

They still celebrated festivals and religious occasions (Hosea 5:7), but there was no heartfelt seeking after God—just liturgy. Isaiah 1:14 says, 'Your new moons and your appointed feasts my soul hates.' The very festivals that were relied on to placate God, were in fact the sharpest provocation to Him. The new moon devouring them in Hosea 5:7 is literally describing a time when the moon is invisible and the night is black. Prophets spoke of the moon going dark as a sign of the day of Yahweh (Joel 2:10; 3:15). It speaks of an eschatological darkness.

Another prophet, Amos, draws the contrast between authentic returning to Yahweh and the pilgrimages to shrines (Amos 5:4–5). What Yahweh wants is for us to come with a contrite heart.

God is clearly angry but this anger is out of love, not hate. As we shall see throughout the book, His relentless harrying of them is designed to bring them to Himself.

A warning

God turns from addressing Israel to Judah. Hosea 5:5 says, 'Judah also shall stumble with them.' Judah were not so immersed in pagan practices but Hosea says to them, 'you too Judah are in danger'. Hosea 4:15 is a prayer for Judah, 'Though you play the whore, O Israel, let not Judah become guilty.'

Hosea 4:15–19 describes the pagan worship and debauchery that Israel stubbornly refused to give up and says to Judah, 'Do not become like them.' God is pleading with them not to go down the same path.

Maybe you are like Judah. You are attracted by sin and all that it seems to offer. But God pleads with you too not to go down this broad path that will lead to destruction (Matthew 7:13–14).

> God pleads with you too not to go down this broad path that will lead to destruction.

In 1986, there was a crash on the M25 due to a thick fog. Cars were travelling at high speed and could not see in time and crashed into other cars. You could hear the screams. Policemen stood on the side of the road leading up to the crash, doing all they could to stop the cars. They even threw traffic cones at the cars to get them to stop. In these verses, if you are still in your sin, Hosea is, as it were, throwing a Gospel cone at you, pleading with you to stop, because there is eternal danger ahead.

Beware of tradition

He warns them not to rely on traditions. Hosea 4:15 says, 'Enter not into Gilgal, nor go up to Beth-aven, and swear not, "As the Lord lives."'

Gilgal and Bethel were places in the North but very near Judah. They were places with an illustrious history but not anymore. Things that were good in the past may become corrupt and unhealthy, so need to be abandoned.

Bethel was the chief sanctuary of the North. It was ten miles from Jerusalem. Bethel was more sacred than Gilgal (Gen. 12:8; 28:11–19a; 31:1–15). Jeroboam I took advantage of sacred traditions associated with it, to rival Jerusalem (1 Kings 12:29), but prophets condemned this as apostasy (1 Kings 13).

The use of 'Beth-aven' in 4:15 and 5:8 is a pun and most certainly refers to Bethel. Bethel means *house of God* but it is no longer a *house of God*. Now it is Beth-aven—house of wickedness.

Gilgal was also a place of great significance in the history of Israel (Joshua 4:19; 5:7–12; 1 Sam 7:16; 1 Sam 11:14–15; 2 Samuel 19:15; 2 Kings 4:38). But by the eighth century, Amos and Hosea tell the people to stay away from them (Amos 4:4; 5:5).

He tells them, do not swear or make oaths by these places. Many heroes of the faith made oaths and said, 'As the LORD lives' (Ruth 3:13; 1 Samuel 20:3; 1 Kings 2:24; 2 Chronicles 18:13; Jeremiah 12:16). In Matthew 5:34, the Lord Jesus forbids making oaths. The point here is we are not to use God's name lightly.

Today we need to be aware of traditions. There are churches, conferences, Bible colleges and organisations that were once places where God's Word was preached and His presence was felt. They were the scenes of real blessing. If you are a Christian, there may be a place you think of which brings back really happy memories— somewhere that reminds you of times when you enjoyed fellowship with other Christians; the singing was glorious; you heard great preaching; met some of your best friends; felt the presence of God. You loved going there. But now they have changed or are changing. Like Mizpah and Tabor, one-time great Christian organisations and events can change; so-called churches that use the name of the Lord Jesus Christ can end up being places that can lead you astray.

We also need to ensure that we do not do things for the sake of tradition but judge everything by the Word of God.

Stubborn rebellion

As well as relying on tradition, Israel was also guilty of stubborn rebellion. Verse 16 of chapter 4 says, 'Like a stubborn heifer, Israel is stubborn; can the Lord now feed them like a lamb in a broad pasture?'

In mind is a cow that refuses to go where her owner leads (Jeremiah 31:18). Obstinate, refusing to comply with her master's instructions. Israel was incorrigible in her evil ways. She had an unbreakable attachment to idols. Her stubbornness made it impossible for God to give her peace and prosperity. Her Master wants to shepherd her and do what is best for her but she will not be led where her Master wants her to go and therefore cannot enjoy what He would give her.

We too are rebels. We hate being told what to do and think we know best. Today, God only wants what is best for us but we think the grass is always greener. Sin seems so attractive but it will always end in ruin.

Too far

By now, Israel had gone too far. Hosea 4:17 says, 'Ephraim is joined to idols; leave him alone.' Verse 19 goes on to say, 'A wind has wrapped them in its wings, and they shall be ashamed because of their sacrifices,' and chapter 5 verse 4 says, 'Their deeds do not permit them to return to their God. For the spirit of whoredom is within them, and they know not the LORD.'

Ephraim was the most important tribe in the North and often a term used to represent Israel as a whole. Thirty-six times in Hosea, Ephraim is used to describe Israel.

Israel has gone after idols: they are wedded to idols; left God to be with idols; bewitched by idols like they are in a trance. No words will get through to them. They have lost their capacity to think straight.

The word 'wind' here is same as *spirit*. A spirit of whoredom has led them astray and taken over them.

Perhaps, at the time, that spirit brought with it a sense of excitement. But now, that spiritual promiscuity has wrapped itself around like a tornado and is sweeping them into destruction.

They are addicted to sin and all its pleasures. It has a stranglehold on them and they are a prisoner of their habits. 'Their deeds do not permit them to return to their God' (5:4). The whole book of Hosea is a study in what it means to return to God. Repentance is always possible, but corruption can so enslave a soul that repentance becomes a practical impossibility. We can get to a stage where we are unable to repent. God hides himself completely from those who continually sin against Him. You can harden your heart until eventually God hardens your heart (Exodus 9:12).

Perhaps it is true of you. There was a time you went to church. Believed these things. Knew they were true. But Jesus Christ and His demands do not fit in with your lifestyle anymore. It bothers you a bit from time to time but the more you fill your life with things, the better it gets. You have spent your life suppressing the truth and it is working. You know what you need to do but you just do not want to do it. It is too hard right now to give things up. There is nothing else to say apart from repent and believe. If you hear His voice, harden not your heart (Hebrews 3:15).

FOR FURTHER STUDY.

1. Who or what is most important in your life?

2. Can you truthfully say, 'I put the Lord first'?

TO THINK ABOUT AND DISCUSS

1. Are we angry when the preacher gives a word of rebuke, or do we examine our lives?

2. Does it frighten or comfort us to know that God sees everything?

6 On the battlefield

Hosea 5:8–15

So far Hosea has taken us to his wedding, the maternity ward, his home, the wilderness, the slave market and the court room. Now in Chapter 5:8–15, we find ourselves on the battlefield.

Sound the alarm

Chapter 5 verse 8 says, 'Blow the horn in Gibeah, the trumpet in Ramah. Sound the alarm at Beth-aven ...'

In mind is a ram's horn or shofar—a metal trumpet of some kind. In the Old Testament these had various uses. For example, in Numbers 10:1–10, it was sounded to call the people to sacred assemblies. But, here, it is being used as a military horn. It is an alarm call to muster the local defence forces because of the threat of invasion. The alarm would be the equivalent of an air raid siren in the Second World War. It is sounded because a day of punishment is imminent; Ephraim are about to be desolated (5:9). They will be crushed in judgement because of their determination to go after the filth of this world and the mockery of God's Word (5:11).

The same alarm is sounded today to warn all who continue in sin. The job of preachers is to warn people about death, eternity, the judgement and urge them to come to Jesus Christ in repentance and faith. Every Sunday up and down our land and all over the world, preachers stand in pulpits and 'sound the alarm' (5:8). As Richard Baxter, the Puritan pastor, put it, they preach as 'a dying man to dying men'.[1]

Despite the seriousness and eternal consequences of it, people take no notice of the alarm. They continually refuse to repent and heed the warnings. God offers them a Saviour who can save to the uttermost all who will come to Him but people wilfully and arrogantly refuse. So, God sends suffering or disaster on nations or individuals to warn them more dramatically to repent. He does this, not because He is cruel, but because He is merciful. If He was cruel, He would not warn us at all, but simply send us immediately to hell. It is His will that none should perish (2 Peter 3:9). C.S. Lewis[2] said that suffering and disasters are like God's megaphone to rouse a sinful, unrepenting world.

An alarm is sounded in these verses to warn the Israelites they are heading for a judgement that will crush them and see them carried off into exile. But there is a far greater judgement to come (2 Corinthians 5:10; Romans 2:5), that will result in heaven or hell. The church needs to raise the alarm and all those not trusting in Jesus Christ need to come to Him in repentance and faith. Disasters, tragedies, death, troubles should drive us to 'look up for the end is near' (Luke 21:28).

> Disasters, tragedies, death, troubles should drive us to 'look up for the end is near'.

All in this together

As we have already seen, when Hosea refers to Ephraim he is talking about the Northern Kingdom of Israel as a whole. Today it would be like London being referred to but the whole of the UK is in mind. However, it is not just the Northern Kingdom who needs to be alarmed; Judah needs to worry too.

Israel by now is under serious threat from the Assyrians and Judah is trying to take advantage of Israel's weakness by annexing its territory. They are making the most out of Israel's troubles by grabbing their land (Hosea 5:10). They are nothing more than common thieves (Micah 2:2; Isaiah 5:8).

On the part of Judah there is no compassion or heartbreak over the plight of Israel—no thought that they were once the united people of God. In 5:9, Hosea uses deliberately archaic language. He says, 'Among the tribes of Israel', which hearkens back to the days of the judges when all twelve tribes were held together by the common bond of being the 'children of Israel'. It is a rebuke for a lack of unity among the tribes of Israel. Furthermore, it is making the point that all the tribes of Israel, North and South, will suffer terribly at the hands of foreigners.

The reference to Benjamin in verse 8 is not to the northern borders but the southern borders of Israel. The three towns mentioned, Gibeah, Ramah and Bethel (or Beth-aven), were all located in Benjamin more or less in a line directly north of Jerusalem. These were place names that straddled the border of the two kingdoms. It was a clear warning that the invader would penetrate Israel to its southmost extremity. It was intended to alarm the Benjaminite cities of Gibeah and Ramah, which lay only just beyond that boundary, even as the doomed Beth-aven lay just within it. When Assyria invades, they will penetrate deep into Israel and out the other side. The invading army will spread throughout the land.

So instead of taking advantage of their neighbour's troubles, Judah needs to be afraid. Both kingdoms are under threat. Israel and Judah must turn to God in repentance and faith or face His withdrawal of protection against the Assyrian threat.

Today we need to heed the same warning. Being in church, not thinking we are as bad as others, having an outward façade of respectability, is not enough to avert the threat of a holy God. The danger is not only directed at 'them out there'.

We can also sit in our 'sound' evangelical churches and pour scorn on more liberal churches. We pride ourselves in holding to the inerrancy and infallibility of the Word of God. But the question is, what are we doing with it? Furthermore, are our services really about worshipping God and glorifying Him, or are they more about making us feel good and addressing our needs, appetites and wants? Are they truly biblical and God centred? Far from feeling proud and looking down on others, we should examine ourselves, be thankful to God for His grace and kindness to us, make the most of our privileges and have a real compassion towards others which drives us to prayer.

Being within the confines of a church, however sound, is no defence against the wrath of God.

The Puritan, John Bunyan, in his famous book *The Pilgrims Progress*, which he wrote while in prison in 1676, describes the glorious scene at the end of the book when *Christian* enters heaven. He also describes *Ignorance* arriving at the gates. *Ignorance* thought he was a Christian but he was not, and on arrival at heaven he gets turned away. His hands and feet are bound and he is thrown out. Bunyan[3] comments, 'Then I saw that there was a way to Hell even from the gates of Heaven.'

The same is true of every church and chapel, every Christian camp, conference and youth group. There is a way to hell from every one of them.

No one to call on for help

Israel and Judah finally realize they are grievously ill; they know they are in trouble—big trouble. And there is no one they can call on for help. The reference to sickness and sores in verse 13 describes the swift loss of power and wealth that Israel and Judah experienced in the latter part of the eighth century. It is difficult to know what events in particular the prophet is referring to. Some see the backdrop to this part of the prophecy as the war between Judah and the Syro-Ephramite coalition (2 Kings 16:1–9; 2 Chronicles 28:5–7; Isaiah 7:1–8:22; Micah 7:7–20). This was when Pekah formed an alliance with Rezin of Syria to try to escape the authority of Assyria. For this they wanted the help of Judah, but Ahaz, king of Judah, refused. So, Israel and Syria joined together to fight against Judah and force Ahaz to join their anti-Assyrian coalition. Ahaz responded to this threat by calling on the help of Tiglath-Pileser III. Isaiah the prophet supported the refusal of Ahaz to join the coalition but considered an appeal to Assyria to be a desertion of Yahweh.

The problem with this viewpoint is that, in this chapter, Judah is portrayed as the aggressor (5:10), whereas during the war between Judah and the Syro-Ephramite coalition Isaiah tells us that Ahaz and Judah were terrified (Isaiah 7:2). It was also during this war that Judah turned to Assyria for help, whereas in this passage in Hosea it is Ephraim (Israel).

That being the case, others think Hosea could be speaking about the desperate payment scraped together for Assyria by Israel's king, Menahem. The king of Assyria invaded Israel and Menahem bought the Assyrians off with a tribute of 1000 talents raised by taxing the people of Israel. This was not only meant to buy off an invasion already begun, but to get external backing for Menahem's precarious kingship—for he was a usurper who had waded through particularly vile slaughter to the throne. His story, which included the butchery of a whole town's pregnant women, is summarized in 2 Kings 15:16–22. Menahem's reign was propped up but within twenty years Assyria proved to be the very nation marked out as Israel's executioner. Israel soon flirted from one great power to another, playing off Egypt against Assyria, and Assyria against Egypt.

It is more likely this passage refers to the general political events of the latter part of the eighth century BC. What is very clear is that when Israel wakes up to its predicament, to save its skin it flies straight to Assyria for help. This is the first reference in Hosea to Assyria. 'The great king' (5:13) is based on an emendation to the text but is probably correct. Whether Hosea is referring to a particular political event or political events in general, Assyria cannot help Israel and Israel has done wrong simply by virtue of seeking the aid of a foreign power. In not seeking Yahweh, they committed apostasy.

What is true of ancient Israel is true of the vast majority today. We turn to anything and everything before God. Perhaps this is true of you. You realize you are not right. You feel guilty

> We turn to anything and everything before God.

and unhappy. You have tried to remedy this by turning to all kinds of things to help you out. You try to entertain yourself or seek after pleasure; you chase money, career, popularity or academic excellence. You make your family your god. Maybe in recognising your 'sickness' (5:13), you have turned to religion or you have told yourself there is no God and have embraced a way of life or a particular world view that you now live for. None of these things will make you better or make you truly happy. Not even church attendance will help, neither will relying on Christian parents or upbringing or some goodness you think you have.

We will all one day stand before the judgement seat of God and we will stand before it alone. None of the things we have gone to for help and support or to take our minds off things or have lived for will be able to help us then. There will be no one to call on for help at the judgement.

God is like moth and dry rot

I wonder how you would describe God. What similes would you use or what comparisons would you draw? In Hosea 5:12–14, God's opposition to Israel and Judah is described by using the harshest and most astonishing metaphors. God describes Himself as a moth and dry rot. He does this to make Israel and Judah realize that something far worse than the Assyrians is coming their way. God is!

Rot describes something that causes decay while moths were a major pest in the ancient world—silently but steadily devouring garments. However, since the metaphor, extended into v. 13, relates to a diseased or wounded body (and not clothing), 'moth' is probably not the intended sense here. Moth could also refer to a maggot in an open wound or puss from the wound. We therefore should envisage here a wounded man, left unattended, whose injuries fester in the most horrible manner.

The meaning is clear. While Israel and Judah were fearing the sound of marching armies and the Assyrians about to take over their country, they should be more worried about the silent process of decay that God was giving them over to.

Dale Ralph Davis[4] tells the story of when they once had a basketball hoop in their backyard. The backboard was composed of pressed board and was not highly weather-resistant. On a particular day after a particular shot, the right side of the backboard came loose and hung down. That was only the final result. The process of decay had been going on for months as the backboard rotted away around the heads of the bolts that held it in place, until the bolts no longer held anything together and that last shot jarred the backboard loose.

Today we live in a noisy world. Everyone seems to have an opinion on everything, especially on God. Rather than someone to be feared, God is a topic for discussion and debate. Governments and politicians, entertainers, commentators, journalists, 'experts', scientists and religious leaders have all put themselves above God. They decide what is right and wrong. They announce whether they agree or disagree on what the Bible says, which bits to take out and leave in, which bits need modernising and sanitising for our era—the parts of Christianity that are acceptable and the bits to be dismissed as relics of a bygone era. They pass laws that oppose the Word of God and even dictate what children are taught in schools about these things. Some get angry with the bits that cut across what they want to do and think, others just mock or dismiss it all as irrelevant in this day and age.

All the while God is observing from heaven, seemingly silent and passive. Far from an irrelevance, the reality is that God is leaving us to it, letting the things we have turned our back on Him for, destroy us, until the day comes when we will all stand before Him and give an account of our lives.

At some point, God hands us over and sin ends up being totally in control. He lifts his hand of restraint and says as it were, 'If that's what you want, have it and let it destroy you' (Romans 1:24, 26, 28).

> At some point, God hands us over and sin ends up being totally in control.

We cannot play around with God or presume upon His grace. He can warn and warn and warn us, but one day He will withdraw His Spirit from us and our hearts will become hardened towards Him, and all we will be able to do is face judgement and eternal damnation. Some cross the line between God's patience and His wrath before they die (Matthew 12:32; Romans 1:24; 1 John 5:16; Exodus 8:32; 9:12).

God pleads for so long but will finally say enough is enough and let us rot and decay. One of our shots will be the last shot that brings the basketball hoop down!

Repent now before it is too late and you will not want or be able to (Hebrews 12:17; Exodus 10:20).

God is like a lion

But, as well as describing Himself as a moth and dry rot, in Hosea 5:14 God describes himself as a lion. Hosea has moved from portraying God as a flesh-eating moth to a flesh-eating lion. The point being, they are already in a lengthy state of decay but the final conquest would come upon them with the ferocity of a lion. After the long rotting and decaying, there will come a sudden violent end.

Israel was desperate to appease Assyria and it was Assyria that was uppermost in their minds. But they needed to realize they were up against a far more terrifying enemy—God! They were at war with God.

It is important to note too that in 5:14 the pronoun 'I' is strongly emphasized. There is a contrast between the power of Yahweh and the power of Assyria. It is completely hopeless to turn to human help to save what God has determined to demolish; no one will be able to come to the rescue.

There may be things, situations and people that you are desperate to please and keep happy; you worry what people think of you. But the main issue is your relationship with God. Jesus Christ said, 'do not fear those who kill the body ... Rather fear him who can destroy both soul and body in hell' (Matthew 10:28). Death, standing before God at the judgement, hell, eternity, are all terrifying. You may try to convince yourself that after death there is nothing, but you know that is just not true. If that was the case, why do we fear death? An animal just finds a corner, curls up and dies. But we know death is not the end. After death is the judgement (Hebrews 9:27), and sinners going to this judgement alone will be condemned to an eternal hell—a place of fire and darkness, where people are weeping and are in so much pain, they gnash their teeth (Matthew 8:12; 13:42; 22:13; 25:30, 41; Mark 9:43). It is a place of distress and misery. All the things we enjoy on earth will be gone forever. It is impossible to imagine how awful it will be; never being able to hear music ever again; never tasting good food ever again; never having your thirst quenched; absolute darkness; horrible loneliness; never feeling loved or cared for. What a terrible plight to find yourself in for all eternity! (Revelation 18).

Worst of all, it will be forever. No chance of escape. No end to it all.

Certain

And all of this is certain (5:9). What Hosea and the other prophets prophesied came to pass. We know that the Assyrians ransacked and ravaged the land. In 722

BC, Israel was completely wiped out and destroyed and Judah became a vassal state (2 Chronicles 28:16–21). In 701 BC, Judah was brought to its knees surviving by a hair's breadth, only to collapse a little more than a century later. The two nations once again simply became the children of Israel with no land.

As certain as Israel and Judah being carried off into exile, is the judgement to come. Just over two thousand years ago, Jesus Christ came into this world and became a man. At thirty-three, He died on a cross, was buried and rose again, and forty days later many people saw Him ascend back into heaven. As the people gazed up into the sky and watched Him return to heaven, two angels asked them, 'Why do you stand looking into heaven? This Jesus, who was taken up from you into heaven, will come in the same way as you saw him go into heaven' (Acts 1:11). In Revelation 1:7, John says, 'Behold, [take note!] He is coming with the clouds, and every eye will see Him.' Jesus Christ is coming back! One day, no one knows when, He will bring all things to an end. The first time He came to this world, He came quietly and humbly; the next time He comes, a trumpet will sound and everyone who has ever lived will be summoned to stand before Him and be judged by Him.

Not a typical lion

Continuing the lion metaphor, but taking us in an

unnatural direction, Yahweh declares that He will turn back and go to His lair where He will await Israel's repentance. Verse 15 says, 'I will return again to my place, until they acknowledge their guilt and seek my face, and in their distress earnestly seek me.'

Lions never behave like this. After devouring their prey, lions do not offer a new chance to its prey. But God is not bound by convention and He is not a typical lion.

Even though God is angry with Israel and is about to come to them in judgement, He really wants them to repent. His heart is for them. It does not have to be like this. Israel have been told to sound the alarm because they are about to go to war with God, but in verse 15 it is as though God is saying, 'Let's sort it out so we don't need to go to war.' Going to war against people is God's last resort. He would rather engage in peace talks. Isaiah 1:18 says, 'Come now, let us reason together says the LORD: though your sins are like scarlet they shall be as white as snow; though they are red like crimson they shall become like wool.'

Maybe you are right now sinning and rebelling against God. Perhaps you are up to your neck in sin and know that you have deeply offended a holy God. You may think that you are too far gone and hell bound. The good news is that right now the lion, that will tear you to pieces if you remain in your sin, is in His lair waiting for you to come to Him in repentance. Apparently, the American evangelist, Billy Graham, once spoke to Winston Churchill about the Saviour but Churchill replied by saying, 'It's too late for me.' But it is not too late.

There is a way back to God from the dark paths of sin
There's a way that is open that all may go in
At Calvary's cross is where you begin
When you come as a sinner to Jesus
(E.H. Swinstead, 1882–1950)

However, if you want to find Him, you have to earnestly seek Him (Hebrews 11:6); you must be serious about Him and seek Him with all of your heart (Jeremiah 29:13). God says in Hosea 5:15, they will find me when they 'seek my face ... seek me early'(AKJV). Pray, read the Bible, meditate upon it, turn away from sin, resist temptation, put yourself in the way of good things and do not give up until you find Him.

For further study ▶

FOR FURTHER STUDY

1. Does the thought that the unconverted are going to hell concern us?

2. It is never too late to seek the Saviour. Look to Him

TO THINK ABOUT AND DISCUSS.

1. Does the thought of Christ's return to earth excite or unsettle you?

2. What do I need to change in my life to live closer to God?

7 Come to God

Hosea 6

Yahweh declares that He would retire to His place and wait for His people to come looking for Him again. Now 6:1–3 calls for them to come to Him in repentance. The invitation is given to return to the Lord. They were in a sorry plight, a pitiful condition, facing total ruin and the only remedy is to run to the One who has taken them to court and declared war on them. The amazing offer is given in Hosea 6:1, 'Come ... to the LORD'.

Come

In chapter 4 and the beginning of chapter 5 we found ourselves in the courtroom. Charges against Israel, supported by damning evidence, were laid out and the verdict of judgement made certain.

In chapter 5:8–15, Hosea takes us to the battlefield

where the Israelites are told to sound the alarm because they are under threat. They are at war. With God!

But, at the end of chapter 5, and more explicitly at the beginning of chapter 6, there is a dramatic intervention. There is still hope.

Hosea 6:1 says, '... for he has torn us, that he may heal us; he has struck us down, and he will bind us up.' God is a strange prosecutor and a peculiar enemy. He does not take Israel to court so that they get what they deserve—to get what is coming to them. Neither does He surprise them with an attack but He warns them of His coming. He calls for the horn to be blown and the alarm to be sounded. His purpose in taking Israel to court or declaring war is that she will turn to Him in repentance and faith.

Throughout Hosea is the threat of judgement. But the longed-for outcome of God's judgements is to show Israel, and us, that if we turn away from God, we will face misery and judgement but if we return to Him we will know peace and happiness. From His heart, God says to us 'Come'.

So come to God. There is no greater word in the Bible, when it emanates from the lips of God, than the word 'come' (Isaiah 1:18; Isaiah 55:1; Matthew 11:28).

But maybe you are worried you will not get a welcome. You think that you have to get yourself better before you come. Some of you are in a relationship or family situation where you have messed up. Some are in emotional trauma; some are in grief and sorrow or the clutches of temptation. Some of you have ruined your reputations; some of you may have committed a *big* sin that haunts you. You are in a mess. But as Davis puts it, 'Yahweh is not a white gloved, standoffish God out somewhere in the remote left field of the universe who hesitates to get his strong right arm dirty in the yuck of our lives.'[1] So, you must come to him. Just as you are.

My dad was a minister in Pontypridd. A tramp called Frank would come in every Sunday night to listen to him preach. He was an alcoholic, reeked of drink, dirty and scruffy. After a while, Frank suddenly stopped coming. A few months later, Dad was in his car and saw him standing, waiting for the bus, in the pouring rain. My dad pulled over and told him to get in. He said, 'Where have been Frank, we've missed you?' Frank said that a couple of the deacons had told him to stop coming to church until he cleaned himself up and stopped smelling of drink! Can I tell you on the authority of God's Word, come to Jesus Christ as you are; in your mess, with your flagons, caped in all your sin and say with the hymn writer, Charlotte Elliott (1789–1871):

Just as I am without one plea
But that thy blood was shed for me
And that thou bidst me come to thee
O Lamb of God I come

The Lord Jesus Christ says, 'Whoever comes to me I will never cast out' (John 6:37). That is not the peg I am hanging my hat on, or the peg I am hanging my coat on, but the peg I am hanging my eternal soul on!

Return

So, with an invitation like this, then our response must be to return. Hosea 6:1 says, '... let us return to the LORD.'

Hosea identifies himself with the people. He says, 'Come let us return.' This is important for all preachers, and in fact all Christians, who tell others about sin, judgement and their need of a Saviour. It's not a 'them and us'. We are all in this together.

> Returning to Yahweh is a major theme of Hosea.

Returning to Yahweh is a major theme of Hosea. The use of the personal name of the Lord, and not the mere general term for God, guided the Israelites thoughts away from pagan gods to the only true and living God. They must forsake all others. They had to turn their back on Baalism. This returning involves true repentance—turning your back on sin and run away from it. You cannot love and indulge in sin and have Christ. You never want to sin and when you do you hate it. William Gurnell said, 'To forsake sin is to leave it without any thought reserved of returning to it again.'[2]

Every truly repentant sinner who returns to God will

receive the warmest of welcomes and be completely reconciled and at peace with God (Luke 15:20–24).

Press on

But we cannot return half-heartedly. In Hosea 6:3 we are encouraged to '… press on to know the Lord …' (6:3). If we are to return to God and want to be reconciled to Him, and really know Him, it involves pressing on; that is, we must engage in an unremitting, enthusiastic pursuit of the Lord.

At the end of Chapter 5 (verse 15), and in line with Hebrews 11:6, we are told that if we want to find Him, we have to earnestly seek Him. We must seek Him with all of our heart (Jeremiah 29:13). This *pressing on* is something that we should do throughout our lives. We should not rest until we know Him and make it then our aim to know Him more and more.

Knowing Jesus Christ is the most important and best thing in the world; it eclipses all else. In Philippians 3 the apostle Paul says, 'That I may know him' (v. 10). He longs to know Christ with ever increasing intimacy. In Philippians 3:13–14 he says, '… forgetting what lies behind and straining forward to what lies ahead, I press on toward the goal for the prize of the upward call of God in Christ Jesus'. Paul says that when it comes to knowing God, he has a steely determination. He forgets what is behind him and does not let his past hold him back. He writes it off as a dead loss, relegates it to oblivion. As Christians we cannot be paralysed by past failures. The devil will tell us that we can never know God intimately. We can never really be at peace with Him. After all the things we have done, there will always be something between us. He will plague us with our pasts and make us anxious about the future. But that is complete rubbish. We are commanded and encouraged to press on.

We press on to know God by putting ourselves in the way of good things. Meet with His people. Read and meditate upon His word. Be obedient to God's Word. Be loving and thankful and kind. Lay aside all sin. If there are relationships, things or places that hinder us pressing on, then cast them aside. If there are darling sins then put them to death. Do not harbour sin in your hearts. Do not put yourself in the way of temptation. And do it now. Don't wait for a 'moment'.

Above all, we pray. Pray on our own. Attend the prayer meeting. And do this without ceasing. Keep up the habit of prayer. 'Give Him no rest' (Isaiah 62:7). We keep on and on and on. Claim His promises and pray them back to Him. Hold Him to His Word.

So many of us say with the apostle Paul at the end of Romans 7, the good that I want to do I do not do, and the bad that I do not want to do is the very thing I do. 'Wretched man that I am!' (Romans 7:24). And we think that is the way it will always be. But Paul also said, 'I press on' (Philippians 3:12).

God's friends search for Him.

Heal

In an allusion to the lion metaphor of Hosea 5:14, God says He will heal what He has torn to pieces, and to the wounds that God was once like a gangrene to (5:12), He will now bandage. The One who, while we remain in our sin, will tear us to pieces, if we come to Him, is the one who will heal us and care for us. In fact, when a repentant sinner comes to God, all the punishments in 4:15–5:15 are reversed.

Maybe you have lived a sinful life and that sinful life has left you wounded. You have messed up your own life and the lives of others. There are things you have done that you cannot put right; you are plagued with regrets and guilt. When you think about God you assume He is out to get you and what you have done means that you will never be able to know forgiveness and be at peace with God. But can I tell you there is forgiveness with God (Psalm 130:4).

However bad you are, however much you have sinned against God, if you come to Him, He will abundantly pardon you. Your messed up life can be healed. At Calvary, Jesus Christ took all our sin upon Himself so that by His wounds we have been healed (1 Peter 2:24).

One day I will stand before God. There will be many people who know me who could present a case as to why I should not be allowed into heaven. People I grew up with, went to school with, went to university with, worked with, my family, friends, who could all point to my sins and say there is no way he should be allowed into heaven. Then there is my conscience that can bring to mind the things I have thought and done that no one else knows. That will definitely condemn me! On top of all that, God's law shows me I have failed on every point. The devil, through all of these things, will accuse me. But, on that awesome day, when I stand before the Judge of all the earth, Jesus Christ will plead for me. He will stand with me and when the devil, the law, my conscience, my past and everyone who knows me condemn me, He will say as it were: 'Look back to before the sun, the moon and all the stars were made. That is when I set my love upon you. Look at those three crosses. On the middle one, I took all your sins upon myself and paid for every one of them! When you confessed your sins to me, I was faithful and just and forgave you. When you called upon me, I saved you. My blood covers all your iniquities.' Healed completely!

The God of heaven heals the broken hearted and restores backsliders (Hosea 14:4; Isaiah 42:3; 61:1).

Life
However, more than just healing is the promise of new

life. Hosea 6:2 says, 'After two days he will revive us; on the third day he will raise us up, that we may live before him.' The original context refers to the restoration of Israel after captivity. Soon the Israelites would be carried off and no one would be able to save them. The situation appeared hopeless. Israel looked dead and buried. But Hosea believed that somehow, though God would destroy His people, He would then revive them. Israel was wiped off the map and wiped out of history but God would restore her and bring her back to life. Ezekiel develops this concept in his dry bones vision (Ezekiel 37:1–14). Ezekiel is taken to a valley of dry bones and asked, 'Can these [dry] bones live?' (Ezekiel 37:3). The answer by God is emphatically they can and they shall.

> Hosea believed that somehow, though God would destroy His people, He would then revive them.

The reference to, 'two days he will revive us; on the third day he will raise us up', is an allusion to the relatively short time before God will redeem His people—when He will bring the true Israel back from captivity. It is like us saying, 'in two- or three-days' time'. In the overall scheme of things, they will have a speedy recovery.

But, as well as the immediate context, it is impossible for a Christian to read this without thinking about the resurrection. The New Testament does not explicitly cite this verse but 1 Corinthians 15:4 asserts that Christ rose from the dead on the third day according to the Scriptures, and no other text speaks of the third day in the fashion Hosea 6:2 does. Israel's resurrection pictures Christ's resurrection.

The Old Testament prophecies are couched in typological patterns. But they have a literal fulfilment in the resurrection of Christ. In fact, in a sense, He is the people of God—their representative. The true Israel is all those who are trusting in Jesus Christ and therefore are in Him. The true Israel, the remnant, would be brought back to life through the death and resurrection of the Lord Jesus.

In Hosea 6, God is both the tearer and the healer. It seems a contradiction, but this contradiction is answered and satisfied in the cross of Christ. At the cross, God tore us apart, but not us, the one who stood in our place. He is the representative of God's people.

Seven hundred and fifty years after Hosea wrote his prophecy, Jesus Christ was arrested in a garden called Gethsemane. The events in Gethsemane at first glance would appear to be the worst in the history of redemption. It was the darkest moment ever. The longed for, promised Messiah had been arrested and bound up by a 300-strong mob, betrayed by one of His own and abandoned by the remaining eleven disciples. He was then tried by Annas,

Caiaphas, the Jewish Sanhedrin, Pilate, Herod, then Pilate again, who sentenced Him to death. After that, He was placed in the custody of Roman soldiers who punched Him, hit Him, mocked Him, spat on Him, whipped Him, squeezed a crown of thorns on His head and then nailed Him to a Roman cross. After six hours on the cross, He died. A Roman soldier pierced His side with a sword and water and blood flow out. His lifeless body was taken down from the cross and buried in a cave. His followers were despondent, troubled, scared and sad. It looked all over. Torn apart. But three days later, this dead Galilean carpenter walked out from the tomb.

When He rose from the dead and conquered sin and death, all those trusting Him did too. What is true of Christ is true of the real Israel, the Church, and every genuine Christian. Thomas Godwin imagined two great giants, Adam and Christ, each wearing an enormous leather girdle with millions of little people hanging on.[3] If we are hanging on Christ's belt, what happened to Christ happened to us.

So, we, who are in Him and were once dead in trespasses and sins (Ephesians 2:1), deserving of being eternally torn apart in hell, may live before Him (Hosea 6:2). Sinners such as us can live in His presence. Like Abraham, we can be friends with God. We can talk with God in prayer as Moses did, '... face to face, as a man speaks to his friend' (Exodus 33:11). Best of all, one day a trumpet will sound and the dead in Christ shall rise and live before Him forever in their new bodies (1 Thessalonians 4:13–17). We will be with Him in heaven.

Refreshing

When God returns to His people it will be a time of refreshing. According to Hosea 6:3, '... he will come to us as the showers, as the spring rains that water the earth ...'. Given the drought the land was experiencing at the time (Hosea 2:12; 4:3), nothing would have been better than the thought of coming rain.

While the majority of us today are not suffering physical drought and are in no need of rain (particularly if you are reading this in Wales!), spiritually it would seem the church in the West is going through a long period of drought. So, instead of bemoaning our plight, longing to live in the past, complaining about the state of the nation and cocooning ourselves in our churches thinking, 'Woe are us', let us come to the Lord, return to Him, press on to really seek Him, and plead with Him that He may come to us as the showers—as the spring rains that water the earth? In other words, plead with God to revive us, revive our churches and revive the land. Duncan Campbell described a revival as a 'community saturated

> Plead with God to revive us, revive our churches and revive the land.

with God'.[4] Surely, we should be pleading with God for times like this! A time when many will be converted, the church will grow and even the nation will be affected so that, as was noted in the *Yarmouth and Gorleston Times* on 10th November 1921, 'The entire town is in the grip of the presence of God. God has become very near.'[5]

Certain

What should spur us on is the certainty that God will keep His promises. Hosea 6:3 says, '... his going out is sure as the dawn ...'

Like the sun rising after a dark night, God will return. To the Israelites, darkness had consumed the land. The new moon had devoured their land (Hosea 5:7). They would go into exile and all would be lost. If we could have stood and watched the exiles being dragged off into captivity and observed the wall-less ruins smoking—sadness sinking into their spirits like never before—they and we would have found it hard to have believed they had any hope at all. But as certain as the dawn follows the night, God will return.

He has said in His Word that if we come to Him, He will come to us. God will keep His promises. We need to hold onto His promises in His Word (2 Chronicles 7:14; Revelation 3:20). Also, remember what God has done in the past.

Maybe today you cannot believe this is possible; you

cannot imagine spring rains watering the earth (Hosea 6:3). You think that society has outgrown God and things have gone too far. But there have been times in the history of the church that have been just as bleak, if not bleaker, and God has gone out to His people.

In 1857, revival came to America as a direct result of prayer. D.L Moody is well known but Jeremiah Lanphier less so. He was a New York businessman who became a city missionary.[6] He had not been a city missionary long before he sent out an advertisement for a noon-day prayer meeting to be held on Wednesdays in the Dutch Church at the corner of Fulton Street in downtown New York. He went to the room that he had hired. Five, ten, fifteen, twenty, twenty-five minutes, half an hour passed. Six others came one after another. They prayed and the next week there were twenty and the famous Fulton Street prayer meeting had begun. During the first week in October, it was decided to hold the meeting daily instead of weekly and within six months 10,000 businessmen were meeting every day to pray for revival. Within two years a million converts had been added to the American churches.

The God of 1857 is still on the throne today. Let us come to Him again, sincerely and earnestly, pray His promises back to Him and plead with Him to return to us.

Frustration

While Hosea 6:1–3 presents a wonderful possibility for

Israel, Hosea 6:4 brings us right back down to earth with a bump! Despite this most inviting of offers, Israel rebuffs God's advances, leaving God to say, 'What shall I do with you, O Ephraim? What shall I do with you, O Judah?' There is frustration at their refusal to return and pursue Him.

Hosea 6:1–3 looks forward to the time when the real children of Israel will return to God in repentance. But, in verse 4, he turns to the sad spectacle of Israel as she is at present, incapable of any such response. Hosea 6:4–7:16 laments the stubbornness of the nation.

Hosea 6:4 underlines how far God has gone in His forbearance with them, 'What shall I do?' It is heart breaking. The Lord God of heaven and earth stooping down to rebellious sinners, pleading with them to be reconciled to Him, but they are stubbornly refusing. Israel's problem was that they were self-sufficient. They were confident they could cope on their own. They did not realize at this stage the call to return applied to them. They did not see their need for God.

Perhaps as you read Hosea you want to scream down the corridors of time to these people and try to get them to see sense. But are we really that much different to them? Is not our problem that we do not feel our need of God? We are too busy for Him. Our careers, families, friends, education are more important. We are now too sophisticated for the God of the Bible. Sin and the world have so much more to offer.

Fitful

The frustration is that Israel and Judah's love is so fitful; their devotion is so short-lived. Whatever good resolutions Israel or Judah made, they were superficial. Their love is like the morning mist (6:4). In Britain, the grass can be wet first thing in the morning but dry by mid-morning. Imagine what it was like in the heat of the Middle East. The dew would have disappeared in no time once the heat of the day intensified.

The love that is referred to in verse 4 is God's covenant love. It is steadfast love. Love that is loyal and sticks through thick and thin. But Israel was incapable of loving God consistently with any sincerity. At best they agreed that what God said sounded fine, but they refused to return to Him with any genuineness. An immoral soul loses the capacity for intimacy, loyalty and love. In the case of Israel, it showed in the cult prostitution and the immorality associated with the cults. It was like Gomer's love for Hosea. She could not stop herself going after other lovers. This was no new thing for Israel but an age-old problem. It was the recurring theme during the time of the Judges. According to Judges 8:33, 34:

> Then it came about, as soon as Gideon was dead, that the sons of Israel again played the harlot with the Baals and made Baal-berith their god. Thus the sons of Israel did not remember the LORD their God who had delivered

them from the hands of all their enemies on every side (NASB 1995).

It was not that they literally forgot the identity of Yahweh or that they could not list the enemies from whom He had rescued them. It means that they knew of Yahweh but He exercised no control over them; He held no grip on their loyalties. They could still answer catechism

> All they knew of Yahweh did not stop them going after Baal-berith as their god.

questions and knew their Bibles but all they knew of Yahweh did not stop them going after Baal-berith as their god.

I imagine, like me, this is sadly the experience of your love for God. In church we can be swayed by a sermon or in the hymn singing. On Sunday morning we would do anything for God, believe these things to be true and want Him. But come Monday at work, the feelings have passed. When it comes to reading your Bible and praying, you start so well. You come from a conference or a camp, start reading a book in the Bible and it all goes so well but within no time, you hit a difficult chapter and you soon give up and prayer goes with it. We need to ask God to strengthen us in our inner being (Ephesians 3:16). If we really love Him, are going to stand as a Christian, overcome temptation, overcome our lethargy in reading the Bible and praying, then we need our weak hearts fortified by the Holy Spirit.

Outward

In Hosea 6:6, God spells out exactly the kind of love and devotion He yearns for. He says, 'For I desire steadfast love and not sacrifice, the knowledge of God rather than burnt offerings.'

This is one of the great texts of the prophets. Jesus used it to expose the hypocrisy of His opponents (Matthew 9:13; 12:7). From it, we should not conclude that God regards sacrifice and ritual worship as inherently bad. He is not saying that He wants to overthrow liturgy and formal worship. Neither is Hosea just a social reformer who is trying to stamp out social sins and impose religious duty on people. What he wants to stress is that the most important thing is to really know God and love God; from that, our worship and behaviour flows. Today it would be as though God is saying, 'I desire devotion not hymn singing, service not sermons,' but of course that is not to say that sermons and hymn singing are not important parts of worship.

We must, above all else, have the right knowledge and love for God (Hosea 6:6). What we believe and how we worship must be directed by the Word of God, the Bible. But doctrinal correctness is not enough; He wants us to love Him and do all the other things we do because we love Him.

Sin

The reason Israel and Judah are behaving the way they are is sin; sin is at the heart of the problem. Hosea refers to three places to highlight the root and extent of this problem.

ADAM

The first place is Adam. Hosea says in 6:7, 'But like Adam they transgressed the covenant; there they dealt faithlessly with me'.

There was a city called Adam but this city is only mentioned once, in Joshua 3:16, as the place where the waters of the Jordan heaped up prior to Israel's invasion of Canaan. Otherwise, it seems to have no significance. However, it most probably had a shrine, as most towns seem to have had throughout Israel during Hosea's time. We can assume, therefore, that Hosea singled out the shrine at Adam because of its namesake. Adam was the first man, the original sinner. The prophet is making a pun on the name of the town and the original sinner. 'Like Adam the man, they break covenants; they are faithless to me there in the town of Adam.'

God placed the first man and woman, Adam and Eve, in a garden called Eden. It was paradise. They could eat of any fruit in the garden except from the tree of the knowledge of good and evil. If they ate from this tree they would die (Genesis 2:17). It was a clear command and warning from God. However, Satan comes to Eve in the form of a serpent, and deceives her into eating the forbidden fruit. She, in turn, gives some to Adam and sin and death entered the world. This is called *The Fall*. The apostle Paul says in Romans 5:12, 'Sin came into the world through one man and death through sin and so death spread to all men because all sinned.'

> Not only did the fall affect Adam and Eve but the entire human race, including you and me.

Not only did the fall affect Adam and Eve but the entire human race, including you and me. Adam and Eve were our representatives, so sin is part of all our nature. The consequences of sin and *the fall* are enormous. It has separated us from God; it makes us dirty; it affects our minds and our actions and pollutes every part of our nature. Evil entered the world; fear entered the world (Genesis 3:10); blame entered the world (Gen. 3:11–13); pain entered the world (Gen. 3:16). Relationships break down (Gen. 3:16). People feel shame (Gen. 3:7). Just making it through life will be a chore (Gen. 3:17). We lost eternal life and instead face eternal damnation. Through Adam's rebellion against God, all Adam's descendants, men and women, boys and girls, are born in sin. We are rebels against God. It all started in that garden, thousands of years ago.

So, through Adam mankind fell. It is the cause of all the problems in the world today and has been from the beginning, during Hosea's time and will be right up to the end. According to Packer[7]: 'It may fairly be claimed that the fall narrative gives the only convincing explanation of the perversity of human nature that the world has ever seen.' The place called Adam was living proof of that and its namesake the reason why.

GILEAD

The second place Hosea refers to is Gilead (Hosea 6:8). Gilead was in the Transjordan region and was famous for a number of incidents in the Bible (see Judges 11). Some think that Hosea is singling out Gilead as a city of evildoers because, when Pekah assassinated King Pekahiah, he was accompanied by fifty men from Gilead (2 Kings 15:25).

However, it would seem more likely that Hosea is citing Gilead because of its connection with Jacob. It would appear that Hosea is working the story of Jacob into his prophecy, a story he will pick up again in Hosea 12:2–4. It was in the hill country of Gilead that Laban caught up with Jacob and accused him of treachery (Genesis 31:25–26). Then at Mahanaim, in the region of Gilead, Jacob prepared to face Esau and had a wrestling encounter with the angel of the Lord (Genesis 32). Furthermore, the last part of Hosea 6:8 actually means 'stained with footprints of blood'. The choice of such an image must be deliberate. The root of the word footprints is also the root of the name *Jacob*. In this verse it also describes the inhabitants of Gilead as 'evildoers' using the word 'awen', the same word that is used for the wordplay for Bethel, 'Beth-aven'. Bethel was the place where Jacob met with God as he fled Esau in Canaan (Genesis 28:11–22).

Hosea is trying to show the Israelites that they are just like Jacob before his encounters with God. Jacob by nature was sinful; he was selfish and cunning. Then he had a vision at Bethel and an encounter with God and was renamed Israel, all in the region of Gilead. However, his descendants, instead of being transformed into Israel, into the people of God, remained Jacob—a name that Hosea has transformed into the grim phrase, 'stained with footprints of blood'. The Israelites had no knowledge or experience of God comparable to Jacob's.

What is true of Israel and Jacob by nature is true of all of us by nature. Every one of us has a sinful nature. It is in our nature to do what is wrong and shameful. After Luis Suarez bit Giorgio Chiellini during Uruguay's World Cup game against Italy in 2014, Alan Hansen said, 'There is clearly a major flaw in Suarez's make-up ... He will also surely have known that he would not have got away with it, yet he still did it.'[8] We can all sit in judgement on Suarez. However, the reality is we all do certain things that we know are not right and have consequences, but we still do them. The reason is that our nature is corrupt. This is why we need God to regenerate us—to renovate our heart, the core of our being—by implanting a new principle of desire, purpose and action.

Shechem

The third place is Shechem (Hosea 6:9). Shechem was a city in north-central Palestine. Rehoboam was crowned there (1 Kings 12:1). Maybe in his mind Hosea has a particular incident: a specific plot to assassinate someone who was travelling to Shechem. It would also appear from this verse that priests act like robbers terrorising the highways. Hosea describes the priests as a gang of thugs who lie in wait for unsuspecting victims to take advantage of.

The most notorious incident to take place there was the slaughter of its inhabitants by Simeon and Levi in retaliation for the rape of Dinah (Genesis 34). So, this verse is a metaphor of ambush and it cannot be accidental that Hosea alludes to a place where Levi, father of the priesthood, was guilty of treachery and mass murder. The assertion that the priests carry out a wicked plan appropriately describes the deceit of Simeon and Levi at Shechem (Genesis 34:13).

All of this was carried out by priests! Those in positions of authority are especially vulnerable to temptation (1 Corinthians 10:12). Sadly, has not more damage been done to the Lord Jesus and His cause by the 'so-called' church? There are so many issues that are hotly debated in the media, by the apparently brightest academics, by talking heads and by politicians: how the world was made; ways of life; leadership in the church; other faiths. So many making real assaults on the living God and ripping the Bible to shreds. But who lets the side down the most? Is it not the 'so-called' church who dumbs down her message, takes the difficult bits out and tells a world that is hurtling full throttle to hell, 'Peace, peace when there is no peace' (Jeremiah 6:14)?

God says, 'In the house of Israel I have seen a horrible thing; Ephraim's whoredom is there; Israel is defiled' (6:10). To God, sin is horrible and walking out on God—spiritual apostasy—is what He hates the most.

Christianity is about love for God. Jesus came and said it is all about the heart. It is not what is on the outside—not about the rules. It is about whether you love God in the first place and then about loving others as much as you love yourself (Luke 10:27). Yes, sin has messed up my life and the lives of others. But the real horror and heart of sin is that it is against God. I do not love Him as I should.

Maybe you think, 'That's not true! I don't particularly

love Him but neither do I hate Him. I'm just indifferent.' But think about how kind He is to you. All the good things you have come from His hand (James 1:17). He made you; sent His Son to die for you and you do not give Him a second thought. Imagine if my wife said to me tonight, 'Alun, I don't love you anymore. You're okay but I just prefer being with other people. I'll do some chores for you and I'm happy to give you a bit of time over Christmas and Easter but I don't really love you!' I'd be devastated. And yet that is how we treat God.

Judgement

The problem with Israel was that this did not seem to bother them; they did not take these things seriously. Maybe that is you. So what if you do not love God? So what that you are a sinner? What is the problem? The problem is that you have to stand before God at the judgement. God will judge all people one day.

> The problem is that you have to stand before God at the judgement.

As far as Israel was concerned, the immediate judgement was going into exile, which happened in 722 BC. And it was not just Israel. Judah in the south would also face God's judgement. Hosea 6:11 says, 'For you also, O Judah, a harvest is appointed, when I restore the fortunes of my people.'

Some critics argue that this verse was added by a later hand and not a genuine Hoseanic text. But there is no reason to doubt that 6:11 is authentic. It is just meant to read as an aside, as in Hosea 5:5; Judah too is headed down the road to apostasy and destruction.

The 'harvest' for Judah is evidently a day of judgement (Isaiah 18:5; Jeremiah 51:33; Joel 3:13; Amos 8:2). Judah will reap what it has sown. They no doubt felt they were better than Israel. More orthodox and correct in their worship of Yahweh. As they watched Israel being carted off into exile, they may have felt quite smug. But *being Judah* is not enough to save them. The only way they can be saved from the judgement and wrath of God is by trusting God and being faithful to Him.

As well as imminent judgement in the form of exile for Israel then Judah, it is also a picture of the final judgement to come. In the same way that the judgement upon Israel and Judah did happen, this final judgement is certain. God has a fixed day in which 'He will judge the world in righteousness' (Acts 17:31). All humans of all ages will be judged. Everyone will get what they deserve (Romans 2:6). All the dead, the great and the small, will stand before God's judgement throne.

Imagine it! Every great historical figure will stand before this throne. Every king, queen and world leader that has ever lived will stand before this throne. Film stars, pop stars, sports men and women will stand before this throne. Tramps, beggars, 'ordinary' people, bankers, hedge fund managers, politicians, Asians, Americans, Europeans, Africans, 'good people', terrorists, rapists, murderers, will all stand before this throne. You and I will stand before this throne. And just as Judah were not exempt because they were Judah, church goers or people brought up in Christian homes, are not exempt. All will stand before this throne.

Everything will be revealed on that day. God says, 'I have seen' (Hosea 6:10). You and I might think that we are getting away with our sin—that no one has seen us. But God has, and one day you will stand before the judge of all the earth and give an account.

And God's judgement is just. God was fair with Israel and Judah. In Hosea 6:5, God's judgement is described as light. It shines on the darkness of their sin and their apostasy. God's light will show sin up for what it really is—shameful and dirty. The light of God's judgement will show us how sinful sin really is; we will see it from God's vantage point. It will show His judgement to be fair.

This judgement should not come as a surprise. God warned them about this judgement through His prophets. In fact, the whole purpose of Hosea telling Israel about the judgement is that they will be ready for it. Today he warns us through His Word, the Bible. Some heed His warnings and are saved—most do not and are damned. His word divides. Life to some and judgement to others (2 Corinthians 2:16).

Sir John William Laing (1879–1978) was a British entrepreneur in the construction industry. He was a fine Christian and a brilliant man. His company built the M1, the Millennium Stadium, the Second Severn Crossing and Coventry Cathedral to name a few. He was one of the earliest employers behind sick pay for workers. He was caring, kind and gave most of his money away. For all his entrepreneurial work and social enterprise, he was knighted by the queen. As he sat in the court of Buckingham Palace waiting to stand before Her Majesty, another gentleman asked him, 'Are you ready to meet the queen?' He turned to the other gentleman and said, 'The more important question is are you ready to meet the eternal King?'[9]

FOR FURTHER STUDY.

1. To repent is more than saying 'sorry'. It is turning away from sin and living a transformed life.

2. Think about the fact that God's promises can be relied upon.

TO THINK ABOUT AND DISCUSS

1. Are we ever too busy for God?

2. Do I look forward to the preaching of God's Word?

8 What are you like?

Hosea 7

Crime is rampant in society (7:1) and none of this has gone undetected by God (7:2). Their sin engulfs them, literally surrounds them. No matter from what angle Yahweh looks at Israel, all He sees is their evil doings. But the problem is that Israel does not see herself in the same way. Things are very bad but Israel is in denial.

The situation

In Hosea 7:1–2, God describes what He sees when he looks at Israel. Ephraim, Samaria and Israel are simply three different proper names for the nation. So, to drive home to Israel what she is really like, Hosea uses six brilliant similes and metaphors.

Scholars agree that Hosea 6:11b and 7:1 belong together and should read, 'When I restore the fortunes of my people when I would heal Israel, the iniquity of Ephraim is revealed and the evil deeds of Samaria.' In effect, God is saying that in order to restore the fortunes of His people and heal Israel, the sins of Ephraim need to be exposed and the crimes of Samaria revealed. Having to face up to reality and the consequences of their sin will be painful. But if she is to be healed Israel has to face up to what she really is and deal with her problems by taking them to God.

An overheated oven (7:3–7)

The first metaphor Hosea uses is an overheated oven (Hosea 7:3–7). The language in these verses is extremely obscure. Hosea's focus seems to be on the crimes of the leading members of society. There is reference to a baker, an oven and dough. The oven is high society, the baker is the king and the leaven is evil.

THE BAKER

The baker is no ordinary baker. He would need to work through the night to have bread ready in the morning. You would expect him to stay awake all night to keep the fires alive and under control, kneading the dough while the leaven does its work. But evidently, from verse 6, he sleeps all night. He is inactive then wakes to find his oven is a raging inferno. The verses describe the debauchery and intrigue of court life. The king is allowing evil and conspiracy to flourish throughout high society and the court.

High Society

It appears that orgies were taking place at the palace. The reference to an inferno could also be an allusion to people burning with sexual desire, and the adultery in verse 4 is probably literal. Adulterous passions burn with the heat of a baker's oven, which is hotter and larger than an ordinary oven. The scene is reminiscent of Daniel 5 when Belshazzar is drinking toasts to his gods from the vassals he had taken from the temple in Jerusalem and of Ben-hadad, drinking himself drunk before a battle (1 Kings 20:16).

As well as drunken orgies, intrigue is rampant and allowed to flourish. Verse 3 says, 'By their evil they make the king glad, and the princes by their treachery.' The verse talks about some unspecified group that gladdens the kings and the princes. It could be a reference to priests but is best left ambiguous. Hosea is vague deliberately and in his mind is probably everyone who is in a position of power, including the priesthood, military and members of royal court.

But there is a double edge to this gladdening. On the face of it, in verse 3, they join the king and high aristocrats in debauchery but verses 4–7 make it clear that they then stab them in the back. The king and aristocrats enjoy and revel in this intrigue when it benefits them, but intrigue will be their undoing too.

Everyone is out for themselves and using whoever and whatever to get what they want.

The king willingly lets himself be diverted from his duties at all hours by those who seek to overthrow him. He brings them near, they gain his trust but they are just ambitious and have a lust for power. Consequently, society is in chaos and decent government is swallowed up by those who only want power; the king is destroyed in a political world that has abandoned God.

The focus of these verses is not on the specific circumstances of any particular conspiracy. As we have seen, Israel's last three decades were of turmoil and intrigue as one conspirator after another hacked his way to the throne only to be murdered in his turn. Of the six men who reigned in those thirty years, four were assassins (2 Kings 15:10, 14, 25 and 30) and only one died in his own bed. The last king, Hoshea, may have escaped a violent end, but he died in captivity.

It is an image of court life that is debased and filled with intrigue. It is evidence that holding high office exposes individuals to increased temptation and the opportunity to indulge their weaknesses. While the Bible says that all who are led astray by alcohol are unwise (Proverbs 20:1), there is no wonder that it sounds a specific alert regarding excessive consumption of alcohol for rulers (Proverbs 31:4–5) and stresses the importance of praying for our political leaders (1 Timothy 2:1–2).

THE DOUGH

The oven is aflame while the baker dozily lets it happen. The picture is of a king allowing the flames of passion and intrigue to burn uncontrollably. Instead of condemning evil, the political leaders delight in it (7:3) and participate in it (7:5). Passion for evil smoulders (7:6) without any need to stoke it (7:4). Sin is allowed to spread and consume everyone (7:7).

These verses illustrate powerfully the dangerous effect of sin. Sin is not simply an action you do or fail to do—that you can choose to do or not to do. Sin is a power that holds you in its grip. Sin feeds sin. Temptation fuels further temptation. The fire of sin burns stronger and stronger until it devours us.

The fire of sin burns stronger and stronger until it devours us.

Think about the patterns of sin in your life. How you commit a sin thinking you could enjoy it for a time and then stop. But you cannot. There are sins we all enjoy and think we will have our fun with them and then, when we are done, we will give them up and at that point may even turn to Christ. But sin is dangerous and if we play with it, instead of us having sin, sin has us.

A frightening example of this is Judas Iscariot. Early on the evening of the Last Supper, John says the devil had already put it into the heart of Judas to betray the Lord Jesus (John 13:2). But by the end of the evening John says, 'Satan entered him' (John 13:27). Satan entered him! What a petrifying thought. However strong the satanic influence, it was only strong because there was a time when Judas opened himself to it. Judas opened the door to Satan. It was not an unwanted invasion but a welcome invitation.

When my son was a baby, I could pick him up and carry him around; even as a toddler and little boy, I would play fight with him and pin him down. But now he is a teenager and I am in my forties, it is getting more difficult, and the day is approaching when he will be able to pick me up and pin me down!

It is the same with sin. People dabble with sins and play with them, but as time goes on, sin takes control and pins you down. The very sin we enjoy and indulge in now, turns on us and leaves us feeling sick (Hosea 7:5). Sin promises so much but always leaves us feeling dirty and guilty. It feels so good at the time but it ruins lives, breaks up families and causes untold pain, because behind sin is the father of sin, the Devil. All he cares about is himself and your destruction.

The real danger, like the leaders in Hosea's day, is we will go so far in our sin that even when we get into trouble, we do not call on God (7:7). God says in 6:11–7:1 in summary, 'I would restore the fortunes of my people … I would heal Israel but they wouldn't.'

If you hear His voice, do not harden your heart

(Hebrews 3:7–8, 15). Seek Him while He may be found, call on Him while He is near (Isaiah 55:6).

A half-baked cake (7:8)

The second metaphor Hosea uses to describe Israel is a half-baked cake (Hosea 7:8–9). The metaphor changes from the cooking in verses 3–6 to the thing that is cooked: a cake. The cake is burnt on one side and not cooked on the other.

If the focus of Hosea 6:6–7:7 is internal politics, the focus of 7:8–16 is her foreign policy. Israel's leadership had not attended to their duties. They had been lax and allowed foreign influence to become predominant. They are meant to be different to other nations because they are God's people, but they are not acting like God's people and turning their back on Him. They are not one thing or the other. The world despises them and God rejects them. The metaphor of the cake is taken a step further when verse 9 says that foreigners eat it. This is a reference to Assyria taking away the material resources of the nation (2 Kings 15:20) and drawing away the people into its religion and ways.

Israel, in these verses, is powerful proof that we cannot serve two masters. The church looks pathetic and becomes weak and good for nothing when it tries to be like the world and win its favour. The more Israel tried to become like the surrounding nations, the less it had to offer. In the same vein, the church becomes impotent and a laughing stock when it tries to incorporate the world, making it unfit for its purpose of being salt and light (Matthew 5:13–16). We should never try to bring the world into the church. We are to be a holy nation (1 Peter 2:9) and our purpose is to show God's character among the nations.

The church in every generation has a difficult act to balance. It cannot retreat and develop a bunker mentality but neither can it melt into its surroundings. The church needs to engage with society. Christians need to live alongside, mix and rub shoulders with their neighbours, friends, colleagues and family. They need to be witnesses in the world and at home in the family. The apostle Paul says, 'I have become all things to all people, that by all means I might save some' (1 Corinthians 9:22). We must avoid unnecessary barriers to the gospel. The Lord Jesus was the Good Physician. He came to heal the sick and to do that He needed to go to where they were. He was the friend of sinners (Matthew 9:9–12). He was accessible to them, drew alongside them. He was compassionate, but totally uncompromising.

We must never aim to be like the world to win the world. The church is at its most attractive when it is different. Christians are radically different and should not try to appeal to the world by making out we are just the same as them—that we can do nearly everything they can do; it is just that we love Jesus too. We have something completely different to offer, something and someone so much more wonderful.

Trying to be two things means we are like a cake that is burnt on the one side and totally uncooked on the other—sickening. In fact, a church in the book of Revelation that was like that actually made the Lord Jesus Christ feel sick (Revelation 3:16). Today, there are many churches who are trying to incorporate society's views and dumb down or adapt what the Bible says in order to appeal to the world around them. We are somehow under the impression that we can have the best of both worlds. We attend church on a Sunday but go to night clubs and get drunk on a Friday and Saturday. We watch the same television programmes and films as everyone else because it does not really affect us, we say. We are Christians on Sunday, and maybe on camps and conferences in the summer, but then we get involved with all kinds of immorality when we're not with our 'church mates'. In our careers we want to get on and if that means working on a Sunday, telling the odd lie, then so be it. But we need to repent of this; turn away from this worldliness; stop living double lives. 'How long will

> We are somehow under the impression that we can have the best of both worlds.

you go limping between two different opinions? If the LORD is God, follow Him' (1 Kings 18:21).

A pathetic, deluded old man (7:9–10)

The third simile Hosea uses is a pathetic, deluded old man. Verse 9 says, '… grey hairs are sprinkled upon him, and he knows it not,' and verse 10 says, 'The pride of Israel testifies to his face; yet they do not return to the LORD their God, nor seek him, for all this.'

The reference to grey hair in verse 9 is different to the reference to grey hair in Proverbs 16:31 and 20:29. There, grey hair symbolizes wisdom and experience. But here it is more like the grey fuzz or mould that appears on bread when people leave it for too long before they get round to eating it.

It is a picture of a man getting old but not wanting to face up to it. He is unaware of the decline. He is a bit like an older man acting like a teenager—attempting the exploits of his youth that he can no longer achieve. A sad mid-life crisis.

In the New Testament, James says it is foolish to look in the mirror and then walk away and forget what you see (James 1:24). The man in Hosea 7:9–10 is a man who cannot accept what stares back at him in the mirror, so stops looking in the mirror.

Israel still wanted to think of themselves as they were in the days of King David, King Solomon and Jeroboam

II, when they were a major power and had known a long period of prosperity. But those days were over. Israel is now a diseased, weakened state but they cannot recognize it or acknowledge where their former strength had come from. They will not return to the Lord. The people have dismissed all calls to repentance (Hosea 7:10; compare with 5:5).

But while we look back at Israel and feel sorry for how pathetic and sad she is, the church today must examine itself for grey hairs. We can be so obsessed with being cool and acceptable that we forget who we are and think and act like something we are not, resulting in us looking sad and pathetic and being totally ineffective.

We need to examine ourselves in the light of God's Word, hold it up before us like a mirror and then pray the promise of 2 Chronicles 7:14 back to God:

> If my people who are called by my name humble themselves, and pray and seek my face and turn from their wicked ways, then I will hear from heaven and will forgive their sin and heal their land.'

A stupid, frantic bird (7:11–13)

THE PICTURE

The fourth metaphor that Hosea uses to describe Israel is a stupid, frantic bird (7:11). The picture is of a silly dove, never settling, never committing, going from one thing to the next. This senseless dove portrays the leadership of Israel frantically seeking for help from a foreign power. Israel is behaving like a stupid homing pigeon that cannot find its way home. It will not realize that Yahweh is the home to which it should fly.

THE NATIONS

God had promised to provide and protect His people. He had an amazing track record of delivering them against the odds. But now, instead of turning to God, though He longs to redeem them (7:13), Ephraim mixes with the nations (7:8). People turn to Assyria, then to Egypt for help (7:11).

Israel was mixing with the nations on religious, political and cultural grounds. She had adopted the nations' gods and rituals. Politically, Israel was trying to make alliances with other nations or had become—or were about to become—vassals of other powers. Culturally, she had adopted the values of these nations.

The background to the events of history corresponding to these charges against Israel were discussed in the introduction to this book. Hosea probably does not have one specific incident in mind but the habitual behaviour of Israel's leadership. Israel sometimes was trying to form an alliance with Egypt, sometimes she bought off Assyria with a tribute (2 Kings 15:19; 2 Kings 15:29; compare with 2 Kings 16:5 onwards and Isaiah 7:1 onwards; 2 Kings 17:1–6). All this was silly and without sense.

As in the metaphor of the baker, Israel's leadership had neglected their duty. From not doing their duty in the first place, they are now like this bird, frantic to find help.

But at the root of Israel's problem was her spiritual adultery and apostasy (7:13). They wandered or strayed from God. Other things had turned their heads and enticed them away. Israel did not want the God who had been so good to her. She was going to anyone and everyone apart from God. They were rebels. They were determined to do what they thought was right in their own eyes and what they wanted to do.

CAN'T GET NO SATISFACTION

But what Israel found out the hard way is that none of these nations they were turning to would be able to really help them. They all used Israel for their own ends, and then turned on them, leaving them high and dry. Eventually the Assyrians, who they turned to for help, would cart them off into exile.

What is true of ancient Israel is true of us today. We go after all kinds of things because they promise to make us happy and fulfilled. They seem so much better and appealing than God. But true happiness and peace is only to be found in God.

A young boy was listening to an organist play the organ. He asked if he could have a go at playing it. The organist said no; he had been playing the organ for years and no one else was allowed or could play it as well as him. But the young boy was persistent and in the end the organist gave in. So, the young Felix Mendelssohn sat down and played. The old organist was amazed: 'I had no idea the organ could be played like that. You played notes I didn't even know were there.'[1] If you are not a Christian reading this, then you have no idea what your life could be like—no idea what true happiness and contentment is. There are notes you do not even know are there.

JUDGEMENT

However, Israel refuses to come to Yahweh despite the fact that in the end they cannot escape him. Whichever way they go, God will catch them with His judgement.

He says, 'As they go, I will spread over them my net; I will bring them down like birds of the heavens ... Woe to them ...' (7: 12, 13).

> Israel refuses to come to Yahweh despite the fact that in the end they cannot escape him.

Yahweh will snare the bird. In chapter 2:6–7, we saw how God would frustrate Israel's attempts to find outside help and put an end to their freedom by making them captives. He would bring devastation to them. They could go from one country to another for help but all the time the net was tightening. They were doomed.

Hosea 7:12 says, 'I will discipline them according to the report made to their congregation.' We cannot be totally sure what the reference to 'congregation' is. It might be the recital of the message of the covenant in the religious assemblies of the North warning that, because of their covenant, it was wrong to go after nations for help. It is to God and God alone they must go (Deuteronomy 30:9–13). But the problem with this suggestion is, would Israel have observed it? More likely it suggests a public assembly convened by the rulers of the North to announce the news that their plans had been frustrated and further calamity was impending. The phrase may possibly relate to the arrival of intelligence regarding the failure of Hoshea's diplomatic approach to Egypt to secure military assistance (2 Kings 17:4), meaning that they would be unsupported to face the might of Assyrian reprisals.

The point Hosea is making is that we can ignore God and live our lives as though He does not exist. We can go after other things and pursue the way of life that we think will suit us best. But we cannot escape God ultimately.

Again, this is true for us today. We will one day have to face God. We will all die. As George Bernard Shaw put it, 'Life's ultimate statistic is the same for all people: one out of one dies.'[2] Our sense of permanence is an illusion. One day will be our last day on this earth. And after death we will meet God at the judgement.

At this point this was still a threat which means that there was still hope. Despite the mess Israel were getting themselves into and the devastation they were about to face, there was still hope. It did not have to be like this. Hosea's prophecy at times can seem like threat after threat after threat—judgement after judgement after judgement. But this is because God is kind and is longing for people to listen to these warnings and fly from this judgement in repentance and faith to the only One who can save them. If He did not want to save us then He would not warn us.

However, Israel stubbornly would not listen. Hosea 7:13 says, '... I would redeem them, but they speak lies against me.' God is gracious but Israel keeps rejecting His grace. As Jonah 2:8 makes clear, those who cling to worthless idols forfeit the grace that could be theirs.

This stubbornness breaks the heart of God. Judgement is His strange work (Isaiah 28:21). He would rather bring you to heaven than send you to hell. Andrew Bonar said, 'At the final judgement, when fire comes down from heaven, it will be wet. Wet with tears that people would not repent.[3]

Self-obsessed prayer (7:14)

The fifth metaphor Hosea uses to describe Israel is a self-obsessed prayer (Hosea 7:14). Israel had not stopped praying. In fact, they prayed all night instead of sleeping (v. 14). But their prayers were all about them. Their prayers were like a child's tantrum: totally selfish and a self-pitying wail in which they complain about their lot. Their prayers are self-indulgent and manipulative.

Israel was copying the way the Canaanite's prayed. In order to attract the attention of the gods and add effectiveness to their prayers, a Canaanite ritual was self-mutilation (compare with 1 Kings 18:28). They also had a ritual of wailing for the deceased. Israel was emulating aspects of this in their prayers and not really thinking about who it was they were approaching.

Frequent and fervent prayer is not necessarily a sign of spiritual health; indeed, it is usually a sign of faithlessness. It can be just an expression of worry and of talking things over and over with yourself, rather than an understanding that we are praying to God and trusting Him. God did not feature in Israel's prayers very much at all. They cried out but not to God; they did not want God.

> Frequent and fervent prayer is not necessarily a sign of spiritual health.

They just wanted someone or something to sort their mess out, do what they wanted them to do and let them carry on as before. Their man-centred lives led to man-centred prayers.

They did not pray to commune with God. It was all

about them. God did not feature in their lives at all. They did not care about their relationship with Him. They refused to repent and continued to regard iniquity in their heart. They were totally materialistic. They cared about grain and new wine.

All of this reinforces the hymn by John Burton (1803–77), which says:

I often say my prayers,
But do I ever pray?
And do the wishes of my heart
Go with the words I say?

I may as well kneel down
And worship gods of stone,
As offer to the living God
A prayer of words alone.

For words without the heart
The Lord will never hear;
Nor will He to those lips attend
Whose prayer is not sincere!

Lord, show me what I need
And teach me how to pray,
Nor let me ask thee for thy grace,
Not feeling what I say.

There is a right and wrong way to pray. There are prayers that God will hear and prayers He will not listen to. We must therefore have a right view of prayer and cultivate a healthy prayer life.

So many people think that prayer is all about them—getting what you want. Whereas it is clear that the Lord Jesus viewed prayer as something refreshing. He had no sins to confess like we do. He did not see prayer as something to do when you need something, but rather saw prayer as a time to spend with His Father. In all that was going on and all that He had to face, He often went to be alone to lay it all out before His Father. This is how we should look on prayer: as precious times spent with God. Times we can just enjoy being in His company. Asking Him to draw near to us; telling Him about our day; thinking about how awesome a God He is; telling Him about the temptation we are struggling with; asking Him to forgive us all our sins. Viewing prayer like this will be so refreshing. It should not be another thing we have to do but rather the highlight of the day. As a Christian I can spend time alone, as often as I want, with the God of heaven and earth!

This is very different to the way Israel prayed. They were just obsessed with themselves—did not think who they were approaching or what praying really was. They were heaping up empty phrases as the Gentiles do, for they think that they will be heard for their many words. Jesus says, 'Do not be like them, for your Father knows what you need before you ask him' (Matthew 6:7, 8).

It is right to cast all our care upon Him (1 Peter 5:7), but at the end, once we know He has heard our prayer, we need to accept He knows best, and if we do not get what we ask for it is because it is not for our good. Even more so, it is to trust Him enough to say, only give me what is in line with your will. 'Please do not give me the desires of my heart if it is going to be bad for me (Psalm 106:15). This is what I want but you know best God, and whatever comes my way, give me the strength I need.' To be able to say 'your will be done', we need to know his will through reading the Bible and the help of the Holy Spirit. When we pray like this, everything changes.

As I cycle to work each day from Twickenham to Fulham, I pray to my Father in heaven. Because He is God and He is my Father, I can pray and then trust Him; I can leave things with Him. I can rest in the will of God and submit myself to that. This is where true happiness is to be found.

Faulty weapon (7:15–16)

The sixth metaphor Hosea uses to describe Israel, is a faulty weapon. (Hosea 7:15–16). A weapon implies a life-or-death situation so this is the most serious metaphor of them all. All of Israel's victories had come when God had protected and equipped them for battle. It was God who strengthened them. Israel was completely reliant on God.

However, in these verses the weapons Israel are using are weak and warped. The bow and the sword they have are useless. This is a reference again to Israel's apostasy and how they had tried to mix true worship with Baalism and the religious practices of the peoples around them.

The weapons were the means God had given them to approach Him: the sacrifices, worship, and prayer He had ordained and the Word He had given to them. But in their hands these weapons had become faulty and warped. They had twisted them and made them into their own ways of approaching God. Like a weapon that is faulty and does not shoot straight, their worship was not reaching God. Their prayers were not getting to Him.

They had invented man-made religion and they regarded iniquity in their hearts. Their worship was profane and their speech was blasphemous.

Likewise today, religions have invented their own ways of approaching God. Even churches have played around with the weapons God has provided. But anything that is not ordained by God in His Word will veer off and miss the target. However sincere we are, if it is not the way laid down by God, our worship and prayers will not get to God and will be rejected by Him. Like ancient Israel, they will be ineffective and doomed and what we think is a blessing will actually be a curse.

Verse 16 says, 'This shall be their derision in the land of Egypt.' This is a deliberate reference to Egypt, the place where Israel had spent 400 years in slavery. Israel is here told to look back to the Exodus, but instead of remembering how great a deliverance they had had, the exile they were facing, because of their apostasy, was going to be like another Egyptian slavery. They will be humiliated and once again Gentile powers will mock Israel.

We may have a religion that suits us or a way of life that justifies what we want to do. We may like to worship God in a way that makes us feel good; dumb down bits of the Bible or get it to say what we want it to; have a brand of Christianity that is not too restrictive and not threatening. All of that might be great now, but all that matters in the end is, is it acceptable to God? If not, it is like a faulty weapon—one that will miss the mark and bring upon us the judgement of God.

For further study ▶

FOR FURTHER STUDY.

1. Our church must not conform to the world, but be conformed to the image of God's Son.

2. Is our church important to the people in our community?

TO THINK ABOUT AND DISCUSS

1. Do I worship God in prayer, or just ask for things or people I am concerned about?

2. How important is prayer to me?

9 Israel has forgotten her maker

Hosea 8

Israel had a presumptive confidence in the covenant. This covenant was the promise God had made with Israel. He chose them out of all the other nations. He made them a great nation. He gave them a land. He said that through them the promised Messiah would come who would be a Saviour for the whole world. But they thought that they could do whatever they wanted and, come what may, He would still be their God. Their confidence was misplaced.

What Israel thought of God

THEY HAD FORGOTTEN HIM

Hosea 8:14 says, 'Israel has forgotten his maker' (v. 14). Moses had repeatedly warned them not to forget these things after they were established in the land (Deuteronomy 4:23; 6:10–23; 8:10–14, 19–20)—but they had. This was not an intellectual forgetting but a moral forgetting. Genuine, true worship of God and rigorous obedience towards Him were completely neglected. They did not want to think about God because if they did, it would impinge on the way they were living. They allowed other things to fill their minds and divert them from God.

According to Morgan:

> He [Moses] saw this nation, and he saw it down the coming years, and he knew its supreme peril would be that God should be forgotten. If they could not intellectually forget God, they could put him out of calculation, they could mislay him.[1]

THEY THOUGHT THEY KNEW HIM

Even though their lifestyles and lack of true devotion to God showed they had forgotten Him, in their own minds they thought they knew Him. Hosea 8:2 says, 'To me they cry, "My God, we—Israel—know you."'

The promise God made to His people and the agreement He had entered into with them had to be received by faith and evidenced in their commitment to the obligations of the covenant. True Israel was those who trusted in the promises of God and out of love for Him, obeyed His commandments. In response to the presumption of the Jews in His day who said to Him, 'Abraham is our father', The Lord Jesus says, 'If you were Abraham's children, you would be doing the works Abraham did' (John 8:39).

Today, the only way you can be sure you are a Christian is if you are walking with Him. 1 John 2:4 says, 'Whoever says "I know him" but does not keep his commandments is a liar and the truth is not in him.' Actions drown out words. The Lord Jesus says in Matthew 7:21, 'Not everyone who says to me, "Lord, Lord," will enter the kingdom of heaven, but the one who does the will of my father who is in heaven.'

According to the Puritan, William Gurnall: 'Say not that thou hast royal blood in thy veins, and art born of God, unless thou canst prove thy pedigree by daring to be holy.'[2]

There are lots of people who think they worship God but they do not. *God* today can be acknowledged with great ceremony, but we forget He must be obeyed and we must live our lives differently. People's lives are full of all kinds of worship. Religion is all around us. There are deeply devout, religious people who carry out all sorts of religious acts. There are lots of people who attend church, particularly at certain times of the year; they find it uplifting. They do good works. But all of this is false worship. None of it has anything to do with knowing the only true and living God; it is just man-made religion—people's attempt to be right with God. It relies on what we do and is geared to make us feel better. It is all about rules and rituals. None of it changes the heart though.

And that is the one area that we do not want to be touched. We want something that makes us feel like we are doing something good but that does not impinge on what we are. We choose a religion to fit around us; a religion that suits us, that makes us feel good about ourselves but does not cut across what we want to do. Once it does, it is too much, too fanatical, too extreme. Once the Bible says something we do not like, Christ has to be got rid of. Once the message offends our pride or is offensive to us morally or intellectually, it has to go. Once it tells us we are sinners and need to be saved we cannot cope with it and throw it out.

> True Christianity is not a religion but a relationship—a relationship with the living God.

The thrust of Hosea, and more importantly what Jesus came and said, is that it is all about the heart. True Christianity is not a religion but a relationship—a relationship with the living God. People like you and me can actually know God. We can have a real sense of fellowship with God, a deep consciousness of his love for us (John 17:26); someone we come to trust, love, pray to, serve, worship. We can know the Lord Jesus as a person, just as well as we get to know other people well (wife, family, friends, colleagues, neighbours). As our relationship with the Lord Jesus develops, we will think and act and talk in a way that Christ would. The Holy Spirit is within us affecting our minds, hearts, will, conscience and very character.

Knowing God is what it is all about. In Matthew 7:23, Jesus says the most chilling words a person will ever hear to come from His lips: 'I never knew you,' and these words were directed at people who would have thought they knew Him—the religious and moral.

MADE THEIR OWN GODS

Instead of worshipping the only true and living God, the Israelites had made their own gods. Human beings are made to worship and if they do not worship the true God, they will end up worshipping something, anything, else. So, 'With their silver and gold they made idols for their own destruction,' (Hosea 8:4b) and Hosea 8.5 refers to the 'calf' of Samaria they had made.

The calf of Samaria was an idol, a bovine representation of Baal or Yahweh Himself. It was probably the calf-idol that Jeroboam set up at Bethel (1 Kings 12:28–29) which Hosea (10:5–6) states the people of Samaria revered.

When the ten northern tribes split from the two southern tribes, thus establishing two kingdoms—Israel in the north and Judah in the south—King Jeroboam built two shrines as rallying points for his breakaway

Kingdom of the North, as counter attractions to the temple in Jerusalem (1 Kings 12:27–30). The one was in Bethel and the other at Dan.

By the time of Hosea, the calf in Dan was no longer under Israelite control; that is why he just refers to one calf. The calf was sponsored by the throne right up to the end of Israel—almost a god in and of itself. The idols referred to here could be the archetype calf of Samaria and replicas of it that people kept at private shrines (compare with Acts 19:24–29).

Throughout their history, Israel repeated the sin of the *golden calf*. Even casual readers of the Bible will know, this was not the first time a *calf* made an appearance in Israel's history. As the people were gathered at the foot of Mount Sinai waiting for Moses to come down from the mountain (Exodus 32:1 onwards), Aaron made a golden calf because the people clamoured for a god like the gods of Egypt.

To us in the twenty-first century who pride ourselves in being sophisticated, hi-tech and advanced, the golden calf may seem completely unconvincing or just silly superstition. I remember singing on Evangelical Movement of Wales camps: 'Some people chop up cedar wood then do strange things I've never understood with half of the wood they cook their food and with half they make their god.' It sounds so ridiculous, and is the point being made and laughed at in Isaiah 44:16–17.

However, while we do not make gods like this, we are more similar than we like to think. We look back at these ancient people and think how silly they were. Why did they not just turn to the true and living God? Why could they not just see sense? But we do not see how foolish we are being, even though our idols may be far more subtle and sophisticated. The calf was probably a symbol of brute strength and sexual potency: power and fertility—qualities that a corrupt society tends to idolize. In that case, ancient Israel and Canaan may be closer to us than we suppose. Today we bow down to fame, power, body image, money and sex, believing they will make us happy, fulfil us and satisfy us. But they cannot. Young people, you may have posters of your idols on your bedroom wall, but what good can they do for you? Do not be enticed and give your life to this world and all that it offers. Even things that in and of themselves are not sinful cannot ultimately satisfy a person. The best the world can offer and the biggest achievements you can possibly have, cannot fulfil your deepest needs.

Disregarded His law

The Israelites also had no respect or regard for God's law. Hosea 8:1 combines the breaking of God's covenant with rebellion against God's law. We cannot call God, 'God', without obedience. Jesus says, 'Why do you call me 'Lord, Lord,' and not do what I tell you' (Luke 6:46).

To break the law of God is to offend Him personally. The whole thrust of Hosea's prophecy is that God is a relational God. He does not want outward ritual or external law keeping. He wants Israel to love Him. And the way they show that is by keeping His commands. Jesus said, 'If you love me, keep my commandments' (John 14:15 NKJV).

Israel was in a mess. Immorality and anti-social behaviour were everywhere (Hosea 4:2), but all of this stemmed back to the disregarding of God's law and their broken relationship with Him. Once this happens everything else goes wrong.

IGNORANT OF GOD'S WORD

The reason why many of them were transgressing the covenant and rebelling against God's law was that they were ignorant of His Word. According to Hosea 8:12, 'Were I to write for him my laws by the ten thousands, they would be regarded as a strange thing.'

Maybe Hosea had Deuteronomy 12 specifically in mind. When Israel settled in the land, God had said there was only one place for them to worship; they were only to offer sacrifice in a central location. God wanted to make worship free from syncretism. Their worship was meant to picture God and His character. This is why the Israelites were meant to worship in the Temple in Jerusalem.

But, in Hosea's day, the people were worshipping at shrines and high places and making idols of calves. The main beliefs of Baal had been accepted as orthodox. God had given His people laws and principles for every aspect of life—sacrifices, feasts, religious practices, diet, military and political life, and the family. But they were not following God's Word at all. The priests

> God had given His people laws and principles for every aspect of life.

had so little respect for the Torah and the people were so badly taught (4:6) that some regarded the Torah as the religious laws of a foreign land. However plainly spoken, they were just irrelevant.

We still have His Word available to us today but people are largely ignorant of it. When I was growing up in the South Wales valleys, young people had a general knowledge of the Bible. Nowadays people have no idea about Noah, Daniel, David and Goliath; they have no knowledge of the Ten Commandments and most importantly know nothing about the life, death and the resurrection of the Lord Jesus Christ.

The Bible is seen as out of date and irrelevant. Imagine though if God was to take His Word away. The Puritan, John Rogers, was once preaching and vividly illustrated this point. He said to his congregation, 'Do you use my Bible so? Then you shall have my Bible no longer.'

Rogers then dramatically pretended to take the Bible away so that the people would have it no longer. The congregation cried out, 'Lord whatever Thou dost to us, take not Thy Bible.'[3] Even though we live in days where the Bible is disregarded and people have no knowledge of it—even in the Church its message cuts across what we want to do, think and live—the worst thing ever would be if God were to take His Word away. We need to preach it from pulpits, expose young people in school to its teaching, model it in our lives and pray that God would turn people and our nation back to it!

If you have grown tired of it, have lost interest in it, forgotten it, then start reading it. Pray and read it until you want to read it. According to the French Benedictine monk, Francois Rabelais, 'The appetite grows with eating.'[4]

What Israel thought of the world

NEED TO IMPRESS

The reality was, Israel had forgotten God. She was now all about trying to keep up with and impress the world. She depended on the Baal fertility cults and on military power for her prosperity, identity and security. Israel looked out at the world and wanted to be like it. She wanted to impress the world and have the world's approval; everything had to be big and impressive.

Hosea 8:14 says, 'For Israel has forgotten his Maker

and built palaces, and Judah has multiplied fortified cities.' The word translated 'palaces' is spaciousness or bigness. We know from 2 Kings 18:13 that, 'In the fourteenth year of King Hezekiah, Sennacherib king of Assyria came up against all the fortified cities of Judah and took them.' According to Sennacherib there were forty-six altogether. The only one to survive was Jerusalem following the message from God to Hezekiah, which opened with the significant words: 'Your prayer to me about Sennacherib king of Assyria I have heard' (2 Kings 19:20). What all this shows is that Israel and Judah put their trust in worldliness, bigness and impressiveness. They had forsaken God, not realising that it was God alone who was big enough for her need. If we have God, we can be content with whatever we have—big or small; if we do not, we find ourselves striving to build big things to take God's place.

This is still true today. On the one hand there are many people who think that to be happy and to feel secure they need to invest their time and energy in their education, career, popularity, homes, possessions, reputations or status. These are the things that the world values and prizes. But how safe will these things keep us on judgement day? The food and drink we enjoy, the nice clothes we wear, our hi-tech gadgets, our houses and cars, one day will all be destroyed. None of them will last forever. So many people set their hearts on the goods and luxuries of the world without any thought for the next world. This is perfectly illustrated in the story of the Rich Fool in Luke 12:16–21. He was a farmer who had a bumper harvest, which made him a very rich man. He had no thought for God or anyone else. Instead he simply ate, drank and enjoyed himself. But one night God said to him 'Fool! This night your soul is required of you.' When a person stands before God, his wealth and riches are of no use. What will it profit a man if he were to gain the whole world and lose his own soul? Or what can a man give in exchange for his soul? (See Matthew 16:26).

Furthermore, do these things really make us happy and secure? They are so transient and fickle. Status, power, popularity, usefulness, can be ours for a while but with the passing of time or a change in mood, one mistake or a false move and they are gone. Matthew Parris described the Foyle's seventieth anniversary literary luncheon in 2001. He says of everyone there, 'Everyone had mattered once, very few did now.'[5] We are all desperate to be someone—to impress. But, however powerful and famous and influential we are or become, it will not last long, certainly in the overall, eternal scheme of things.

> However powerful and famous and influential we are or become, it will not last long, certainly in the overall, eternal scheme of things.

The church herself can be guilty of this desire to be impressive and have approval. In our evangelism and worship, we think that we need to be like the world to attract the world. While we should do everything we can, as well as we can, we should not try to use worldly ways to attract the world.

In attempting to reach and win the world for the Lord Jesus Christ, do we trust completely in the weapons He, as our commanding officer, has given us—prayer and preaching? We will never be able to compete with the world on their terms. They will always be able to do things *bigger and better*. We just need to preach the majesty of a holy God and the glory of the Lord Jesus Christ, pray without ceasing and live holy, Christ like lives—and then trust the rest to God.

WORLDLY LEADERS

Allied to Israel's desperate need to be accepted by the world and to impress it, was the way they went about appointing their leaders. Hosea 8:4a says, 'They made kings, but not through me. They set up princes, but I knew it not'.

No doubt behind this verse is Israel's political instability in the latter half of the eighth century BC. During this time, they wrestled the whole process of appointing kings from Yahweh and sought help from other nations instead of God. There was a total abandonment of Yahweh in the political realm. They appointed kings and rulers not known to Yahweh. They did not trust Yahweh and thought they knew best. In describing another time in Israel's history where a similar attitude prevailed, Davis puts it: '"A king—or bust" not "In God we trust."'[6]

Today we vote in leaders and set up regimes as though supposedly they are answerable only to ourselves. God is an inconvenience, an irrelevance. If God does not fit in with us then He has to go. 'We do not want this man to reign over us' (Luke 19:14).

The problem is that all earthly kings and empires come to an end. The Psalmist says, 'Unless the LORD builds the house ... Unless the LORD watches over the city ... It is in vain' (Psalm 127:1, 2). This world, and all that is in it, is transient and will one day come to an end. All the governments and kingdoms of this world are in God's hand. Kingdoms rise and fall at His command. Daniel 5:21 says that the 'Most High God rules the kingdom of mankind and sets over it whom he will'.

World leaders and those who have power and influence are full of their own importance, and seldom do any of them acknowledge God. As they rule their countries and pass laws and make their plans and policies, almost never do they consider God. They seem to think that their power is in their own hands alone.

The moral law Is subject to the vote, or to the climate of modern opinion.

However, human power is short lived. At the time of Hosea, Assyria was the superpower. At the moment, America seems to be the world's dominant power, but one day—maybe one day soon—it will not be. One day the good and the great, along with all people outside of Jesus Christ, will be terrified because this world they have lived for, and whose pleasures they have indulged in, will come to an end.

What the world thought of Israel

To Israel, the world is very important, but as far as the world is concerned, it has chewed Israel up and spat her out. The fertility cults and foreign alliances are proving to be hollow. Israel's military establishment is soon to be overwhelmed and even now the land is suffering the effects of famine. Hosea uses three images to convey the message that all of Israel's efforts to gain the favour of the nations has only resulted in her being made helpless and pathetic before these very nations.

USED CUP

The first image is a used cup. Hosea 8:8 says, 'Israel is swallowed up; already they are among the nations as a useless vessel.'

In mind is a cup or container that has been emptied of all its drink. Imagine today buying a cup of coffee on the way to work. The plastic cup is useful for as long as it holds the drink but once you have finished your coffee, the cup has served its purpose and just needs to be thrown away. The cup is no longer of value to anyone. The surrounding nations were only interested in draining from Israel all the wealth they could get from tributary payments. Once that was exhausted, they had no interest in protecting Israel but were happy to discard her. All the money that Israel had doled out to Assyria and Egypt and others had done them no good. She was as useful to them as a used plastic coffee cup!

LONELY DONKEY

The second metaphor Hosea uses to describe Israel is a lonely donkey. According to Hosea 8:9: 'For they have gone up to Assyria, a wild donkey wandering alone.' In likening Israel to a donkey, Hosea is playing on words; it is a pun. In Hebrew, the words *Donkey* and *Ephraim* have the same consonants which tie the words together. Both the lonely, solitary donkey of the desert and Israel are in search of a partner. Israel has gone to Assyria for aid but, instead of gaining an alliance, it remains a lonely creature left to fend for itself.

PAYING PROSTITUTES

Hosea 8:9 says, 'Ephraim has hired lovers.' Here, Yahweh compares Israel to a man who tries to gain love by giving money to prostitutes, only to discover he has squandered his money and gained no love in return. In the prophecy of Hosea, Israel mirrors Gomer, who has behaved like a prostitute. But here Hosea, as the prophets freely do, alters his metaphors to suit his message; the point being that the nations are like prostitutes, offering their friendship and protection for a price. That price was high and was costing Israel dear.

In verse 10 he goes on to say, 'Though they hire allies among the nations, I will soon gather them up. And the king and princes shall soon writhe because of the tribute.' 'I will gather them' probably means God will gather the nations together to make war against Israel, but the royal house was already putting pressure and demands on the people to enable them to buy off other governments—the most striking example being the tax imposed by Menahem (2 Kings 15:19–20). Long before Israel was delivered their final blow and carted off into captivity by the Assyrians, there was a huge burden on the people as the leadership sapped the nation's wealth by giving it to foreign powers.

> Nothing much has changed from Hosea's day to ours.

Nothing much has changed from Hosea's day to ours. Christians' desires to be like the world and to have the favour of the world is just the same today as it was in

Hosea's day. Likewise, the world's treatment of us is also the same.

People spend their whole life chasing the world and all that they think it has to offer, but will never find true happiness, fulfilment and contentment. We listen to a piece of music, love it, play it again and again and again. Then we are sick of it. We fall in love but then get bored. We live by distracting ourselves. We need something: cash, significance, sex—whatever it takes me to get through getting up, getting through, getting off, getting up, getting through ... We live in a high-tech age but technology will not fix your marriage; technology will not sort out your addiction; technology will not sort out your selfishness. There are lots of people who we regard as 'making it' who prove that the world can never really fulfil and will always end up letting us down. The actor Jim Carrey said, 'I wish everyone could get rich and famous and have everything they ever dreamed of so they would know that's not the answer.'[7] We can gain the whole world only to find the world is not enough.

Israel, and all of us who look to the world for satisfaction, fulfilment and happiness are like a man wasting his money on prostitutes but never finding fulfilment or love: a used cup; a lonely donkey.

What God thought of Israel

The most important thing, though, is what does God

think of Israel; what did God think of Israel's dangerous self-reliance, its self-appointed kings, its expensive allies, its man-made calf, and its own version of religion. The people did not stop to think what God made of all this. They had not troubled themselves at all with God's view and standpoint.

Man-made religion is useless

The first thing God wants them to know is that their man-made religion is useless. He says,

With their silver and gold they made idols for their own destruction. I have spurned your calf, O Samaria. My anger burns against them. How long will they be incapable of innocence? For it is from Israel; a craftsman made it; it is not God. The calf of Samaria shall be broken to pieces (8:4b–6).

There is a sarcastic overtone to this. Their religion was man-made just as their idols were man-made. In fact, their gods were made by the local metal worker! They were not God. God is Israel's maker but Israel had forgotten that and made her own gods. After all her experiences, the fact that Israel could embrace such idolatry is beyond comprehension. This idol that they are worshipping is just a piece of metal! Like the calf of Aaron was ground to powder (Exodus 32:20), this calf will be smashed to pieces.

But, as well as the futility of it all, the effect their

sacrifices have on Yahweh is the reverse of what they intended. Instead of accepting their sacrifices, He rejects them; He remembers their sins instead of forgetting them. According to Hosea 8:11, 'Because Ephraim has multiplied altars for sinning, they have become to him altars for sinning,' whereas v. 13 says, 'As for my sacrificial offerings, they sacrifice meat and eat it, but the LORD does not accept them. Now he will remember their iniquity and punish their sins ...'

Israel is full of religious activity but it is all meaningless.

The altars they made to atone for sin only increases sin. In fact, the altars for sin offerings have become altars for sinning. Israel is full of religious activity but it is all meaningless. The religion Israel had invented had bits of Yahweh in it, but it was mixed with idolatry and Baalism, which allowed the Israelites to have sex and enjoy themselves all in the name of honouring the gods. It was a religion that fitted around them. This kind of worship is valueless and sickening to God. It is a false theology of easy grace. Do whatever you want, whenever you want. But instead of removing their guilt it was compounding it.

While we today are not bowing down to idols or involved in ritual orgies, there are many who say they are religious, even Christian, but their religion is one that fits in with them. We are happy with religion as long as it does not cut across our way of life. We need something that makes us feel good, eases our conscience but allows us to do as we please. We want a religion where we can be Lord and God.

Moreover, we need to check ourselves to make sure that our church services and how we worship God and evangelize is not centred on making us feel happy and relaxed in our services rather than pleasing and honouring to God.

And considering we live in an apparently sophisticated, scientific, enlightened society, we are far from free of superstitions. Bands, beads, routines and rituals—people who read their horoscopes or touch wood not to tempt fate are all too common. I was on a cruise recently and on the ship, there was no *deck 13*. It went from *12* to *14*. I was chatting to someone in my office who told me how well things were going at the moment, then immediately touched some wood. But if we really think about it, how on earth can any of these things affect our lives?

While we may invent our own religions, world views and ways of life, at the end, when we face God at the judgement, our lordly choices are not the last word. What God says is all that matters. Damningly he says to Israel, 'I have spurned your calf' (8:5).

WARNING

To be all religious but unaware that your religion is taking you to hell, is serious. Or to have adopted a way of life, as politically correct, modern and liberal as it may be, but is destroying you, is fatal. Hence, in Hosea 8:1 a warning goes out: 'Set the trumpet to your lips! One like a vulture is over the house of the LORD, because they have transgressed my covenant and rebelled against my law.'

In the immediate context, the Israelites were unaware of the danger that was about to come upon them. The watchmen should sound the alarm because an enemy is swooping down on Israel like a vulture or eagle. A vulture is an unclean bird and so the picture is of something hideously unclean at the very Temple of God. The shofar needs to be blown as urgently as though that were happening.

The house of Yahweh, or house of the Lord, is almost always a reference to the tent of meeting (Exodus 35:21; 36:8–39:43) or the Jerusalem Temple. While it is true and fitting within this context to see the Israelite priests or pagan deities compared to vultures at the shrines of Yahweh, it could also be that Hosea has the whole of Israel in mind here. Elsewhere in Hosea 'house of Israel' is a reference to the whole of Israel (5:1; 9:4, 8).

Israel was religiously, politically, socially and morally unclean and in danger. The reality was that the Assyrian invasion hovered over Israel, ready at any moment to swoop down and attack with terrifying speed and power because the people had broken God's covenant.

The problem was they were too deluded to see it. In Hosea's day the people gazed complacently at the house or household of the Lord (like the disciples admiring the temple in Matthew 24:1), not noticing the ominous clouds in the sky above it. It was high time someone pointed it out. *Set the shofar to your mouth! Someone is over the house of Yahweh like a vulture.*

AN ANGRY ENEMY

Hosea 8:4b–6 emphasizes how angry God is. The broken grammar and uneven lines of these verses portray Yahweh as vexed in the extreme and almost apoplectic with anger over the perversity of Israel's representation of their God that mixes Yahweh and Baal. God is almost speechless with anger. He is so angry that He is now their enemy. They have made an enemy of God. Verse 3 says, 'Israel has spurned the good; the enemy shall pursue him.'

Romans 8:28 says that all things work together for good to those who love God. These verses in Hosea show the opposite is also true. All things now work together for bad to those who do not love God.

The Israelites have spurned the goodness of God. They have rejected the goodness of the Torah, so they are now reaping what they have sown. They are getting what they have worked for. Verse 7 says, 'For they sow the wind, and they shall reap the whirlwind. The standing grain has no heads; it shall yield no flour; if it were to yield, strangers would devour it'.

Some see the first part of this verse as a proverb. Whether that is the case or not, the reference to reaping and sowing is not incidental. Baal worship was a fertility cult that promised good harvests. Baal was supposed to make the land plentiful, which is why the Israelites worshipped Baal and tried to incorporate the worship of Baal with their Yahwehism. But they will have no harvest.

Ancient farmers sowed seed by hand. In these verses they are trying to sow seed or harvest crops in the worst conditions. They cast seed in high wind and have to watch as their seed is blown away. The gales would scatter the sheaves of a farmer who tried to cut and bundle them in a windstorm.

False religion pays disastrous dividends and cannot succeed.

Furthermore, the verse is a pseudosorites—that is a rhetorical device. There will be no harvest but, even if there was, foreigners would come and take it.

It is not just literal fields in mind here but also the political and religious ideology on which Israel has placed its trust. The point Hosea is making is that false religion pays disastrous dividends and cannot succeed. Attempting to keep everyone happy, and mix different religions and ways of life together, will result in ruin.

God demands exclusive loyalty. He likens His relationship to His people as a marriage, as shown with Hosea and Gomer, and He wants us to be exclusive to Him. He is a jealous God (Exodus 34:14). In going off with other gods, Israel have made Him their enemy. He will turn everything against them. The evil Israel has pursued, will now overtake them. God Himself shall also pursue them as an enemy would. The language of Hosea 8:14 recalls Sodom and Gomorrah (Genesis 19:23)— wicked cities that were destroyed by fire.

Verse 13 says that '… they shall return to Egypt'. This does not literally mean they will all end up back in Egypt. Some did, as refugees, but Assyria was the main conqueror. In saying 'they shall return to Egypt', God means their removal from the land and the nullification of the covenant promises. God had once delivered them from Egyptian slavery. In total they spent 400 years there but God looked down from Heaven, heard their cries for freedom, had compassion on them and through Moses delivered them. God sent Moses to tell the Pharaoh to let His people go but the Pharaoh refused. God sent ten plagues, to change his mind but each time the Pharaoh refused until the last plague, the death of the eldest son. God sent an angel of death to Egypt to kill the eldest son in every Egyptian household. However, Moses told the Hebrew people to kill a blemish-free lamb and daub its blood on the sides and top of the door frame of their houses. When the angel saw the blood, he would know to *pass over*. The blood of the lamb saved them, and God's people left Egypt that night. Pharaoh's army pursued to retake them but God parted the Red Sea, the people crossed over and the waters closed on Pharaoh's army. God saved them, but now they have turned their back on Him repeatedly, so He is in effect sending them back into slavery. Refugees in Egypt, but mainly in exile in Assyria. Same horse, different jockey.

God's anger, God as an enemy, fire and exile, all point towards the final judgement and the way God judges people today by handing them over to their sin. Revelation 6:12–17 describes what will happen at the end of time. It symbolically describes the physical catastrophes which will take place at the end of the world when the unbelievers face the wrath of God. People will be so afraid that they will try to hide in caves and want the mountains to fall on them. The question will go out, 'Who can stand?' (Revelation 6:17).

Before this final judgement, even today, God sends judgements. Some are to warn people to repent, others usher people into eternity. God controls everything, even natural disasters, and uses them to warn people that there is a God in heaven to whom we must all answer. God is, as it were, shouting down from heaven, offering the opportunity to repent.

We cannot play around with God or presume upon His

grace. He can warn and warn and warn us, but one day He will withdraw His Spirit from us and our hearts will become hardened towards Him All we will be able to do is face judgement and eternal damnation. A time will come when He says, *enough is enough.*

No other way but Jesus Christ

The Israelites were incapable of innocence (8:5). They had lost all decency. But that is true of every one of us. We have all messed up. We have all rebelled against God. Every one of us is selfish and all out for *me*. We are dirty and flawed and keep committing and falling into the same sins time after time after time. There is only one who is innocent. We need to trust Him. The warnings that are found in Hosea, far from driving us away from God, are meant to make us run to Him.

The NIV reading of verse 8:5 suggests it could be an appeal: God is appealing to Samaria, 'spurn your calf'.

Turn, turn from your sin to a pardoning God!

For further study ▶

FOR FURTHER STUDY

1. Can people around me see by the way I live that I am a Christian?
2. 'We can gain the whole world only to find the world is not enough'. Do you believe that?

TO THINK ABOUT AND DISCUSS.

1. Do I worship a cold, man-made idol, or the living God?
2. How often do we think of heaven?

10 Do not rejoice, O Israel

Hosea 9

The book of Hosea is difficult to understand and it is hard to decipher any clear structure. Even so, we must not view Hosea's prophecy as an anthology of sermons that can be read in isolation but rather as a unified literary work. As far as Hosea 9 is concerned, it is reasonable to think it is an adapted message that Hosea first delivered on the occasion of a harvest—perhaps a failed harvest.

The autumn festival of Sukkoth (Feast of Booths) was a time of joy at the end of harvest. It is twice called a Feast of Yahweh (Leviticus 23:39–43), which was supposed to be observed on the fifteenth day of the seventh month. It is possible that the specific feast Hosea has in mind here is an alternative version of the Feast of Booths. It was probably the festival of the fifteenth day of the eighth month that was established by Jeroboam I in order to ensure loyalty of the Israelites to the northern shrines

(1 Kings 12:32). This feast was mixed with Baalism and generated artificial piety.

Like the Feast of Sukkoth, it would have been characterized by feasting, fun and dancing.

A coming disaster would have been the last thought to enter anyone's mind. Yet at this point Hosea probably steps forward to demand the revelry cease, and to call the people to face up to the way things really were. In 9:1 he says, 'Rejoice not, O Israel! Exult not like the peoples; for you have played the whore, forsaking your God. You have loved a prostitute's wages on all threshing floors.'

'Rejoice not' reads like a reversal of what would have been a typical harvest proclamation. You would have expected something like: 'Rejoice, Israel for Yahweh has given you a harvest' (compare with Joel 2:23–24), but Hosea is here turning a proclamation of joy into a lament.

It is hard to get people to think about judgement when everything is going well and everyone is having a good time. Few people like to warn or be warned of God's judgement. We live in an age where we are never to think a serious thought. It is all about entertaining ourselves and being happy. We do not want to hear anything bad. Hosea would have come across as a party pooper. The person who says, 'Stop the party,' sounds like a killjoy. Unless of course the venue is on fire; then he is a life saver. According to Davis, 'Israel's God may love us too much to be nice. His word may pursue us relentlessly until we hear it. He may even ruin a nice occasion if it will get your attention and lead you to repentance.'[1]

Israel was in trouble. They were hurtling full throttle towards judgement and exile and they needed to know that—and fast. Verse 1 goes on to say, '... for you have played the whore, forsaking your God. You have loved a prostitute's wages on all threshing floors.' The reference here to *prostitute's wages on threshing floors* has a double meaning. It refers to the immoral acts that often accompanied the party atmosphere at harvest but it is also to be taken figuratively. The fertility cult was intended to ensure a large harvest. The benefits of the cult were both sexual license and agricultural prosperity, which is why it was so attractive to the Israelite. God did not really hold the slightest interest for Israel. Her only loyalty was to her carnal appetites. The people had forsaken God; therefore, God had now forsaken them. Consequently, their threshing floors and wine presses will not feed the people anymore. If they do not want the Lord, they will not be allowed to remain in the Lord's land.

Perhaps everything seems to be going your way and life for you right now is good. There may be things that are important to you because you think they will bring you happiness and contentment. Exam results, career, family, relationship, money, popularity, social media— whatever. They may be going well or you may think you must spend your time and effort on making them better.

But none of these things really matter in relation to eternity and will not last.

The focus for the Israelites was having a good harvest but the harvest is not the harvest that really matters. Revelation 14:14–16 describes a harvest at the end of the world, and this is the harvest Israel should—and we need to—focus on. The harvest is a picture of judgement day when the Lord Jesus Christ will divide every human being into two groups: those who trust him and those who do not.

When Christ reaps this harvest, everyone will be there; from all over the globe and throughout history, everyone will be summoned to stand before God. Whether you like it or not, or believe it or not, one day you and I will stand before the judgement seat—not the judgement seat of public opinion, not the judgement seat of modern thinking, not the judgement seat of social media—the judgement seat of God! As we are standing there, the books will be opened and the records of the life of every person will be read out. Those who have not trusted Christ will be condemned to hell forever. Imagine it! No wonder Hosea wants to stop the party!

Fools for god

Fools

The people laughed at Hosea and thought he was a fool (Hosea 9:7–8). It is very similar to Amos who was told by the people to 'get out' (Amos 7:10–13). They did not kick Hosea out, they just called him mad. Their attitude is one of, 'Who in his right mind thinks this?'

This has always been the attitude of the world to prophets and preachers. Noah was thought of as a fool. Isaiah was mocked: they accused him of *do and do and do; rule on rule on rule* (Isaiah 28:10). In Acts 26:24, Festus accuses the apostle Paul of being out of his mind. The Lord Jesus Christ was accused of being demon possessed (John 7:20; 8:48). To the world, the prophet is a fool, the man of the Spirit is mad.

> To the world, the prophet is a fool, the man of the Spirit is mad.

If you are not a Christian, perhaps you look at the Church, or particular Christians you know, and feel sorry for them. In the West, Christians today are viewed as a pathetically small group. In some places Christians are persecuted; in other places they are made fun of and left out of things. What Christians believe is seen as old fashioned, out of date and ridiculous. Christianity goes against the trend of society and is seen as completely unimportant to the overwhelming majority of twenty-first century people. You may look down on Christians. You think, 'What fools!' However, what really counts is not what people think of the prophets but what God thinks of them. The world calls them fools but God is with them.

This is why Jesus told the disciples to welcome a prophet's persecution and misrepresentation (Matthew 5:12). I'd rather be Hosea, Isaiah, Amos, the apostle Paul and Noah right now than to be those who laughed at them and ignored them but are now in torment in hell.

WATCHMEN

While the world calls the prophets, *fools*, God calls them *watchmen*. The prophets were often referred to as watchmen (Jeremiah 6:17; Ezekiel 3:17; 33:2–7). They were the ones looking out for the people and warning them of impending danger. That is the role of preachers and all Christians today. To tell people about the wrath to come and urge them to turn to Jesus Christ to save them.

But they will only operate as a watchman if the people heed their warnings. In verse 7, God is saying in effect, 'Yes the prophets are mad, you have driven them to it with your sin and hostility.'

Hearing the prophets' message and then rejecting it will become a snare (v. 8). Instead of being a means of salvation, it becomes a downfall to the unrepentant. The apostle Paul says in 2 Corinthians 2:15–16, 'For we are the aroma of Christ to God among those who are being saved and among those who are perishing, to one a fragrance from death to death, to the other a fragrance from life to life.'

But it was not just prophets and it is not just

preachers—all Christians are called to be fools for God. We are to be different. Israel's problem was that she tried to gain a good harvest by the same means that the other nations employed—the fertility cult. The lost harvest served as evidence that they are not like other nations and should not try to be. The harvest had failed because of their prostitution against God.

The Lord Jesus compares the church to salt and light. In the ancient world salt was needed to keep meat and food as fresh as possible for as long as possible. He says Christians are meant to be to the world what salt is to food and meat. They are to be in the world, like the salt was rubbed into the meat, and do it good. But when salt loses its flavour, it becomes entirely worthless (Matthew 5:13). In the same way, when the church tries to be like the world and just blends in, then it becomes ineffective. We are called to be in the world but to be different. Stand up and stand out for Jesus Christ. This will inevitably result in the world thinking we are fools. But far better to be called a fool for God than be called a fool by God.

Sin corrodes

Hosea 9:10 describes how it all started so well for Israel but how sin has now corroded her. At Mount Sinai, Israel became a nation (Exodus 19); God met Israel in the wilderness (Exodus 14-19); He fought for His people and they took the land, a land flowing with milk and honey

(Exodus 3:17); And then God gave them rest. This home for Israel was a picture and pointer to God's ultimate plan.

At the beginning of Hosea 9:10, you can sense God's delight and anticipation in this great early venture with His people; there is zest and enjoyment, not cold charity. This is made clear in the analogy Hosea uses: grapes in the wilderness and the first fruit on the fig tree in its first season. You would not expect to find edible grapes in the desert and such a discovery would be a real feast for a Bedouin traveller, whereas the first fruit on the fig tree in spring would be especially delicious to people in the ancient world. This was because they could not transport fruit over long distances, so could not enjoy fruit except when it was locally in season. It would have been especially delightful if you had not had a fig all year. By the end of the season, when everyone had eaten their fill of figs, the pleasure would have worn off. The point in both analogies is that in her youth, Israel was a special source of delight to God, but the mood of the verse turns. The people who had been so highly favoured went to Baal-Peor.

Baal-peor was the location of a shrine to Baal in the plains of Moab some twenty kilometres (twelve miles) northeast of the Dead Sea. According to Numbers 25:1–9, after Balaam failed in his efforts to bring a curse down on Israel, the Israelites brought one down on themselves by yielding to the enticement to have sexual relations with

Moabite women, who were sacred prostitutes in the cult of Baal-Peor. A plague began in Israel and the plague did not come to a stop until the priest, Phinehas, took a spear and ran it through the bodies of an Israelite man and Moabite woman that he apparently caught in the act. This reminds us that Israel began its apostasy to Baal before it even entered the Promised Land and emphasizes the need for drastic action to be taken to bring this kind of immorality to a halt. It is also striking that Hosea is highlighting the fact that Yahweh condemns Israel for sins at a certain location. Yahweh is interested in specifics. Nothing escapes His eye.

However, not only did things start well for Israel and then go wrong, but this is even more true of how everything changed from what God intended originally. God placed the first man and woman, Adam and Eve, in a garden called Eden. It was paradise. They could eat of any fruit in the garden except from the tree of the knowledge of good and evil. If they ate from this tree they would die (Genesis 2:17). It was a clear command and warning from God. We do not know how long Adam and Eve lived in the idyllic paradise. Genesis 3:8 infers that before Adam and Eve fell, each evening God would come and meet with them.

Then the Devil comes to Eve in the form of a serpent, deceives her into eating the forbidden fruit and she in turn gives some to Adam. Adam and Eve, therefore, disobey God and sin and death enters the world. We lost eternal life and instead face eternal damnation.

But, as well as Genesis 3 recording what the root problem is and where everything went wrong, every day our nature confirms the Fall is true. You know you are not right. Like me, you are a sinner.

Sin makes a person do awful things. It stops you thinking straight. You cannot play around with it. Hosea 9:9 says, 'They have deeply corrupted themselves as in the days of Gibeah.' It is a reference to the story in Judges 19–21 in which a Levite's concubine was raped and murdered at Gibeah. The Levite, to obtain revenge, cut her body into twelve pieces and sent the pieces to the tribes of Israel to provoke their outrage, and so began a civil war and a series of grotesque atrocities. Hosea declares that the people of his day have fallen to the level of the most corrupt generation of Israel's history.

> Sin makes a person do awful things. It stops you thinking straight.

Sodom and Gomorrah, two notoriously evil cities (Genesis 19) could teach Gibeah nothing. If a person or people or country keep sinning, God eventually hands them over to what they want. And the consequences are awful. Evil becomes good and good becomes evil (Romans 1:18–32).

This is why we must take drastic measures to kill sin, or

sin ends up being totally in control. It is the devil's lie, a total illusion that you believe you can stop sinning when you decide. You cannot! Repent now before it is too late or you will not want or be able to (Hebrews 12:17; Exodus 10:20). If you do not kill sin, sin will kill you.

Sinners in the hands of an angry God

Not only does sin corrode, sin also makes God angry. In verses 2 and 3, 6, 11–13 and 15–17 of chapter 9, God's anger towards sinful Israel is expressed. There are four ways God's anger is clear in these verses.

GILGAL

It was at Gilgal that Joshua gained his first foothold in the Promised Land (Joshua 4:19). At Gilgal David was welcomed back from exile (2 Samuel 19:15). And Gilgal was the place where Saul's reign was inaugurated (1 Samuel 11:15).

But, in Hosea's day, Gilgal was the quintessential city of Israel. It contained every evil that the book of Hosea condemns. It was a cult centre (Hosea 4:15; 12:11). So much so, this was the city that prompted God to declare Israel His enemy. In fact, at Gilgal, God had begun to hate Israel.

Hate is a strong, harsh Hebrew word for rejection (3:1; 11:1 onwards; 14:4). It shows that God can have no dealings with sin or those who continue in it and refuse to repent. He rejects it and hates it with every fibre of

His holy being. God is longsuffering and slow to anger (Psalm 103:8) but there gets to a point where enough is enough—when sin seems to spiral out of control.

BAD HARVEST

As a result of their sin, God will send them a bad harvest. Verse 2 says, 'Threshing floor and wine vat shall not feed them, and the new wine shall fail them.' Verse 16 goes on to say, 'Ephraim is stricken; their root is dried up; they shall bear no fruit ...' These verses describe famine conditions and the failure of the Baal cult to secure a good harvest. Israel will bear no fruit in the land. Famine would be the last stroke of divine punishment before captivity.

NO CHILDREN

But as well as a failed harvest, Israel's women would be barren. Verse 11 and 12 says, 'Ephraim's glory shall fly away like a bird—no birth, no pregnancy, no conception! Even if they bring up children, I will bereave them till none is left. Woe to them when I depart from them!'

In these verses there is another seeming paradox. It talks about the women becoming barren but then refers to them bringing up children. God is saying that because of their sin, the women will be barren. But even if they could get pregnant their children would not survive (v. 16). The point is that God's wrath is inescapable.

There are references to child sacrifice in verses 13

and 16. The cult of Baal was hideous and a complete paradox. This is something that is brought out in Psalm 106:28–30. On the one hand its objective was to enable women to give birth to many healthy children. But the same cult consumed children in ritual sacrifice. While these verses do not explicitly charge the Israelites with child sacrifices, the judgements of barrenness could be a response to such atrocities.

I am sure these verses raise many questions in our minds but however obnoxious these things are to us, it shows how much more obnoxious our sins are to God. How these things seem to us is what the stench of our sin is in God's nostrils; how it smells to Him. It repulses Him.

The thought of sacrificing children outrages us. And yet, 7 million unborn children have been aborted in the United Kingdom; this is more than the number who died in the Holocaust. If an unborn child is discovered to have a cleft pallet, they can be aborted the day before they are born. How can we have disability rights when we carry out screen tests to detect Downs Syndrome with the intention to abort? Someone has said that inside the womb is the most dangerous place to be in Britain today.

Exile

Because of their sin, Israel's glory shall fly away—wealth, power, self-respect, reputation and children. Looking back to the metaphor of Israel as an adulterous wife, Yahweh says He is going to put them out of His house (v. 15). His house was a place of plenty, provision, security and safety. But they had believed Satan's lie that they would be better off without God—freer. However, in the end, they have been enslaved by sin and self. This will happen when God sends them into exile. It will be sudden and impossible to prevent. Their glory will just fly away like a bird (v. 11).

Verse 6 says, 'For behold, they are going away from destruction; but Egypt shall gather them; Memphis shall bury them. Nettles shall possess their precious things of silver; thorns shall be in their tents'. Verse 3 says, 'They shall not remain in the land of the LORD, but Ephraim shall return to Egypt, and they shall eat unclean food in Assyria.' and verse 17 says, 'My God will reject them because they have not listened to him; they shall be wanderers among the nations.'

Yahweh found Israel like grapes in the desert but now the imagery is of nettles and thorns. Everything will be reversed. God had brought Israel out of the wilderness into an abundant land, but now they would go back to be wanderers in the desert. He had brought them out of Egypt, but now they would return to an Egypt-type state. He had freed them, but now they go back to being slaves. For her religious flirtations she would pay the price of having scattered her favours everywhere: captive in Assyria and fugitives in Egypt. The reference to Yahweh's land and unclean foods is synonymous.

They are rejected from Yahweh's land and therefore the people will have to eat unclean food in a foreign land.

So, what relevance has all this got for us?

Every move we make, every breath we take, God is watching us

As God saw everything that was going on in Gilgal, so He sees everything that we do—and it makes Him angry. The fact that Yahweh condemns Israel for sins at a certain location is because He sees everything, and Yahweh has seen our sins too, at all the particular locations where we have sinned. Today, God seems silent but the silence of God does not indicate the absence of God. Just because God is not uppermost in our minds today and He does not feature much on our agenda at all, does not mean to say that He is not actively watching and keenly aware of everything. He is observing it all from heaven.

> Today, God seems silent but the silence of God does not indicate the absence of God.

Every one of us has got guilty secrets. Some of them are so shameful. You may be quietly hoping and thinking you have got away with it. But you have not. God has seen everything. What you have done and where you have done it. It is all recorded, as are all the injustices and corruption that goes on around us.

A boy in my school once pushed another boy to the

floor and while he was on the floor, kicked him. Before he did so though, he looked around to see if anyone was watching. The problem was that upstairs in the English classroom, the Head of English was looking down, watching it all. The boy looked around but did not look up. That is our problem. We look around to see if anyone is watching before we click on a website, commit an immoral act, gossip, lose our temper, cheat, steal, whatever. But we do not look up. God sees our sins. All of them. He knows them all specifically and remembers them all. 'Thou God seest me' (Genesis 16.13, KJV).

JUDGEMENTS

As with the failed harvest in Hosea's day, God sends judgements today. God's Spirit will not always strive with man (Genesis 6:3). In the book of Revelation, God's judgements are depicted as seven trumpets (Revelation 8 and 9) and seven bowls (Revelation 15 and 16). Human wickedness does not go unnoticed in heaven. The trumpets are to warn people to repent, whereas the bowls are the actual outpouring of these judgements.

To some, judgements come as God's trumpets to warn and remind them that this world is under a curse as the result of the Fall and there is a God in heaven with whom we have to do business! For others, these are bowls that usher them into eternity where they will stand before God. Some will be ready, most will not.

THE FINAL JUDGEMENT

But, as well as sending judgements on people and nations to warn and point us to God, there is also the final judgement. God warned and warned Israel until finally they were sent into exile. Similarly, God warns and warns us but one day the trumpet of God will sound, the Lord Jesus will return (1 Thessalonians 4:16) and we will all stand before His judgement seat. At the judgement, God will decide whether we go to heaven or hell.

It is impossible to envisage how awful it will be. What a terrible plight to find yourself in for all eternity! According to Hendriksen [2]:

> The pleasure mad, arrogant world, with all its seductive luxuries and pleasures, with its antichristian philosophy and culture, with its teeming multitudes that have forsaken God and have lived according to the lusts of the flesh and the desires of the mind, shall perish. The wicked suffer eternal despair.

No wonder the Bible urges us to flee from the wrath to come! (Matthew 3:7).

BE AFRAID

Some will read this and say how wrong it is to motivate by fear, but that is nonsense. What matters is whether there is a true basis for fear. If there is reason to tremble, we should tremble. God is warning Israel for their own good. What would be wrong is if He did not warn at all and let them go straight to destruction. The hymn writer, John Newton (1725–1807), says in his hymn, 'Amazing Grace', 'Twas grace that taught my heart to fear'.

In his famous sermon, 'Sinners in the hands of an angry God' Edwards[3], preaching on Deuteronomy 32:35 said:

> Nothing but his hand that holds you from falling into the fire every moment. It is to be ascribed to nothing else, that you did not go to Hell last night, that you were suffered to awake again in this world after you closed your eyes to sleep ... God's hand has held you up.

No access

Worst of all, Yahweh Himself will abandon them. God very soon will no longer be there. He is about to withdraw his presence. Israel will have no access to God.

Hosea 9:5 says, 'What will you do on the day of the appointed festival, and on the day of the feast of the LORD?'

Verse 4 says,

> They shall not pour drink offerings of wine to the LORD, and their sacrifices shall not please him. It shall be like mourners' bread to them; all who eat of it shall be defiled; for their bread shall be for their hunger only; it shall not come to the house of the LORD.

It is important to note that even though Israel had embraced Baalism (so they could have the excitement of an orgy and all the other fringe benefits, as well as hedging their bets for a good harvest) they had not completely rejected Yahweh. Although apostate, they considered themselves to be orthodox and desired Yahweh's favour. They thought that keeping the festivals and offering sacrifices was enough to appease Yahweh. Religion gave them their identity; they were a people, had traditions and a land. Religion penetrated everything except the conscience. It was a charm against trouble, a compelling pattern of festivals, stories and customs that gave shape to life.

Ritual cleanliness was important to Israelites. A dead body in a house made all who ate there unclean. Those who were mourning must deal with the burial of a dead body. That was not a problem when you could go to the temple and be cleansed. But in exile, away from the temple, you would remain unclean. Their food would be contaminated and their bread unfit as an offering to God (Deuteronomy 26:12–14). Exile, and famine, would make ceremonial rituals impossible. So, the fact that they could no longer sacrifice to Yahweh and there would be no festivals, mattered. The sacrifices they offer would either not be acceptable or they would have nothing at all to offer as sacrifices. All of this would leave them totally adrift. God was abandoning them. He was leaving them to it. They had no way to access Him.

When we sin, we think how nice it would be if God were

to leave us alone. Maybe, as you read this book, you resent the fact that you feel God stops you from doing certain things. He troubles your conscience and you just want to shake Him off. But imagine if He left you? Imagine if He said to us today, 'I will love them no more' (Hosea 9:15). God says, *'Woe to them when I depart from them'* (Hosea 9:12). It is an awful thing when God leaves you alone. It is haunting (1 Samuel 13:15; 15:34–35a; 28:25b).

> It is an awful thing when God leaves you alone. It is haunting.

You cannot play around with God. Hell is full of people who said, 'When I have done this and when I have done that, I will sort things out.' But today is the only day promised as a day of salvation (2 Corinthians 6:2). You may die tonight. However, you may live another seventy years but have no interest in Christ at all after today. He may be calling to you now but tomorrow your heart may be hardened. He may never pass your way again. If you hear His voice, harden not your heart (Hebrews 3:15).

O Lord ...

In verse 14, we have a truncated prayer of Hosea. He says, 'Give them, O Lord—what will you give? Give them a miscarrying womb and dry breasts.'

Hosea seems to pause in his prayer. It is like he does not know what to ask for. You can sense a strangled cry—a gasping sob welling up from the heart. He loved God and God was His. But he also loved the people and they were his too.

Israel was about to be condemned to a wandering existence: a well-earned judgement. They had ogled one nation after another. They had dismissed as mad fools God's look-out men, the prophets, and had forsaken the Lord for Baal. Therefore, they would return to 'Egypt' and to slavery.

Hosea wants to pray for them but does not know what to ask. In order that the miseries of the day of judgement are as limited as possible, he prays for wombs that miscarry and breasts that are dry. He reluctantly prays for adversity to come upon them to bring them to repentance.

What about us? What should we pray, for ourselves and our communities and nation?

The good news is this. The exile was final for Israel, but what is true of that generation is not true for us; it is still a day of grace. The way we have lived and the sins we have accumulated mean we deserve to be exiled from God, in hell forever. But, on the cross, the Lord Jesus Christ was willing to suffer the exile for us. He cried out 'with a loud voice, saying, "Eloi, Eloi, lama sabachthani?" which means, "My God, my God, why have you forsaken me?"' (Mark 15:34–35). He was abandoned, exiled by God, feeling the guilt of millions of sins and the white-hot anger of a holy God.

However, because the Lord Jesus was abandoned, 'exiled' for us, the wrath that God should pour out on us, was poured out on Him. When he cried out, 'My God My God, why have you forsaken me?' God's answer in effect was, 'because in the twenty-first century there will be people who will need a Saviour. You are abandoned so they do not have to be.'

So, what should we pray? For ourselves and for others? Surely whatever it takes to bring us and them to repentance and to come to trust the One who was exiled for us on that cross. Conviction of sin; hardships; a bringing of an end to ourselves and themselves? Just that we all would fly to Jesus Christ!

Jerry Bridges prayed, 'God whatever it takes, I want Christ to be my Saviour.'[4]

FOR FURTHER STUDY.

1. Does the thought of standing before the judgement seat of God concern or encourage you?

2. How is my life different to that of an unbeliever?

TO THINK ABOUT AND DISCUSS.

1. Is our love for God deeper than our love for the things of this world?

2. Do I fear rejection if I speak of my faith to family and friends?

11 Time to seek the Lord

Hosea 10

Hosea's ministry began during a period of prosperity. Israel enjoyed a time of luxury with abundant harvests. But instead of thanking God for her prosperity, Israel used her wealth to build altars to other gods. In fact, the nation's prosperity led to unfaithfulness.

How did it get to this?

Again, in this chapter Hosea bombards us with lively metaphors (10:1, 4, 7, 11). In verse 1 he says, 'Israel is a luxuriant vine that yields its fruit. The more his fruit increased, the more altars he built; as his country improved, he improved his pillars.' God often refers to Israel in the Bible as a vine (Isaiah 5:1, 2, 7; Jeremiah 2:21; Ezekiel 15, 19:10–14). When Jesus said I am the true vine (John 15:1 onwards), the vine of Israel was the background. The pillars, mentioned in verse 1, are probably totem poles, shrines to other gods—possibly local fertility symbols. There was a direct correlation between her growing prosperity and her growing apostasy: '... the more his fruit increased, the more altars ...' (v. 1).

Israel could not have been given a better opportunity or received more privileges. Hosea 9:10 says when God first found Israel—that is, when He first formed her as a nation—she was like grapes in the wilderness. Now Hosea winds forward the story to a time when Israel had become a luxuriant vine, spreading through the Promised Land. Psalm 80 uses similar imagery, describing how God brought a vine out of Egypt. He cleared the ground for it by driving the nations out of the Promised Land. Under God's care it prospered.

However, by the time of Hosea's prophecy, while Israel is producing a lot of fruit, it is not the fruit that matters. The vine took up valuable soil—soil that could be used by a productive plant, rather than one like Israel that gave benefit only to itself and not to its owner. God could not have done more for His vineyard but the vine kept producing sour grapes—fruit that had gone rotten. It is reminiscent of the wild grapes in Isaiah 5:1–7. The fruit Israel is producing are the fruits of an idolatrous religion.

Israel was living proof that it is far harder to cope with prosperity than with suffering. The more we have, the easier it is to forget God. It is hard to have things before they end up having us. They absorb us and take over our lives. We start to live for them. No wonder Solomon said:

> Remove far from me falsehood and lying; give me neither poverty nor riches; feed me with the food that is needful for me lest I be full and deny you and say, 'Who is the LORD?', or lest I be poor and steal and profane the name of my God (Proverbs 30:8–9).

It also shows that we can presume upon the kindness and mercy of God. We can have so many gospel privileges—the Bible, faithful churches, Christian family, good preaching, sound Christian books—and yet take all these for granted and go after sin.

Divided heart

It was not that Israel did not love God, or at least think they loved God. They just loved other things more. They did not love God with all their heart (Mark 12:30). Verse 2 says, 'Their heart is false ...' and verse 4 says, 'They utter mere words; with empty oaths they make covenants.'

Their hearts were deceitful. They were in a covenant with God, had made promises to God but were not faithful and true to Him. They pretended to worship God; they worshipped Him with their lips but their hearts were far from Him (Isaiah 29:13; Matthew 15:8). They said they loved Him but the way they behaved proved otherwise. When Gomer went off with her lovers, she would no doubt still have said, 'I love Hosea I just want my lovers too.' This is sadly the case among a lot of Christians today. We are not out and out for God. We try to fit Him around our lives. We go to church on a Sunday but God does not really affect our lives. He is a bolt-on.

Our approach to the Lord's Day is a good test of how much we love God. As well as paying the tithe, in the Old Testament one of the barometers by which the spiritual life of the nations

> Our approach to the Lord's Day is a good test of how much we love God.

of Israel and Judah could be judged was their observance of the Sabbath. Today many Christians go to church once a Sunday because there is no 'rule' about going twice and find all that kind of talk legalistic. We keep His day but mix it with everything else we want to do as well—sport, television, whatever. If we loved Him with all of our hearts, we would want to be in church to hear about Him, worship Him and meet with His people.

I am sure there will be people who will say that this is legalistic mumbo jumbo; that we should be able to enjoy our Christian liberty. God does not want to spoil our fun and wants us to have life. But it cannot be healthy if we want to get away with spending as little time with God as possible and do the bare minimum we can get away with and justify.

Describing Christianity in his own day, J.C. Ryle says:

It is a Christianity in which there is undeniably

something about Christ and something about grace and something about faith and something about repentance and something about holiness, but it is not the real thing as it is in the Bible. Things are out of place and out of proportion.[1]

He goes on to say:

It has long been my sorrowful conviction that the standard of daily life among professing Christians in this country has been gradually falling away ... separation from the world are far less appreciated than they ought to be and that they used to be in the days of our fathers.[2]

We need to get serious about God again and seek Him with all our hearts, not with divided ones. He has promised that those who seek Him with all their hearts will find Him (Jeremiah 29:13). According to Duncan Campbell: 'This awareness of God is the urgent need of the church today.'[3] It would be great if we could say as Paul did, 'God is really among you' (1 Corinthians 14:25).

No one tells me what to do

It is hard to know which is worse, arrogance or apathy. Israel had swung between the two, shown by their fluctuating attitudes towards the monarchy. They pinned all their hopes on a king and princes (13:10). Then they cheapened it with debauchery and tore it apart with assassinations (7:3–7). Finally, during the chaotic years after the death of Jeroboam II, the people became cynical; they shrugged the monarchy off as meaningless along with everything else, from God downwards. They felt none of the kings had legitimate claim to the throne. Hosea 10:3 says, 'For now they will say: "We have no king, for we do not fear the LORD; and a king— what could he do for us?"' The people of Israel rejected all authority. They had no reverence for Yahweh as their king or respect for the kings who ruled over them. They declared they were free from all authority. Everyone did what they thought was right in their own eyes (Judges 21:25).

When there is no fear of the Lord, a country has a political system with no integrity. Injustice and people not keeping their word and breaking their promises soon follow. Hosea pictures the situation as weeds which take over a farmer's field. The corrupt political and religious system bears bad fruit and weeds (10:4).

An attitude of cynicism and everyone knowing best is prevalent today. There is a loss of confidence in the political system and a widespread feeling of, 'What does the government ever do for us?' and 'You can't trust any politicians.' While this might be understandable, and sadly may too often be the case, there is also no fear of God or regard for His Word. What matters is what we think. No one tells us what to do! Justice no longer towers over us all but springs from the thoughts, policies, ideas and feelings of the moment. This humanistic approach, at best, takes its estimate of morality and justice from ground level—from whatever happens to be society's current mood and practice. In describing society during his time as Prime Minister, Tony Blair said, 'The mood was merciless in its pursuit, indifferent to anything other than satisfying itself.'[4]

Society in no time can end up with people thinking nothing of cheating others for their own private gain. Laws are passed for selfish motives and interests. Everything is about 'Me'. We turn our back on God and do our own thing. False morality strengthens its hold on the community, Christian values are choked and smothered, and a wild crop of sin and ungodliness spreads. Things will only get worse and worse unless we return to the Word of God. And the Church, while engaging with society and being as winsome as we can, must not try to keep it happy and indulge it. We must be people of the Book.

> Society in no time can end up with people thinking nothing of cheating others for their own private gain.

No help to you in the end

But while people feel they can do what they want, live for themselves and act as though there is no God, in the end they will have to answer to God and all they have lived for and set up will be no help to them. Israel had invested so much in her altars and pillars but these same altars and pillars will be destroyed; God will break them down.

It happened to ancient Israel and the same will happen to us, and it is not just religious altars. It is all the altars we have erected. All the things we worship and give ourselves to instead of God. We are answerable and our guilt before God has not gone unnoticed. Our man-made religion, world views, way of life will be of no use to us then. God will have the last word. What He thinks is all that matters. His verdict is the one that counts. Hosea 10:2 says, '... now they must bear their guilt. The LORD will break down their altars and destroy their pillars.'

THE CALF

This is clearly illustrated in the *calf* that Israel erected (Hosea 10:5, 6).

Samaria was the capital of Israel and represented all of Israel. After the death of Solomon, the Kingdom of Israel divided, Judah in the south and Israel in the north. Jeroboam I became the first king of the Northern Kingdom. His subjects regularly made pilgrimages to Jerusalem, right at the heart of the rival regime. This meant money for the South. So, Jeroboam I set up two rival shrines, one in Bethel and the other in Dan, in order to stop people going to Jerusalem. By Hosea's time in the history of Israel, the shrines had fallen into enemy hands, so only one remained—the calf at Samaria. Dan had fallen with the rest of the northern territories before the armies of Tiglath-Pileser (2 Kings 15:29).

Hosea does not refer to the shrine as Bethel (House of God) but by its nickname, *Beth-aven*, which means 'house of wickedness'. The house of God had become the home of wickedness. The people merged Baal and Yahweh together. In their minds, they worshipped at the Baal cult but remained loyal to Yahweh.

The calf or bull was a symbol of fertility and power. Yet ironically, they worry about its safety (10:5). In reality they should tremble before God but instead they tremble for the calf. They should fear God because He is majestic and holy, but they are more worried about a calf that is impotent and unable to move on its own accord, and about to get carried off to Assyria (10:6).

Their carefully crafted belief system was failing; it was a religious system with no future. Israel's glory was about to vanish. They would mourn, but their mourning would spring from disappointment and wounded pride rather than repentance. It would be a worldly grief, not godly grief that leads to salvation and brings no regret (2 Corinthians 7:10).

In the Hebrew, the reference to the 'great king' (10:6,

ESV) is given a scornful twist to read 'king Jareb' in the KJV, which translates: 'a king who finds fault'. Israel thought they were being so clever and savvy in making alliances with worldly powers. But Hosea—as so often with his play on words—in a single word has shown up the hopelessness of attempting to buy off so seasoned an aggressor. The 'king' they have gone after will chew them up and spit them out.

We can look back on ancient Israel and pity them but we are no better today in the twenty-first century. We build our own 'calves' that we trust in and worship at. Liberalism, religious toleration, power, popularity, wealth, looks, intellect: these are the things we bow down to but one day God will destroy them. They will do us no good and be worthless. In fact, they will be our ruin and downfall.

All the good and the great we look up to today, who seem so powerful, will be brought low. There will be a rapid end to all thoughts of human self-sufficiency. Hosea 10:7 says, 'Samaria's king shall perish like a twig on the face of the waters.' He will be like a twig just carried along with the movements over which it has no control. The king of whom was said, 'under his shadow we shall live among the nations' (Lamentations 4:20), would prove to be no massive oak, deep-rooted and reassuring, but a twig on the surface of a torrent, overtaken by events and whisked helplessly away.

We need to realize and understand that God is sovereign. You can bash yourself against omnipotence but the success rate is nil. Kings rise and fall at His command. 'The Most High God rules the kingdom of mankind and sets over it whom he will' (Daniel 5:21).

DESOLATION

If Hosea's picture of the calf is of turbulence, the next one he paints in verse 8 of shrines and altars, deserted and overgrown, is ominously still. It is a picture of desolation: thorns, thistles and broken walls. The one-time great empires are desolate. Great men and women are no more.

This is powerfully illustrated in Revelation 18 where it describes every department of this world's existence being destroyed. The kings and mighty men, the men of influence, will weep and mourn over the world (Revelation 18:9–10). They yielded to her temptations and enjoyed her luxuries but now they are terrified at her torment and are amazed at the fact that judgement could fall so suddenly (Revelation 18:10).

Merchants are pictured mourning over the world because no one buys their produce anymore (Revelation 18:11–17). The food and drink we enjoy, the nice clothes we wear, our hi-tech gadgets, our houses and cars, one day will all be destroyed. None of them will last forever.

Seafaring men also mourn (Revelation 18:18–20).

These comprise of the captains; the passengers, intent on business; the sailors; exporters; importers; and fishermen. They see from afar the smoke of the world's flames. They recall its former greatness and splendour and they can hardly believe their eyes when they see her total ruin.

Whoever we are, living for the world, and all that it offers, will be no help to us in the end. One day it will all go up in smoke.

SHAME

All who are not trusting in God will know unbearable shame. Hosea 10:8 says, '... they shall say to the mountains, "Cover us," and to the hills, "Fall on us."'

Hosea again uses a nickname, 'Aven', which means iniquity. These holy places are the sin of Israel and God's last word on man-made religion. They sum up human arrogance, stubborn independence and rebellion against God, all of which heap judgement upon us. Hosea is describing in these verses the plight of the land but also points towards the fact that the plight of the people will be far worse. Furthermore, Israel's judgement looks forward to judgement for all humanity. In the end all who are not

> Israel's judgement looks forward to judgement for all humanity.

right with God will want the mountains to 'cover us', and the hills to 'fall on us'.

This cry is taken up twice in the New Testament. Firstly, to predict the horror of the fall of Jerusalem in AD 70, following Israel's choice to crucify the Messiah (Luke 23:30). Secondly, to portray the terrors of the last judgement (Rev. 6:16). At this time there will be an earthquake, the sun will become black, the moon become like blood, and stars will fall from the sky. It will be terrifying for everyone who is not safe under the throne of God. The kings of the earth, princes, great men, commanders, the rich, the strong, slaves and the free—in fact every kind of person—will be so afraid that they will try to hide in caves and want the mountains to fall on them. The question will go out, 'Who can stand?' (Revelation 6:17). It will be an awful day when the hearts of many will fail them for fear (Luke 21:26). It will be a day when everyone will be summoned to the judgement and everything we have done will come to light.

Think

THINK BACK ...

Hosea reinforces what he has to say with a reminder of Israel's past history. He wants them to think back. He reminds them of Gibeah (Hosea 10:9). The event at Gibeah took place during the time of the judges; a time when everyone did what was right in their own eyes (Judges 17:6; 21:25). Gibeah was a town occupied by the tribe of Benjamin. A Levite or priest during the time of the judges was on a trip and on his way home with his concubine. As night-time neared, he found that he was not going to be able to reach home that evening. He reached Gibeah and tried to find somewhere to stay for the night. But no one would open their home to him apart from an old man who came from the fields and invited him to stay. However, depraved youths gathered and demanded he send the Levite out for homosexual sex with him. The old man resisted and in the end the concubine was sent out. The men used her all night. She staggered back to the house in the morning and fell on the doorstep. By the time the Levite emerged, she was dead.

The shock of this event resulted in her body being cut into 12 pieces and sent to the 12 tribes of Israel calling on them to do justice. They demanded that the tribe of Benjamin hand over the men of Gibeah but they refused, which resulted in civil war. The number of Benjaminites killed was 25,000, leaving only 600 survivors. It was a time when the twelve tribes perilously came close to becoming the eleven tribes (Judges 20).

By trying to get them to think about what happened at Gibeah, Hosea is trying to impress upon the people of his day that something similarly awful is about to be repeated. Gibeah's crime was not the exception. Gibeah was one of the worst incidents; it was an unrestrained expression of sin in the hearts of the people, but Israel has not moved on—they had continued to sin. They continued with the same pattern of behaviour and operated at this level consistently.

Israel's violent history relied on military power and violence for security. They maintained the Gibeah mind-set. During the time of King Saul, Gibeah was a fortress place. Archaeology shows that some of the walls were 1.2 metres thick. This is what Israel trusted in.

> As God's people we must not trust in ourselves but in Him and keep turning to Him for forgiveness, help and strength.

There are lessons today we can learn from Gibeah. It shows us how evil sin is and that there are huge consequences. It proves the power sin has over us and that in our own strength we cannot overcome it. Left to ourselves, we would keep falling deeper and deeper and more tangled up in our sin. As God's people we must not trust in ourselves but in Him and keep turning to Him for forgiveness, help and strength.

AND MORE RECENTLY...

However, Israel did not have to go as far back as Gibeah to be made to think. Hosea 10:14 says

... therefore the tumult of war shall arise among your

people, and all your fortresses shall be destroyed, as
Shalman destroyed Beth-arbel on the day of battle;
mothers were dashed in pieces with their children.

This is a reference to some terrible siege that the people knew about. Beth-arbel may be what is now the modern Irbid, located thirty kilometres south-east of the Sea of Galilee. As to who Shalman is, we can only guess at. He could be a person mentioned in the Assyrian annals of Tiglath-Pileser III, named Salamanu of Maob, but, in all likelihood, Shalman is short for Shalmaneser of Assyria. So, the one mentioned here could either be Shalmaneser V (727–722 BC), whose march to besiege Samaria could have taken him through Beth-arbel (the Arbela of Maccabees 9:2 near the west shore of the lake of Galilee). Alternatively, it could be Shalmaneser III of the previous century (859–824 BC), who campaigned against Syria, Hauren and Israel in 841 BC and whose route could have included this Arbela or another Arbela near Pella, east of Jordan.

While we cannot be sure who exactly Shalman was, we do know what those names meant for the people in Hosea's day—the same as Hitler to us today. To make it even worse, a conqueror's atrocities against mothers and children (10:14b) were clearly all too common (2 Kings 8:12; 15:16; Psalm 137:8–9; Isaiah 13:16; Amos 1:13; Nahum 3:10). These events were fresh in the memory of every Israelite and would have brought special sharpness to the present warning.

Again, Hosea is trying to focus Israel's mind and get them to wake up to their impending judgement. Unless they repent, something similar was about to happen.

Think ahead ...

As well as encouraging Israel to think back, by bringing recent events to their mind, Hosea tells Israel to think ahead.

God has an appointed time when he will judge Israel again. Verse 10 says, 'When I please, I will discipline them, and nations shall be gathered against them when they are bound up for their double iniquity.'

This judgement is a sure thing. He goes on to say in verse 15, 'Thus it shall be done to you, O Bethel, because of your great evil. At dawn the king of Israel shall be utterly cut off.'

The judgement will be as sure as the sun rises. The king will not be able to postpone the day of reckoning any more than he could stem the torrent of verse 7 that was to sweep him away!

The reason for this judgement is their sin. According to verse 10, '... they are bound up for their double iniquity'. The Israelites are tied to the choices they are making and have made.

Sin ties the sinner to their choice. 'Double iniquity'

could be a reference to Israel's worship of Baal and to their worldly alliances in its politics, both of which are major accusations in this chapter. Alternatively, it could be a reference to the repeated or persistent acts of Israel's disobedience, like the three transgressions and four of the first chapter of Amos. It is the fact that they keep committing the same sins time and time again.

Whereas this judgement in the past has come in the form of what happened at Gibeah and by fellow Israelites, it will be by foreign nations this time. The fulfilment is recorded in 2 Kings 17:6 and 24–41.

That the judgements threatened by God through Hosea and the rest of the prophets all came to pass, should hammer home to us the certainty of the judgement to come, promised in the New Testament. Each of us will stand before the judgement seat of Christ (2 Corinthians 5:10). It is appointed unto man once to die and after that the judgement (Hebrews 9:27).

In August in 1756, George Whitfield preached in William Grimshaw's Yorkshire parish. Whitfield preached in the open air to a massive throng. His text was Hebrews 9:27. 'It is appointed unto men once to die but after this the judgement' (KJV). He paused and was about to proceed but was cut off by a wild curdling shriek from the middle of the congregation. Grimshaw hurried to investigate and after some minutes returned to tell Whitfield that 'an immortal soul has been called into eternity'. This news was announced to the people. After a few moments Whitfield again announced his text: 'It is appointed unto men once to die...'[5]

But it has not got to be like this

Even though Israel is hurtling full throttle to judgement and ruin, it need not be like that.

WE GET WHAT WE PUT IN

In verse 13, the picture is of a harvest and a farmer reaping what he had sown. You cannot plant apple pips and expect to harvest pears. Israel was only getting out what she had put in. If you plant fruits of lies, you will get grapes of poison. The fruit of lies looks nice and tastes nice but it is poisonous. Israel was ploughing iniquity, lies and injustice, so she would have to reap what she had sown. And the harvest was fast approaching! Sin seems so appealing and compelling, but it is corrosive, addictive and destructive. It always ends in pain and shame.

Israel had turned their back on God and set up other idols and worshipped and bowed down to them instead. They were relying on military strength and alliances with other nations to keep them safe. But judgement was coming and they were about to find out that the things they were bowing down to and that were so important to them, and the things they were trusting in to protect them, would not be able to save them.

The ultimate harvest is the judgement of God. On that day we will all reap what we have sown. Many live their lives indulging in sin, living for themselves, pleasure, lust, money, possessions, career, popularity; all that has mattered is 'me'. But at the judgement none of these things will help us; in fact, they are the things that are ruining us. The things we trust in to keep us safe will all be burned up.

The only ones who will stand at the final harvest are those who have repented of their sin and are trusting in the Lord Jesus Christ. They will reap

> The things we trust in to keep us safe will all be burned up.

what He has sown for them—the righteousness of His perfect life and the complete cleansing and forgiveness of His atoning death.

WE HAVE TO SERVE SOMETHING

Israel wished to be free to do what they wanted and not have to bow to the Lordship of Yahweh, but the reality is that we all have to serve something. Hosea 10:11 says, 'Ephraim was a trained calf that loved to thresh, and I spared her fair neck; but I will put Ephraim to the yoke; Judah must plow; Jacob must harrow for himself.'

Israel and Judah (v. 11b), inadvertently, had chosen the yoke of slavery, thinking this yoke would bring them freedom. But, on the contrary, it brought hardship, which was compounded by her retreat into obstinacy. She was like a stubborn heifer (4:16). The yoke of verse 11 would no longer be the well-fitting one of God's ideal design but the harsh, heavy collar of slavery. Israel now had the yoke of judgement.

Yoke of Christ

They could have been under a completely different yoke; the yoke of God. The threshing referred to here was a comparatively light task, made pleasant by the fact that the creature was unmuzzled and free to eat (Deuteronomy 25:4) as it pulled the threshing-sledge over the gathered corn. This owner's pride in his beast and his consideration for it (Proverbs 12:10), together with the creature's obedience and contentment, provides one of the many affectionate touches in these troubled chapters—along with another with the same imagery of a man and a beast (Hosea 11:4).

However, this idyllic scene, by necessity, had to change. For the good of the animal, and its growth to maturity, there must be a transition to hard and testing work (compare with Hebrews 5:8; 12:6). While it may seem harsh and difficult, the yoke is there to serve the best of ends. Being obedient and serving God may at times be difficult and costly, but this is where true happiness, satisfaction and contentment are to be found and experienced.

A map or sat nav helps me get to where I want to go. If I follow its instructions, it restricts me to certain roads. There are particular roads I need to go on and lots of other roads I must not go on if I am to get to where I need to go. I have never had map rebellion. I have never told the map that it is being unfair and restricting my freedom by not letting me go on every road. By following the map, I will get to where I need to go and not end up frustrated and lost.

In Matthew 11:28–30, the Lord Jesus invites us to:

Come to me all who labour and are heavy laden and I will give you rest. Take my yoke upon you and learn from me, for I am gentle and lowly in heart, and you will find rest for your souls. For my yoke is easy and my burden is light.

He tenderly and lovingly invites us to come to Him and to let Him be our teacher. Of course, there will be things that we cannot do and restraints that we will find hard, but the things He tells us in the Bible not to do, and the things He encourages us to do, are all for our good. It is for my good that I read the Bible and submit myself to what it says. Living for me, thinking all the time about me, worrying about me, trying to please me, is tiring and will always lead to discontentedness and messing up. The hardest thing to do is to deny 'me'. I love me. I live for me. It is all about me. But at the same time 'me' is my biggest problem. I am a slave to my lusts. I am self-conscious. I get stressed trying to keep up with my job. I am tired of keeping up with fashions and other people. My personality sometimes really gets on my nerves. Oh, to be free from being me!

Dying to self is liberating. C.S. Lewis said, 'It is not thinking less of yourself but thinking of yourself less.'[6]

Jesus Christ is not out to make us unhappy or to deny us things for the sake of it. He made us, knows how we are wired and what is best for us. The Lord Jesus is kind. I do not know about you but living for me, embracing the world's way of doing things, has made me weary and heavy laden. But Jesus invites us to come to Him and by putting His yoke upon us and learning from Him, He will give us rest.

> Jesus Christ is not out to make us unhappy or to deny us things for the sake of it.

TIME TO SEEK THE LORD

This was not meant to be all doom and gloom. The whole purpose of Hosea's prophecy was to get across to Israel that it was time to seek the Lord. In verse 12, Hosea gives positive and practical advice on how Israel should seek the Lord. His invitation is generous and urgent. 'Sow for yourselves righteousness; reap steadfast love; break up your fallow ground, for it is the time to seek the LORD, that he may come and rain righteousness upon you.'

Digging up

If they were going to seek the Lord and find Him, they needed to break down fallow ground. Verse 12 says, '... *break up your fallow ground* ...'. The picture is of a vegetable patch that has been worked on every year into a well-trodden footpath. It needs to be broken and softened. Returning to God would be hard work. Israel needed to soften their hearts. *To break up fallow ground* means they would need to break bad habits. Sin at first is fun and pleasurable but it can take hold. It is a dangerous, controlling power that takes effort and the help of the Holy Spirit to overcome.

This is not easy. Every action is one step towards a habit. We must not feed our temptations. Rather we must weed out sin. Farm our hearts every day. Saying no to sin is like part of us dying. We must put sin to death (Colossians 3:5). Be ruthless with it. Do not give in to it.

Planting

But it was not just a case of weeding out sin. They needed to sow righteousness (v. 12). To do this, Israel needed to use the provision in the covenant for sin, namely the atonement symbolized in the sacrifice. They needed to turn from their sin and turn back to God. Israel needed to cultivate new habits of righteousness to replace the hard soil in their hearts. If Israel did this, they would reap steadfast love. They could enjoy the love of God.

Returning to the image of Hosea and Gomer in the first three chapters, Gomer could return to her husband and enjoy his love again.

For us today, we need to meditate on God's Word, worship Him with His people, pray, and meet around the Lord's Table. Christians cannot neglect the means of grace and expect to harvest good fruit and become more like Jesus. To keep the weeds out we must grow lots of flowers. The only way we can do this is by abiding in Christ (John 15). Without Jesus, the branches have no life. You do not get life back from the fruit but from the stem; the fruit simply shows there is life. Christians need to go back to the stem. Abiding in Christ means to keep His commandments (John 15:10) and if we do this, God will rain righteousness upon us. Our battle against sin will lead to joy; the joy of knowing God. The parable of the Sower (Matthew 13:1–23) shows that if we are to have a good heart, we must have the Word of God planted in our hearts and mix it with faith. Believe it, trust in it, live off it and do not allow the cares of this world, or persecution, destroy it or allow our hearts to become hard towards it.

Even though we may feel dirty and too bad for God— that we are caped in our sin and have gone too far—God can take the hardest, most fallow ground and cultivate it into a beautiful garden. We may be spiritually bankrupt, overdrawn and in a mountain of debt in terms of our sin and filth, but God can make us spiritually wealthy.

Gibeah proves this. As we have seen in Judges 19–21, Gibeah is *Sodomburgh* (compare with Genesis 19). Sexual perverts abuse a woman through one long night of terror until dawn brings relief in death. There is no sorrow or repentance in Gibeah—nor indeed in all the tribe of Benjamin. The tribe is so rebellious, so insistent that Gibeah's perverts do not receive justice, that a disastrous civil war ensues. That is the situation in Judges 19–21. Gibeah is synonymous with sin and degradation of the worst kind. People would have said, 'Can anything good come out of Gibeah?' But in 1 Samuel 11 this place of wickedness and destruction has become the source of salvation and deliverance. He is able to restore the years that the locusts have eaten (Joel 2:25) The Spirit of God can make such a difference (1 Samuel 11:6). God is able to bring light into darkness. What is impossible to us, is possible with God (Luke 18:27). He can do far above what we can ever imagine (Ephesians 3:20).

Surely all of this means it is time to renew our allegiance to the kingdom (1 Samuel 11:14).

JUDAH

Even though the focus is on Israel in the north, there is a word for Judah in the south. Hosea 10:11 says, 'Judah must plow; Jacob must harrow for himself.'

As Judah looked at Israel, in some ways it was tempting for her to rejoice in Israel's troubles. But she should see in Israel's fate a warning of her own future. Israel was not Hosea's only audience: Judah needs to listen too.

As Christians we need to make sure that we love God with all our hearts and not let the world and all that it offers and promises, turn our heads and infiltrate our churches. Neither must we ever adopt a spirit of self-righteousness and looking down on others.

For all of us, it is time to seek the Lord!

FOR FURTHER STUDY.

1. Do we possess so much that we feel no need of God?

2. Do we feel safe in the 'hollow of God's hand?'

TO THINK ABOUT AND DISCUSS.

1. What things in my life need to change?

2. Is the Lord's Day really His Day, or do I want it to be mine?

12 The heart of God

Hosea 11:1–11

Hosea 11 is one of the most poignant passages in the entire prophecy of Hosea, possibly even the whole Bible. It reveals the heart of God.

It contains an oracle from Yahweh on Israel's apostasy which draws heavily on two components of Old Testament history. The first component is the Exodus. Hosea 11:1–5 focuses on this and threatens that God will undo the Exodus. The second component is the destruction of Sodom and Gomorrah. Hosea 11:6–12 contains the possibility that Israel will become like the cities of the plain, Sodom and Gomorrah; that is, eternally annihilated. However, Yahweh recoils from this and promises a new Exodus. Throughout the entire chapter, seven things about the heart of God are revealed.

A tender heart

The first thing to say about the heart of God is that it is a tender heart.

CHOSEN

The children of Israel were tenderly chosen by God. Hosea 11:1 speaks of the day of Israel's adoption. Here God changes the metaphor from Israel as His wife to Israel as His child. There are a number of passages where God calls the people of Israel *His children* (Deuteronomy 14:1; Isaiah 1:2; 30:9; Jeremiah 3:14, 19, 22; Hosea 1:10) and Ezekiel 16:1–6 describes the young nation as a female child. Here the word 'child' can refer to a girl or boy anywhere in the age range from infancy (Exodus 2:6) to adolescence (Genesis 21:12).

Israel was in her infancy when they were in Egypt. Hosea 11:1, therefore, refers to the Exodus event, particularly Exodus 4:22–23. This was when God commissioned Moses to go to Pharaoh and told him to say: 'Thus says the LORD, Israel is my firstborn son, and I say to you, "Let my son go that he may serve me ...' This is the first time in the Bible God reveals himself as a Father, with Israel as His son. He is calling His son to freedom and setting His love upon him. The divine election of Israel is in mind. This arose out of God's grace not Israel's good qualities. Israel was not chosen because they were better than other nations; they were not chosen because they were good. They were chosen, elected, because God is kind and tenderly cast His love upon them.

Election is one of the key doctrines of the Bible; that

before creation God chose for salvation a great number of our fallen human race and sent Christ into the world to save them (John 6:37–40; 10:26–29; 15:16; 17:2, 6, 24; Romans 8:29–30). *Election* is also illustrated in the life of Abraham, Jacob and Esau and the calling of the disciples.

This doctrine has caused some controversy throughout church history, but it is unnecessary. Some argue that it is 'not fair'. But there is no one anywhere who has deserved to be saved and yet has not been. God does not punish anyone unjustly. We are all sinners by nature and deserve God's wrath but God, in His mercy, saves some and, in His justice, condemns others. The one who is condemned is receiving only what his sin deserves. It is important to remember that no one is sent to hell because they were not elect. People are in hell because they would not come to Jesus Christ. No sinner has ever come to Jesus Christ and been turned away. No one will be able to say on judgement day to Jesus Christ, 'I called to you but you would not listen.' Even though election is on every page of the Bible, it is equally true that 'Whosoever shall call on the name of the Lord shall be saved' (Acts 2:21 KJV), and that God takes 'no pleasure in the death of the wicked but that the wicked turn from his way and live' (Ezekiel 33:11). Whoever wants to, can come to Jesus Christ! Far from being a hard, callous doctrine, election reveals a tender-hearted God who lovingly chooses to save His people.

Election and *predestination* are things that are ultimately beyond our comprehension. The same Saviour who came to save the elect is also the same One who, when He looked out at Jerusalem said, 'O Jerusalem, Jerusalem, the city that kills the prophets and stones those who are sent to it! How often would I have gathered your children together as a hen gathers her brood under her wings and you were not willing!' (Matthew 23:37). This was not a cold, calculating Saviour who thought, 'Well these are not the elect and so them 'not coming to me' is simply part of the eternal redemptive plan." He was heartbroken and says He would have loved to have gathered them, but they would not. How do we reconcile election with a God who is heartbroken with the unrepentant? I do not know; my mind is tiny and God is infinite. Who can know the mind of God? (1 Corinthians 2:11, 16; Job 38:4–13); all I know is that if I am a Christian, it is because God tenderly chose me and if I am not a Christian then if I come to Him, He will never turn me away.

> How do we reconcile election with a God who is heartbroken with the unrepentant?

The late Rev Derek Swann said that there was a time when he fought against God's sovereignty and predestination but then he began to live off it! When someone asked Spurgeon how he reconciled God's sovereignty and man's responsibility, he said that you don't need to reconcile friends.[1]

Instead of arguing with it and protesting against it, just come! Come now. Come as you are, your tale of sin confessing. Your past will be forgiven and forgotten; you will have a guide, a friend and protector through life, and a glorious hope for the future! All who come will find mercy (John 6:35, 47–51, 54–57; Romans 1:16; 10:8–13).

If you are reading this book, have listened to sermons, read your Bible, had the gospel explained to you but you feel nothing; you cannot see it. Then cry out to God that He would reveal these things to you and make them real to you. Cry out with the hymn writer, Fanny Crosby (1820–1915):

Pass me not oh gentle Saviour

Hear my humble cry

While on others thou art calling

Do not pass me by.

CARE

As well as choosing Israel, God also tenderly cared for Israel. In verses 3 and 4 He says,

Yet it was I who taught Ephraim to walk; I took them up

by their arms, but they did not know that I healed them.

I led them with cords of kindness, with the bands of love,

and I became to them as one who eases the yoke on their jaws, and I bent down to them and fed them.

A better translation of the beginning of verse 3 is: 'It was I who taught Ephraim to walk, taking them by the arms' (NIV). Rather than the picture being of a father picking up the child, the image is of a father teaching his child to walk, bending over and holding the child's arms; supporting the child's first staggering steps; picking him up when he stumbles and falls; making everything better when he hurts himself.

In these verses it is like we are given a glimpse into the family photo album; Israel walking out of Egypt, God helping them to get 'steady on their feet' and picking them up every time they fall. God looks back with fondness in a similar way that a father remembers his child's first steps, patching up the grazed knee, lifting their child up for a kiss. At that point the album showed the bright promises of Israel's youth.

The second half of verse 3, '... but they did not know that I healed them', has Exodus 15:22–26 in mind—the story of the bitter water at Marah, which Moses miraculously purified after praying to Yahweh. God compared the bitter water of Marah to the plagues He brought on the Egyptians. Hosea's allusion to this incident implies that the Israelites quickly forgot both how the Egyptians were afflicted and how God repeatedly restored health to Israel in the wilderness

(Numbers 21:6–10). They also forgot how God cared for them as they left Egypt. He is making the point that He will continue to be Israel's healer so long as they are faithful. But they are like some scornful adolescent who has forgotten, or simply does not want to know. Verse 4 continues with the theme of how Yahweh cared for Israel. This verse could be translated in different ways. The word 'yoke' has the same consonants as 'child'. Therefore, given the context, it could be better to translate verse 4 as the NIV does: 'I led them with cords of human kindness, with ties of love; I lifted the yoke from their neck and bent down to feed them.'

Verse 4 could even be translated as, 'I led them with cords of a human, with ropes of love.' The image therefore would be of Moses as the intermediary between God and the nation, Moses as God's human face for Israel. The people had dealings with Yahweh through Moses rather than with Him directly (Deuteronomy 5:22–33). Moses was the one who interceded with Yahweh to be merciful to Israel (Exodus 32:11–14). Sinful Israel could not stand before a holy God on their own. They needed a mediator. This is true of us today. We enjoy full access to God. We can pray directly to him and be intimate with Him. But it is all

> Sinful Israel could not stand before a holy God on their own. They needed a mediator.

through the Lord Jesus Christ. Moses was a type of the mediator to come.

Moreover, the picture could be of Yahweh lifting Israel into His arms and nuzzling her into His cheek and bending down to feed her; God tenderly stooping down and gently giving her food.

Alternatively, it could be that the metaphor has changed from Israel as a child, to Israel as an animal. That being the case, 'jaws' in verse 4 could imply a farmer needing to adjust some kind of bit or harness device that either went into the animal's mouth or around its jaws. If that is the case, the line describes an adjustment of the yoke and an easing of the burden, not a complete removal of the yoke. The point then is not liberation from all duties but liberation from the harsh conditions Israel experienced in Egypt. But for her own sake, God did not remove all yoke from her but gently put her under His yoke and under His tender care.

Whichever way the verse is translated, what is clear is that Israel's problem was that they did not realize their privileges and how good God had been to them in choosing and caring for them. Neither did they see God as someone to enjoy and delight in. Israel assumed that God was being cruel in some of the ways He dealt with her and in the things she was forbidden to do.

This lack of understanding of God's tender care is one of our problems today too. We see God's laws and ways as hard and difficult and that somehow God is out to spoil our fun. We feel we are being denied things that would make us happy. But imagine a sick child whose father forces him to take medicine or a child who demands sweets all the time but the father refuses. The child thinks the father is being cruel. Whereas any onlooker can see the father is acting in love. This is the tender care that Israel rejects.

God has our best interest at heart, and the laws He lays down for us to obey, the things He forbids and the way He directs our path are for our good. He wants us to enjoy Him as this is the only place true happiness is found. According to Owen:

> Set your thought on the eternal love of the Father and see if your heart is not aroused to delight in him. Sit down for a while at this delightful spring of living water and you will soon find its streams sweet and delightful. You who used to run from God will not now be able, even for a second, to keep at any distance from him.[2]

A broken heart

The second thing to note about the heart of God is that it is a broken heart. Israel's early promise after they left Egypt faded quickly and their sin and perversity kept coming to the fore. Hosea 11:2 says, 'The more they were called, the more they went away; they kept sacrificing to the Baals and burning offerings to idols.'

Israel discovered their identity as God's son through the Exodus. The problem was, almost immediately, they kept forgetting. The people did not live as liberated sons but as vulnerable orphans who thought they needed the protection of other gods. Even though Yahweh had delivered them from slavery in Egypt, they were ungrateful to Him. As they wandered through the wilderness, God provided food and drink for them every day, but even then, Israel complained about the lack of variety in the diet, particularly when there was a plague after they gluttonously consumed quail (Numbers 11).

Some interpret the beginning of verse 2 to mean: 'They (Israel) called to them (Egypt), that is how they (Israel) went from them (Egypt)'. This would mean that in the Exodus itself, Israel was already committing apostasy by yearning for Egypt (Numbers 11:4–6) and carrying Egyptian paganism with them. The second half of verse 2, with its reference to Baal, would therefore mean that Hosea is describing the apostasy of the Exodus in language more relevant to the cult of his day. His point is that the cult of Hosea's generation was a continuation of what they began as early as the Exodus. It started with the golden calf (Exodus 32) and led to the Israelites falling into the fertility cult of Baal of Peor (Numbers 25), right up to the time of Hosea. This has been their age-old problem.

While this is no doubt true, verse 2 is probably better

interpreted to mean that the more God called out to them, the further they ran from Him. Even though they were a rebellious and stiff-necked people (Exodus 32:9), in His kindness, God sent prophets to Israel to warn them of the danger they were in if they continued to rebel and to plead with them to repent. But the more the prophets called, the further away Israel went.

They took God for granted and presumed upon His kindness. They forgot that all good gifts come from above (James 1:17) and developed a sense of entitlement. The more prosperous and successful God made them, the more conceited and ungrateful they became. The more God gave them, the less they wanted God. They assumed God would always be there for them, and they could do whatever they wanted. They mistook the patience of God for weakness.

Furthermore, Israel knew that they were disobeying God; they knew that they were sinning against Him. When He called to them, they were afraid, so they ran further away. It is like a father taking their young child out for the day. The child runs off so the father calls them back for their safety but the child is afraid of the father's voice and does not want to be punished so runs further away.

Israel did not trust or understand the grace of God. They did not understand that their God would not treat them as their sins deserved but would lavish on them undeserved kindness if they would only come to him.

However, it is not just Israel. The Scriptures are full of sinners running from God. Maybe you are running from God. But you do not need to run from Him, rather run to Him. The Reformer, Martin Luther, had a tough time at school in Magdeburg. He had no friends or protectors and used to tremble in the presence of his severe

> Maybe you are running from God. But you do not need to run from Him, rather run to Him.

masters. He painfully had to beg for his food with his companions, wandering through the neighbouring villages at Christmas time, going from house to house singing in four parts the usual carols. He described how once he stopped before a peasant's house, that stood by itself at the extremity of the village. He says, 'The farmer, hearing us sing our Christmas hymns, came out with some victuals which he intended to give us, and called in a high voice and with a harsh tone, "Boys, where are you?" Frightened at these words, we ran off as fast as our legs would carry us. We had no reason to be alarmed for the farmer offered us assistance with great kindness; but our hearts, no doubt, were rendered timorous by the menaces and tyranny with which the teachers were then accustomed to rule over their pupils, so that a sudden panic had seized us. At last, however, as the farmer continued calling after us, we stopped, forgot our fears, ran back to him, and received from his hands the food intended for us.' 'It is thus', adds

Luther, 'that we are accustomed to tremble and flee when our conscience is guilty and alarmed. In such a case we are afraid even of the assistance that is offered us, and of those who are our friends, and who would willingly do us every good.'[3]

Maybe that is you right now. God calls you but you run away from Him trembling. Yet He wants you to repent and turn to Him. Instead of needing to run away from Him, He waits in His lair for you to come running to Him. He will welcome you with open arms (Romans 10:21; John 6:37).

Israel continued to reject this grace and this broke God's heart. In these verses we see the broken heart of a doting Father, shot through with pain. If you are reading this and have suffered the pain of betrayal from a family member or bereavement, then you have some very small understanding of the heartbreak Israel caused God. It is a pain that Hosea felt in some way in the way he was treated by Gomer; the heartbreak of being married to an adulterous wife.

An angry heart

While God's heart is tender and broken, His heart is also angry with them because they are determined to turn away from Him (vv. 5, 7). They will not repent but are 'bent on turning' from Him. In Deuteronomy 21:18–21, the punishment for a persistently rebellious son was death. Moreover, the fifth Commandment states,

'Honour your father and your mother ... that your days may be long, and that it may go well with you in the land that the LORD your God is giving you' (Deuteronomy 5:16). The Israelites had to be obedient to their parents to learn the pattern of being obedient to God.

However, Israel would not obey God and, because of their disobedience, they would not be able to stay in the land. They would be exiled. The Exodus would be undone; that is, slavery in Egypt would be the pattern for a second period of enslavement in an alien land. But, even though some Israelites would go as refugees to Egypt, this time the slavery would be in Assyria not Egypt. They would be under the tyranny of the King of Assyria instead of the Egyptian Pharaoh. Different country but similar plight

There is a bit of a wordplay in verse 5 with the verb 'return'. Israel would not *'return'* to Egypt but instead would go to Assyria because they refused to *'return'* to Yahweh. Their refusal to *'return'*, or repent, is why they will end up *returning* to a state of slavery.

Verse 6 poetically portrays the Assyrian armies slashing through the cities of Israel. God will put an end to their boasting and empty talk by frustrating the plans and counsels of Israel.

This angry God is coming to them in judgement and what they are relying on and living for, will not be able to help them. The Israelites depended on an apostate theology in which they assimilated the worship of Yahweh to a Canaanite cult under the ambiguous title 'God on High'. But verse 7 says, '... and though they call out to the Most High, he shall not raise them up at all'. Hosea makes a mockery of this name with the term 'Not-on-High' (compare with 7:16). The 'god' they are worshipping is 'not on high'. Yahweh is. And He's angry.

This is true for us today. Everything we trust in, look up to and rely upon—ourselves, careers, family, status, wisdom of the world, possessions, celebrities, sport stars, kings and queens, presidents, leaders—are not really 'on high'. God is.

A holy heart

The fourth thing to say about God's heart is that it is not like our hearts. His heart is holy (v. 9). Sin does not fade from His memory. It is not that God is in a bad mood at sin and needs to cool down. When we commit a sin, we feel guilty and do not feel able to pray right away because we think God must be really angry. We leave it a few days, or even longer, and as the shame fades from our memories we feel it fades from God's memory too.

> God's anger is not like ours. It is a righteous, holy anger.

But God's anger is not like ours. It is a righteous, holy anger. He hates sin as much today as He did thousands of years ago. He remains as righteously angry with unconfessed sin that was committed twenty years ago as He was when it was first committed.

'Come in wrath' (11:9) could be translated, 'come into the city'. God is too holy to enter the city. He would have to destroy it. Therefore, His refusal to enter the city is an act of both judgement and mercy.

A torn heart

The fact that God's heart is holy and angry, but at the same time tender and broken, means His heart is torn. Perhaps in one of the most poignant verses in the whole of the Bible He says:

> How can I give you up, O Ephraim? How can I hand you over, O Israel? How can I make you like Admah? How can I treat you like Zeboiim? My heart recoils within me; my compassion grows warm and tender (v. 8).

In human terms, these words expose to us the mind and heart of God. As daring as this may seem for us to say, in these verses Yahweh enters what can only be described as distraught self-questioning. God's heart recoils within Him. According to the NIV, God says, 'My heart is changed within me,' whereas the New American Standard says, 'My heart is turned over within me.' He is like a father who is at his wits end over what to do with a wayward child. Yahweh is at a loss as He tries to resolve His compassion for Israel with the punishment demanded by their sin.

All human analogies fall short at this point and we should not press the language too hard. Hosea is putting things in human terms to help us understand. We must be careful to safeguard above all else the character and being of God and know that God does not self-doubt. But neither are we to have a cold theology, all neatly thought through and sewn up. While the impassibility and foreknowledge of God should never be abandoned, a text like this should be allowed to speak to us in the power of its raw emotion. We cannot come away from these verses without beholding a holy, majestic God; the creator of heaven and earth, who in some way is swayed by impulse and emotion. These verses strike us with the openness of God, and His love becomes a vivid reality and not a sterile abstraction. We must be careful to be doctrinally correct and thoroughly Biblical, but we must never take the warmth out of love and the fire out of anger. We will never fully grasp and plumb the depths of the heart of God!

He cannot bear to think of them suffering the same fate as the five cities referred to here.

Admah and Zeboiim, together with Bela, were the other cities of the plain, in addition to the more famous Sodom and Gomorrah (Genesis 14:2). These cities represented the depravity that God annihilated in the destruction that is recounted in Genesis 19 and is recalled in Deuteronomy 29:23.

As is Hosea's style, by mentioning Admah and Zeboiim rather than the more 'infamous' Sodom and Gomorrah, which other biblical writers seem always to do (compare with Isaiah 1:9–10; 3:9; 13:19; Jeremiah 23:14; 49:18; 50:40; Lamentations 4:6; Ezekiel 16:45–56; Amos 4:11; Zephaniah 2:9), he is being deliberately obscure and elusive and demanding of his reader. He wants his readers to recognise the allusion to their far-less-famous sister cities. Hosea is making his readers and listeners really think.

The question remains as we consider God's torn heart, what did He do? Did He give Ephraim up? Did He hand over Israel? Did He make them like Admah or treat them like Zeboiim?

The answer is no. At Admah and Zeboiim there was an overthrow. But this time the overthrow is within God himself.

A big heart

And the reason for that is because God's heart is big. In verse 5, Israel refused to return to God or repent. Yet now God turns; He turns away from His anger. But how can God be determined to judge in verses 5–7 and determined to save in 8–9? Because God is not like us.

His heart is big—bigger than the problem of our sin and rebellion.

Verse 9 says, 'I will not execute my burning anger; I will not again destroy Ephraim; for I am God and not a man, the Holy One in your midst, and I will not come in wrath.' This literally means, 'I will return to ruin Ephraim' or 'I will turn from ruining Ephraim'. It conveys a really torn heart. But this big problem was resolved in the even bigger heart of God in such an amazing way that His mercy does not compromise His judgement.

Yahweh will not vent His fury as He did with Sodom and Gomorrah. These cities were so bad that they had to be wiped off the face of the earth. But Israel, even though they are no better, will not suffer the total, irreversible annihilation that Sodom experienced.

There is an allusion to Abraham's negotiations with Yahweh in which he called upon divine mercy and forbearance (Genesis 18:22–33). That is, what God ultimately could not do with the cities of the plain—save them from total annihilation—He is determined to do for Israel. And the reason is that there was one righteous man. That one righteous man was his Son, and it is because of Him that the true Israel, all those who put their trust in Him, will be delivered.

The move from wife analogy to son analogy is not a coincidence. Christ sums up in His person all that Israel was called and meant to be. Hosea knew (not fully) that his words had significance that transcended his own time. As so often with the Old Testament writers, Hosea wrote better than he knew.

Israel was in the wilderness for forty years (Numbers 32:13); the Lord Jesus was forty days in the wilderness (Matthew 4:1–11). Jesus gave His law on the mountain (Matthew 5–7) just as God gave the Torah at Mount Sinai (Exodus 19, 20, 24, 32–34). The Lord Jesus miraculously fed His followers in the wilderness (Mark 6:30–44) just as Moses gave the people manna (Exodus 16).

> The Lord Jesus miraculously fed His followers in the wilderness just as Moses gave the people manna.

However, most strikingly, in line with Hosea 11:1, when the Lord Jesus was a baby, He departed from Egypt (Matthew 2:13). Jesus did what Israel failed to do. The original children, 'sons', of God who had originally been called out of Egypt at the time of the Exodus had proved to be disobedient and false. But the Lord Jesus, the only begotten Son of God, came back out of exile in Egypt and proves to be the true Son of God.

He then grew up and lived a perfect life, the life you and I and ancient Israel could never live. And then at thirty-three, He died an atoning death. As we have seen, in Deuteronomy 21 the death penalty falls on the disobedient son. Galatians 3:13 uses Deuteronomy

21:22–23 to describe the cross of Jesus. At Calvary, God sentenced His own Son. Instead of pouring His wrath on us, He poured it out on his own Son. On the cross, Jesus was turning away the wrath of a sin-hating God. The wrath that God should pour out on us, was poured out on Him. On the cross Jesus was paying the wages of sin. He had no personal sin of His own but, as a representative, He bore so much sin. He paid the price of the sins of everyone who will trust Him.

At Calvary, the bigness of God's heart found a solution to His torn heart. His desire to save sinners does not compromise His justice. The cross reveals a heart that is big and full of love. On 28th April 1996, Martin Bryant went into holiday resorts in Tasmania with an assault rifle and killed thirty-five people.[4] He went into restaurants and parks and men jumped in front of their wives and children to save them. One was called Jason Winter. Jason Winter's son will never be able to wake up and wonder, 'Did dad love me?' You and I can never look at the cross and ask, 'Does God love me?'

While the nation of Israel did go into exile, the true Israel will be delivered, as was the remnant who threw in their lot with Judah and whose descendants returned with them from Babylon (1 Chronicles 9:1–3). It is this remnant who are the continuing Israel that we meet in the New Testament and are the seeds of the church (see Romans 11). And all of this because of a big-hearted God.

A strong heart

This can be accomplished because God's heart is strong. He is 'lion hearted' (Hosea 11:10–11).

The metaphor recalls Numbers 24:8–9. God is pictured as having the heart of a lion, a lion who will deliver His people into a new Promised Land. He is a ferocious lion but His ferocity will restore not destroy Israel.

Hosea sees a time when the lion will roar and, while it will make the people tremble, instead of fleeing from God, they will return to Him. It is a roar that will bring them home. In contrast to Hosea 7:11, Israel is no longer like a silly dove wandering to and fro; it will fly directly to Yahweh. As He roars, birds will come to Him rather than flee. It looks forward to a day when God's people, the true Israel, will turn to God with their hearts, as without a change of heart they will just repeat the past. Here they are pictured as no longer being wanderers among the nations (9:17) but 'trembling' they go after the Lord who will return them home.

This can only happen because of God's strong heart. His heart is stronger than ours. He is determined and resolved to overcome all sin and evil on behalf of His people so they can come to Him.

The Lion's roar could refer to several things. On the one hand it could be the overthrow of Babylon, when the Israelites returned from the exile. However, the text envisages a general return not only from Egypt and Assyria but also from the west—regions of the Mediterranean. It could be the spiritual homecoming of God's sons (Hosea 2:23; 1:10; Romans 9:25–26), while some believe that it includes the great turning of Israel as predicted in Romans 11:12, 25 onwards.

We must remember though that the Lion roars whenever the gospel is spoken or preached. We need to pray that as He roars people will come to Him. His roar can conquer the hardest heart.

FOR FURTHER STUDY.

1. I must never stop praying for those I love to come to repentance and faith in the Lord Jesus.

2. Do we feel God at times is distant, although He is very near?

TO THINK ABOUT AND DISCUSS.

1. Do we only think of the cross at Easter or is the Lord's sacrifice constantly in our thoughts?

2. Is the knowledge of God's presence a comfort to us or is it a challenge to our way of life?

13 A history and geography lesson

Hosea 12

In this chapter, Hosea gives us a history and geography lesson. He wants us to learn lessons from people and places in history.

Judah and Israel

Ambiguous

Hosea 11:12 is ambiguous. It is not clear whether it is saying Judah is faithful, or not. According to the Septuagint, the Greek translation of the Old Testament, 'Judah is known and is faithful to God.' But according to the original Hebrew, it can appear that Judah still 'plays fast and loose' with God.

In all likelihood, Hosea is being deliberately abstruse. He does not use the word *Yahweh*—God's covenant name—but the generic term for God. The point Hosea is raising seems to be, 'Judah is faithful to a deity but is it Yahweh, the Lord?' The NIV translation of the second half of Hosea 11:12 brings this out, 'And Judah is unruly against God, even against the faithful Holy One.' They are still religious but wavering in their devotion to Yahweh and turning to the Canaanite cults. Therefore, it would appear that while Ephraim (Israel) is mainly being rebuked, there is a warning here for Judah too. Israel is unfaithful but is Judah any better? It is for the Judean readers to decide. They must examine themselves.

LIES EVERYWHERE

The expression that Yahweh is being surrounded by lies is quite unusual. Maybe in mind is some shrine or altar that was originally dedicated to Yahweh, but which now the Israelites have literally surrounded with sacred images to the fertility cult. What is clear is that there is so much falseness, hypocrisy and apostasy.

Ephraim are on a downward spiral. Their religion is meaningless (4:6; 7:14; 8:11 onwards). This in turn leads to moral anarchy (See 4:1 onwards), pleasure-seeking (4:10 onwards), duplicity in politics and diplomacy (7:6, 11), double dealing (12:1b) and in the end, friendlessness (8:8–10) and ruin.

Assyria and Egypt

Hosea 12:1 says, 'Ephraim feeds on the wind and pursues the east wind all day long; they multiply falsehood and violence; they make a covenant with Assyria, and oil is carried to Egypt.'

God made a covenant with Israel and Israel swore promises to Him (Deuteronomy 29:12–13; Joshua

24:21–22), but now they are off making treaties with
Assyria and Egypt. They have compromised their
principles in order to accommodate relations with
foreign powers. They have broken their marriage vows
to Yahweh.

The reference to oil being carried down to Egypt is a
tribute paid to seal the deal.

The flimsy and elusive nature of these commitments
is emphasized with the image of Ephraim feeding on the
wind and chasing it. A meal of wind is never going to
nourish and sustain you, and however much you chase
after the east wind, you will never be able to bring it
under your control.

Some experts say that the translation *'feed'* is
incorrect here. They maintain that when the word is
used of a human it means *to shepherd*. The picture,
therefore, is of a shepherd trying to control the wind in
the way that he normally controls his herds and goes
in pursuit of strays. It is futile but also dangerous. The
east wind in Palestine is the destructive sirocco. Israel
is trying to manage something dangerous and as a result
will get caught up in a whirlwind.

Today we would use the expression, 'playing with
fire'. Ephraim is trying to control what is uncontrollable.
Assyria and Egypt will never satisfy Israel and never do
what Israel want and need them to do.

Jacob

As well as places, God also wants Israel to learn from people and He draws their attention to Jacob (v. 2).

OVERVIEW

Jacob was Abraham's grandson. Isaac, Abraham's son had twins, Jacob and Esau. God gave Jacob a new name, *Israel*. This is the name his descendants became known as. The story of Israel the nation parallels the story of Israel the person.

The picture we have of Jacob in the Bible is of a desperate, greedy, selfish, deceitful, unlikeable man transformed by the grace of God. The nation of Israel had picked up the worst traits of their ancestor and during Hosea's generation were, in the main, untouched by grace. Hosea wants to remind Israel of what Jacob was like by taking them through some of the stages of his life and showing them what can happen when God and man take hold of one another.

GRASPING

Hosea starts the story in the womb. Verse 3 says, 'In the womb he took his brother by the heel, and in his manhood he strove with God' (Compare with Genesis 25:22–26). Jacob was born grasping the heel of his twin brother Esau. This gave him his birth name, Jacob, *'he-is-at-the-heel'*. For years Jacob's dealings with other people were to confirm all that was sinister in the name: someone who ruthlessly pursues what he has not got; someone who steals up from behind to outwit and overreach you. The grasping of the heel depicts the whole history of conflict between the two brothers. Esau, who was bargained out of his birthright and tricked out of his blessing, cried, 'Is not he rightly named Jacob? For he hath supplanted (Jacobed) me, these two times ...' (Genesis 27:36, KJV).

DECEIT

Jacob is an idiom for deceit. He twice cheated Esau.

Firstly, he cheated him out of the birthright, which involved all the prerogatives and inheritance rights that went with being the eldest son.

Then secondly, he cheated him out of the covenant blessing. As the blind, old Isaac came towards the end of his life, he had to pass on his inheritance and bless his elder son. This of course was Esau and not Jacob. In Genesis 27, we read how Isaac told Esau to hunt wild game and prepare a meal during which Isaac would bless him. But Isaac's wife, Rebekah, overheard this and came up with a plan to deceive her husband. While Esau was out hunting, she got Jacob to kill two domestic goats. She then prepared the meal while Jacob dressed in Esau's clothes and wrapped animal skin around his arms so he smelt and felt like Esau, who was naturally hairy. Isaac said, 'The voice is Jacob's voice, but the hands are the hands of Esau' (Genesis 27:22). 'Are you really my son, Esau?' he asked. And Jacob answered, 'I am' (Genesis 27:24). So, Isaac blessed Jacob and the promise of God passed to Jacob. God's people came from Jacob's line. The promised Messiah came from Jacob's line and not from Esau.

Jacob was a deceiver; Israel the person was a deceiver. And now the worst traits of their ancestor had come to the nation of Israel. Hosea 12:7 says they are like 'a merchant, in whose hands are false balances, he loves to oppress'. The word *merchant* is literally 'Canaanite'. Canaanites used dishonest scales and loved to defraud. God cast the Canaanites out of the Promised Land so that there might be a place on earth in which the goodness of His reign could be on display. God chose His people Israel to be a light to the nations but now His people are 'Canaanites', or as we would say, pagans. They are no different to the world around them. They would do whatever it took to get ahead. They may escape the Israelite justice system but they will not escape God's justice.

Relied on his own wits

Because Jacob had cheated Esau, he had to flee for his

life (12:12). He went to live with his mother's brother, Laban, in the land of Aram. It would be hard to find a meaner man in the whole of the Old Testament than Laban. He was a slippery, conniving, calculating, double-dealing man. But even Laban found he had met his match in Jacob.

Jacob fell in love with Rachel, Laban's daughter. Genesis 29 tells the story of how Jacob spent seven years tending sheep for Laban, earning a dowry to win Rachel. But in fact, Laban tricked Jacob and married him to his elder daughter, Leah, instead. So, Jacob worked a further seven years to earn the right to marry Rachel.

Altogether, Jacob spent twenty years with Laban, where he relied on his natural wiliness and, together with hard work, it enabled him to make his way well. He amassed and accumulated wealth and wives and goods. But after twenty years with Laban, this natural guile had hardened into pride and selfishness.

MET WITH GOD

But there were two crisis points in Jacob's life which changed him. One of these crisis points took place as he fled from Esau on the way to Laban, and the other as he fled from Laban and returned to the Promised Land and prepared to meet Esau again.

During both these crisis points, God met with Jacob and these two meetings would transform him, even though the first one did not straight away. Jacob's first meeting with God took place at Bethel. His second was at Peniel, twenty years later. Hosea recalls these encounters in 12:3–5. It is important to note that Hosea does not use these accounts in chronological order but makes use of them for his stylistic purposes. In the beginning of verse 4 he talks about Jacob's encounter at Peniel, whereas at the end of verse 4 he talks about Bethel. Hosea places Bethel at the end of his retelling of the story to create a contrast between the grace Jacob received and his life of conniving, scheming and struggling.

BETHEL

The first meeting happens as he is on the run from Esau, who is ready to slay his brother because he has lost all the material value and prosperity involved in the covenant blessing.

On the run from Esau, he collapses at night and begs God for help. At this point he has nothing but God's promise to hold onto. This covenant-keeping God comes to him and speaks to him. He gives him a vision of heaven opened, of the heavenly stairway, which showed that God was gracious and Jacob had access to God. Furthermore, Jacob received from God the assurance that he would inherit the promise given to his fathers, Abraham and Isaac (Genesis 28:13).

Jacob calls the place Bethel. Elsewhere in the prophecy,

Hosea refers to Bethel by its nickname, *'Beth-aven'* (Hosea 4:15; 10:5) which means 'house of wickedness', because that is what it had become. But here Hosea calls the place *Bethel* which means 'House of God'.

Hosea wants to stress that Jacob had a meeting with the living God. In verse 5, Hosea says, 'the Lord, the God of hosts, the Lord is his memorial name'. He emphasizes God's name. It was the majestic God of the whole earth who Jacob met there, not a golden calf (Hosea 10:5; 13:2). This was what Israel needed above all else—not to go after idols who would never satisfy or save them. They need to meet with God.

PENIEL

But the most important encounter was the one Jacob had at Peniel. Everything else in his life were steps that led to this event.

Jacob had to leave home running for his life, marked out by deceitfulness and apprehension about what the future might hold. Twenty years have passed and Jacob is still on the run and has nowhere to go but back home (Genesis 31). Jacob has had hard times—and prosperous ones—and now he is on his way back to his land, the land of promise, the land of which God had spoken to Abraham and Isaac about. So, he prepares to meet Esau again, not knowing how Esau will react.

Just as he is about to step back into the land of

promise, Jacob hears that Esau is coming to meet him accompanied by an army of four hundred men. Laban and Esau were the two men that Jacob needed to fear. Laban was no longer a threat, but here was Esau and he must be faced. Jacob would need all his trickiness, but the night before he expects to meet Esau, God meets with him (Genesis 32:22–32).

WRESTLED WITH GOD

It was not an ordinary encounter. Jacob wrestled with a man who is God (Genesis 32:24–30). Jacob wrestled with a pre-incarnate appearance in the Old Testament of the Lord Jesus Christ. This is known as a *Theophany*. They wrestle all night. As dawn is breaking, Jacob overcomes the man and wrestles a blessing from God. This is the moment when God gives him the name *Israel* which means 'fights with God'.

ALONE AT NIGHT

He was alone with God in the dark of night (Genesis 32:24). God worked through Jacob's circumstances to bring him to this very place and this very hour. Jacob is a man with a past that has caught up with him and that he now has to face. God needed to get Jacob alone; He was about to get Jacob to face up to himself and the state and need of his heart. It was not merely outward circumstances which troubled Jacob's mind, but the spiritual realities behind them. Jacob needed to realize that, despite all that had happened and all that he now had to face, his problem was sin.

As a result of his sin, Jacob was alone. But he was not completely left alone. He was left alone with God, and we know from the account in Genesis that this was an intimate encounter. Jacob wrestled with God (Genesis 32:24). If you wrestle with someone, you have to get very close to each other. All alone, in the dead of night, Jacob was about to have a one-on-one meeting with the living God.

> Jacob needed to realize that, despite all that had happened and all that he now had to face, his problem was sin.

HANDLED BY GOD

Jacob was handled by God. Hosea 12:4 has the word, 'prevailed'. In the account in Genesis 32, in verse 25 it has the words, 'touched', 'out of joint', 'wrestled'. It is *earthy* and *real*. It is an account of God assuming human form and laying hold of a man, crippling and disabling him.

He did not smash Jacob, which He could easily have done—rather it was a gentle touch. He touched the hollow of his thigh. He wanted Jacob to stop resisting. The thigh is so important for a wrestler. If a wrestler has a sudden injury to his thigh or hip, all he can do is wrap his arms around his opponent and hold on as hard as he can.

All Jacob could do was take hold of God. Jacob was crippled and helpless in His hands. God humbled him. God was puncturing Jacob's pride, self-confidence and self-reliance, and all he could do was wrap himself around God.

Have you been handled by God? Has He brought you to an end of yourself? Has He brought you through your circumstances and situation, where all you can do is take hold of God and wrap yourself around Him?

NAME

During this encounter, God asks him his name. He had been asked this many years ago by his father, Isaac, and had lied. On that occasion, in order to receive the blessing, he had to con Isaac into thinking he was Esau. But now in his encounter with God, he has to face up to who he really is. He is asked directly by God, 'What is your name' (Genesis 32:27). The Amplified Bible says, 'And [in shock of realization, whispering] he said, Jacob' [supplanter, schemer, trickster, swindler[!

PRAYER

Jacob's encounter with God at Peniel was real and physical (Genesis 32:32). It was also a prayerful encounter. Real prayer is a very serious and solemn matter. It involves man taking hold of God.

Hosea 12:4 said that Jacob wept and made supplication. He would not let God go until He blessed him (Genesis 32:26). Jacob wrestled with God and this is the pivot around which the whole story turns and how Jacob is changed.

This is what real prayer is: wrestling with God. Not letting Him go until He blesses us. We lay the whole situation out before God and tell Him everything we have on our hearts. According to Olyott:

> We pray ourselves empty. We go over it and over it again and again until we have nothing else to say. We hold nothing back. With tears we have confessed every sin we know about and all our foolishness. We have told him every mistake, every worry, every fear, every ache and pain, every difficulty we face.[1]

God blessed him there

The encounter transformed him. He had left home in sad and spiritually depressing circumstances more than twenty years earlier. His mother's impatience to hurry on the blessing of God for him, together with his own readiness to snatch at every seeming advantage, had meant estrangement from his ageing father, and enmity from his twin brother, Esau.

He had left home as Jacob but he now returns, after this encounter, as Israel (Genesis 32:28). This name is very different. It speaks of tenacity without sneakiness. Instead of grasping, 'he strives'. His preoccupation is with God not man. This is made clear in the first two lines of Hosea 12:4. Jacob's character has been transformed. He is still Jacob but has now been touched by grace. His initial aggression and will to win is now redirected towards the nobler end of having power with God. His arrogance has been broken but not his eagerness, and he is now begging and pleading and 'grasping' for grace. God has taken hold of Jacob and remoulded him.

Jacob can face anything now, even Esau, because he has met God face to face. He is right with God and so everything else, whatever happens, will work out for his good.

THE POINT

The whole point of Hosea referring to Jacob is to encourage his descendants to learn the lesson of history. "So you, by the help of your God, return, hold fast to love and justice, and wait continually for your God" (Hosea 12:6). God is saying to Israel, you are like Jacob: grasping and deceitful. But Jacob sought God's grace and became Israel. Like Jacob, wrestle with God. Weep over your sin and seek His favour.

If Israel repents, they will be like Jacob in the best sense not the worst sense. Hosea wants to make them think, and us. Is deceit the way forward? Does Jacob become a great nation because he is a grasper?

The desire is for Israel and us to be a grasping people, but ones that grasp for God. It is a heartfelt challenge.

Return to God for our name is not Jacob/Israel for
nothing. If you have been more Jacob than Israel, so was
Jacob! But God was gracious to him and changed him
and can do the same for you. What should we do when
we feel unmoved by the gospel? Unmoved by grace?
Unmoved by the thought of God? We grasp, we fight, we
wrestle!

But sadly, the Israelite's response to all of this is in
Hosea 12:8: 'Ephraim has said, "Ah, but I am rich; I have
found wealth for myself; in all my labours they cannot
find in me iniquity or sin."'

They were very similar to the Church at Laodicea
(Revelation 3:14–22) whose attitude was, 'we need
nothing'. The Lord Jesus Christ had no words of
commendation for the church at Laodicea. They had
absorbed the complacent spirit of an affluent society.
They were totally ignorant of their real condition. They
thought they were doing fine, that they were rich, but
in fact they were 'pitiable, poor blind and naked' (Rev.
3:17). They were neither hot or cold but completely
indifferent towards Jesus Christ.

We need to ensure that we are not like Laodicea or
ancient Israel but like Jacob and take hold of God and
plead with him to take hold of us. Wrestle with Him!

Moses and the Exodus

Because of Israel's stubborn refusal to repent and lay

hold of God, God's answer is another flashback to the past; this time to the Exodus. He starts by reminding them of who He is by using familiar words from the opening salvo of the Ten Commandments (12:9). He reminds them that He brought them from Egyptian slavery into a land that was occupied by Canaanites, but God defeated them and gave His people the land as a gift. God wants them to think back to where He brought them from, to show them if they carry on in their sin and rebellion toward God, they will end up in a situation like they were in Egypt.

> God wants Israel to think back to where He brought them from.

The appointed feast referred to is the *Feast of Tabernacles* or *Booths*. It was an annual holy week in which Israel recalled the wilderness wandering by leaving their homes and spending a week in tents hastily constructed, temporary, lean-to shelters or booths (Leviticus 23:33–44). It was to remind the people again of what it was like for their ancestors in the wilderness and how God brought them through it and into the Promised Land. Hosea is saying to them though, that the discomfort of the booths would become a permanent condition. Verse 9 is looking ahead to Israel once again going into captivity and being dispersed and scattered. They would become like their ancestors, hopeless wanderers.

Furthermore, in the wilderness, Israel learnt that 'man does not live on bread alone' (Matthew 4:4 NIV), but by trusting in an all-sufficient God. Israel needed to learn the lesson: in God we trust. But Israel was trying to be like other nations. God did not save Israel to make them into more Canaanites. He redeemed them to be a holy nation, set apart. If they continued in their quest to be like other nations, He would do to them what He did to the Canaanites and drive them out of the land (Judges 1:1–2:5).

But this does not need to be the case. If they will only listen, there is healing. Even in driving Israel out of the land and threatening them that they will once more dwell in tents, it is to bring them to their senses so they will seek the Lord their God again. In the wilderness, God will not abandon her. He wants to meet her there. This chimes with Hosea 2:14–15.

This is the spirit of the whole book. The heart of God is that they return to Him, but it will be met with stubborn refusal on the whole and there is no attempt to hide that possibility or to mask its fatal consequences.

Prophets

As the chapter closes, it has the broken, disjointed sound of agitation and distress. Abruptly, God moves from the Exodus and wilderness history to the activity of the prophets (12:10).

God spoke to the people through His prophets. The words in this book are not Hosea's words. As with all the other true prophets, these are the words of God.

These prophecies came in strange and varied ways. At times God speaks with the precision of a lawgiver and the clarity of wise teacher. But at other times He chooses to dazzle us with visions or provoke us to think with parables. What He says can seem puzzling and almost like *riddles*. Every time though, the prophets were sent to make the people think. They confronted them with the signs of the times and with the living God.

Hosea's message was not new; he was simply preaching the same message as the other prophets, including Moses (12:13). The prophets can trace their lineage back to Moses (Deuteronomy 18:15–22). So, by rejecting Hosea they were rejecting Moses.

The fact that Moses is not mentioned in verse 12 is probably to emphasize that it was not really Moses who spoke, but God. In using the phrase, 'By a prophet', twice in verse 13, Hosea is making an important point. Moses was not just great because he stood up to Pharaoh but because he stood before God and knew Him face to face. At the burning bush, Mount Sinai, the giving of the Law and Covenant, Moses stood before God.

Moses has come and gone, Hosea has come and gone, Jacob has come and gone, but God still speaks. Hosea 12:4 says, 'He [Jacob] met God at Bethel, and there God spoke with us.' Jacob met God but as well as speaking to Jacob, God speaks to us. The God who spoke at Bethel still meets us in His Word today. Every Sunday in church, as we listen to faithful preachers of God's Word, those sermons are our Bethel. The Lord Jesus is our Bethel and He meets us in His Word.

However, what we do with all of this is important. It is fatal to have prophecies and reject or abuse them. Ephraim was incapable of learning the lessons of history, whether recent or more distant (v. 14). The people spurned Hosea and the other prophets, who warned them of the calamitous outcome of their disobedience. They provoked God and showed flagrant disregard for (His Word) the Torah and profanely gave Baal honour in the shrines of Yahweh. Their guilt is worthy of capital punishment and Hosea probably has in mind actual crimes. They will not get away with it.

> It is fatal to have prophecies and reject or abuse them.

If we have been enlightened by the truth, we need to exercise this truth and have an appetite for it. We need to act on it. Live off it. Trust in it. Having it and not doing anything with it, trampling on it and ignoring it, is dangerous.

You cannot afford to take any chances with your never-dying soul or treat the things of God lightly and presumptuously. A story is told of a man who sold everything he had to buy a precious diamond. He was on the deck of a ship one day tossing the diamond up in the air and catching it, tossing it up in the air and catching it. A lady approached him and told him how foolish he was being and how he needed to take care of something so precious. He laughed and told her to stop worrying, that he had been doing it for ages and it was fine. He threw the diamond up again but suddenly the boat jerked and the diamond fell into the water. The man screamed on top of his voice, 'Lost! Lost! Everything is lost!' Maybe you are playing with your soul and you have been doing it for ages and its fine. But God will suddenly say that your soul is required of you and you will spend eternity screaming, 'Lost! Lost! Everything is lost!'

Gilgal and Gilead

Finally in this history and geography lesson, Hosea turns our attention to Gilgal and Gilead (12:11).

GILGAL

Gilgal appears in two other places in Hosea. Firstly in 4:15 where it is a shrine like Bethel (Beth-aven) that only leads people into apostasy. Secondly, in 9:15 where it is the example of everything that is evil in Israel.

This would be more recent history and geography for Israel to consider. It would be fresh in their mind.

He names actual places, like Gilgal and Gilead, that are ripening for judgement to drive his message home.

Hosea pours scorn on their pious superstitions, punning on the venerated Gilgal with the disrespectful *'gal'* — *'a stone heap'*. The sacrifice of bulls does nothing to appease Yahweh because the very altars of Gilgal are defiled. Altars were characteristically made of simple, undressed stone and as such would resemble a heap of rocks. In an agricultural field, a heap of rocks is not a good thing but an impediment that must be removed in order for ploughing, growth and harvesting to take place. Thus, Gilgal is an obstacle to preparing a harvest of righteousness.

GILEAD

Hosea mentions Gilead only in one other place (6:8) as the place where Laban caught up with Jacob.

Taking this verse as uttered by Hosea in the closing period of his ministry, Gilead was already occupied by the Assyrians and so it is appropriate to take the reference in both clauses as being the past—the very recent past.

Gilead was in the Transjordan, whereas Gilgal was near the southern border of the Northern Kingdom. Two places that were far and near. What was true of them would tell the story of the nation as a whole.

It also tells the story of the world, of history and of us. Wherever there is iniquity and whoever is involved, God one day will bring it to nothing.

FOR FURTHER STUDY.

1. As we look back over our life, has there been an occasion when we could only cling to the Lord?

2. How important is prayer in our Christian life?

THINK ABOUT AND DISCUSS.

1. God speaks to us through His Word, but do we listen to what He wants to say?

2. How have we changed since coming to faith in the Lord Jesus?

14 The wages of sin

Hosea 13

Chapter 13 is the climax of Hosea's prophecies of judgement and doom but not the climax of the book. The Northern Kingdom will fall in 722 BC, never to reappear, but readers of the New Testament know that greater things were to lie beyond this tragedy. In chapter 14, the book will conclude by appealing to the people to return to Yahweh.

Personal and exclusive

The first thing to note is that God demands from Israel exclusive loyalty. Verse 4 says, 'But I am the LORD your God from the land of Egypt; you know no God but me.'

This verse alludes to the Exodus and the first Commandment. Hosea makes lots of references to the Exodus, but this and the prophet's response in verses 15–16 contains the last reference to it in the prophecy.

Hosea slightly changes the first Commandment though from, 'you shall have no other gods' (Exodus 20:3), to 'you know no God but Me'. This is a deliberate modification. Hosea wants to focus on the word 'know'.

Yahweh insists on a personal relationship and exclusive loyalty. He is a jealous God (Exodus 20:5). This is the main thrust of Hosea's prophecy. Like a husband whose wife has cheated on him countless times, the way Israel are acting towards God has hurt Him. It has broken His heart.

Started so well

The second thing to note is that it had started so well. According to verse 1, 'When Ephraim spoke, there was trembling; he was exalted in Israel.'

Ephraim is usually a reference to the whole of the Northern Kingdom but here it specifically means Ephraim as the leading tribe of the North. At one time Ephraim was a formidable entity (Judges 8:1 onwards), but now he has fallen and his fall is representative; if Ephraim can fall, what chance have the others got? It underscores the instability of the economy and politics. Human fortune is such that it can turn giants of one era into weaklings of the next.

It is all down to me

The problem was that Israel thought they did not need

God and that everything they had was down to them. They became smug and ungrateful (13:6). They focused on the blessings and benefits of God instead of God Himself. When they were fed by God, they were satisfied; when they were satisfied, they became proud; then they forgot Him. It was a chain of events that began with God feeding them and ends with them forgetting God.

Their mind-set was, 'I have what I have because of me.' But without God they were nothing (13:6). Even when they were in the wilderness, God looked after them so well that, for them, it was as if they were living in their own pastureland.

This mentality can be seen among Christians and in churches today. We turn to God when we are in need but, once our prayers are answered or the problem is sorted, then we forget Him and act as if it was all down to us. Even when God adds to our numbers and our churches grow, we somehow even manage to make that about us. We put it down to, and talk up, our evangelism strategies, outreach events, style of our preaching, programme of meetings, or just how we are.

Perhaps God has blessed you with a nice home and a good job. Our attitude in this should not be that I can spend what I have because I earned it, but I owe what I have because God gave it to me. Perhaps you have a lovely family with everyone doing well. Again, this should not fill us with pride but gratitude to God. Every good and perfect gift comes from above (James 1:17). It is the Lord who gives and it is the Lord who takes away; blessed be the name of the Lord (Job 1:21).

Cause of death

Because of the state they are in, Hosea looks at Ephraim as though she is already dead. According to verse 1, '... but he incurred guilt through Baal and died'. The cause of death is twofold:

IDOLATRY

As a result of them turning away from God and going after idols, Ephraim died. The main reason as to why Ephraim has fallen is the cult of Baal. For Hosea, the apostasy, crime and immorality of the people stemmed from this one fundamental deviation from the Torah (first five books of the Old Testament).

Today we have our idols. Sport, television, popularity, image, career, family, money, fame, status, possessions, education, power; and as Chesterton observed, '... the most horrible is ... the god within you'.[1] What good will any of them do you in the end? How will 'god self' help you when you stand before God at the judgement?

> How will 'god self' help you when you stand before God at the judgement?

All these 'gods' and idols will let you down and fail you in the end. Your career will end; your looks will go; in sport you will not quite make it or will not be as good as you were and your skills and speed will not be as sharp; popularity will be forgotten; and any power you have will not last.

Verse 2 goes on to say that they:

Make for themselves metal images, idols skilfully made of their silver, all of them the work of craftsmen. It is said of them, "Those who offer human sacrifice kiss calves!"

Hosea makes repeated allusions to the Exodus, and the reference to 'calves' calls to mind the golden calf (Exodus 32:8). 1 Kings 12:20–33 details Jeroboam's establishment of the shrines at Dan and Bethel and says that Jeroboam established a feast at which Israel would go to Bethel and sacrifice to the calf idols. This was forbidden, as the only place the Israelites should worship was at the Temple in Jerusalem. Jeroboam was establishing a man-made religion, even though it was presented as the worship of Yahweh. Only God can prescribe how He is to be worshipped.

The second Commandment clearly says that we must not make an image of God (Exodus 20:4–6). The Puritans maintained that churches should be as stark as possible. Nothing should draw our attention away from worshipping God in spirit and in truth. There should not be any ornaments or artefacts that we could be tempted to worship or use as charms. We do not need visual aids, smells or bells; the only focus should be on the Word of God. This is why the pulpit should be central and raised.

Christian art should not have any images of God the Father, God the Son or God the Holy Spirit. We should not have crucifixes that could encourage or lead us to worship the cross, sentimentalize it or treat it superstitiously. And the cross of Jesus Christ certainly was not adorned and expensive!

KINGS

As well as Israel going after idols, the other cause of death was that they put their faith in kings instead of God. In verse 10 God taunts them, 'Where now is your king, to save you in all your cities? Where are all your rulers—those of whom you said, "Give me a king and princes"?'

This verse describes the crises in the latter stages of Israel's history. Israel's royal government was in a deplorable state. As we have seen, king replaced king in rapid succession. There was sheer desperation among the people for effective rulers. The reference to kings, judges and princes all describe members of the government. Yahweh's point is obvious. None of them will do Israel any good in the coming crisis of the Assyrian invasion.

When the nation of Israel first lived in the land, they were ruled over by God himself, but eventually they asked for a king, to be like the nations. They rejected God's kingship in favour of human kingship. They wanted a king they could see and who was 'real'. But these human kings were a disappointment and, almost without exception, led the people away from God.

Verse 11 says, 'I gave you a king in my anger, and I took him away in my wrath.' As well as a reference to the anointing of King Saul, Israel's first king, in mind here is the whole history of the Israelite monarchy. In addition, if they reject God as their king, the king He will give them to rule over them is the Assyrian king and the one He 'took' away is the Israelite monarchy. This is brought out in the Vulgate, the fourth-century Latin translation of the Bible, which has the verb in the future tense, 'I will give you a king in my anger'. They will realize once and for all that a human king cannot protect them, and certainly cannot protect them when their enemy is God.

Sin abounding

The fifth thing to note in this chapter is that sin abounded. Idolatry, rejecting and ignoring God, trust in kings and thinking it is all about 'me', results in sin abounding. They sin repeatedly. Verse 2 says:

> Now they sin more and more, And have made for themselves molded images, Idols of their silver, according to their skill; All of it is the work of craftsmen.

They say of them, 'Let the men who sacrifice kiss the calves!' (NKJV)

While some Israelites may have stooped to human sacrifice, it would seem Hosea's reference to human sacrifice here is not literal human sacrifice. It is best to read this verse as a condemnation of the routine idolatry and apostasy of the people, especially as it occurred at Bethel. It is doubtful whether he would make a passing reference to such a heinous kind of idolatry. Human sacrifice is not the kind of thing you mention as an aside, especially if it was regularly practiced. Furthermore, the relevant portion of the Hebrew text is ungrammatical and some emending is necessary. The simplest emendation, which is supported in most of the English versions, eliminates from the text the idea of human sacrifice.

Romans 1 sheds more light on the type of thing that was happening in ancient Israel. Once human beings reject God and exchange the truth of God for a lie, God hands them over to their sin. People then start worshipping the creature rather than the Creator and relationships become perverse; wrong is right and right is wrong, and people indulge in all kinds of sin. If you keep sinning, God will give you over to your sin and you will end up sinning in unimaginable ways!

People who are fearfully and wonderfully made in the image of God (Psalm 139:14) use their God-given talents and skills in the service of their idols, going to great expense to create their idols, thus increasing their culpability all the time. Their depravity is summed up in three shocking words: *Humans kiss calves'*

Stored

While Israel kept on sinning, God had taken note of it all and was storing it all up. Most of Hosea's ministry was conducted during good days: the economy was booming and the nation enjoyed peace. It was all too easy to draw the conclusion that sin does not matter. People who sinned seemed to prosper, but their sin was being stored up. Verse 12 says, 'The iniquity of Ephraim is bound up; his sin is kept in store.'

> People who sinned seemed to prosper, but their sin was being stored up.

Once again, Hosea's use of imagery is powerful. To arouse a complacent, 'couldn't care less' Israel, he pictures unforgiven sin as a well-kept store of trouble for the future. God had not failed to notice what was happening nor was He indifferent towards their sin. The fact that He had not judged them already was because of the 'riches of his kindness and forbearance and patience' (Romans 2:4–5). He was giving them opportunity to repent, but their continued hardness of heart and impenitence was just storing up wrath.

There are two other references in the Old Testament to being bound up, or locked up, which are helpful in understanding what Hosea is actually saying here.

In Zechariah 5:5–11, the prophet sees a container that is said to hold the iniquity of the land. When the cover is removed, he sees a woman named 'Wickedness' sitting in the container. Angels then seal the container and carry it off to 'Shinar' (Babylonia) where a house will be built for it. While this text is subject to various interpretations, it is fairly certain the idea is that the evil of Israel must be returned to the land of their exile, to a pagan people who would esteem 'Wickedness' as a goddess. It is not possible to prove that Zechariah was building upon the metaphor of Hosea 13:12 but, since the two passages are so similar, even to the point of following Hosea's practice of using a woman to symbolize the evil of Israel, Zechariah helps us understand Hosea here. Hosea is saying the evil of Israel must be contained and removed. Future tense is probable. This implies that the metaphor of the 'hidden' sin stands for the coming exile, an act of judgement that is also an act of grace since it leads to the separation of Israel from her sin.

The other reference to *locked up* is used in 2 Samuel 20:3 for isolating women so that they might not have sexual relations with men. It is similar to Hosea 2:6–7 where Israel is hedged in so that she may no longer gain access to her lovers. The point seems to be that the fertility cult would be closed in order to put an end to Israel's adultery and so that she would no longer bear children for Baal.

Two things are important to note in all of this. Firstly, sometimes God takes drastic action to make us stop sinning. Hardships, changes to our circumstances, health, relationships—some have even been struck down (1 Corinthians 11:30). Secondly, our sin has not gone, or is not going, undetected. God is watching it all and is storing up wrath.

We need to repent and turn away from our sin.

The wages of sin

NOTHING TO SHOW FOR IT

In the end they will have nothing to show for their sin. The people have become nothing because of their idolatry. They are like morning mist, dew that goes early away, chaff, smoke from a window (v. 3). This was not really a window but a chimney that may or may not have been in the roof of an Israelite house. The chimney could be a lattice or frame in the wall. The point is they will disappear quickly.

All the pleasure that sin offers will be over very quickly. The initial feeling after you sin is not guilt or remorse but disappointment. Sin promises so much but always leaves you feeling dirty and empty.

IT WILL ALL GO WRONG

Furthermore, sin sooner or later will go wrong. To illustrate this, Hosea abruptly returns to the metaphor of the woman. Verse 13 says, 'The pangs of childbirth come for him, but he is an unwise son, for at the right time he does not present himself at the opening of the womb.'

In the Bible, birth pangs are frequently used as a picture for sudden, unavoidable agony associated with divine punishment (Isaiah 13:8; Jeremiah 13:21). In Romans 8:22, the pangs of childbirth are used to illustrate the suffering before the coming of God.

The analogy Hosea uses is of a birth that threatens to go fatally wrong. The great attraction of the Baal cult was more children, more calves and more crops. In response, Yahweh declares that their cult would be shut down and that the 'pregnancy' of Israel would be fatal.

Metaphorically, Israel's adultery produced a child to whom she cannot properly give birth. The child is breech and both the mother and child are likely to die. In Hosea's metaphor the mother and child are doomed— that is the institutions of Israel and the people. The son is not wise enough and does not realize the enormity of what is happening as his life is ebbing away. He does not realize the seriousness of the situation. King Hezekiah of Judah would one day use this very metaphor, not in blank despair, but in desperate appeal to God. God answered his prayer with a miracle (2 Kings 19:3

onwards), but in the Northern Kingdom there was no leader of that calibre or faith.

Sin is killing them, as individuals and as a nation, and they do not realize it. The same is true today. Adultery, drunkenness, drug addiction, greed, gossip, materialism, spending what we cannot afford, the breakdown of the family and the like are destroying society and yet we carry on. Society is birthing generations that do not know or care about God. As a result, society will destroy itself and the people in it.

> We try to find solutions to our own and society's problems anywhere apart from turning to God.

Yet we do not seem to see it or want to face up to it. We try to find solutions to our own and society's problems anywhere apart from turning to God. Too many churches look on and try to make their message palatable and to fit in with society as much as possible. No wonder numbers are dwindling and the church is ineffective. If the church stops preaching Jesus Christ and Him crucified (1 Corinthians 2:2), she has got nothing else to say.

HORRIFIC

The wages for sin will be horrific. This is pictured here as drought, being stripped of all treasure and ripped apart by the sword. Hosea 13:15–16, which is concise and staccato in form, describe what the conquest will really entail.

Drought

It is better to interpret the verse as referring to 'rushes' instead of brothers. Brothers does not fit with the context and has no reference point. These *rushes* are a metonymy for wetlands and pools of water—conditions in which cattle and sheep could thrive. In Genesis 41:2–3, 18–19, Pharaoh sees seven fat cows and seven thin cows coming up out of the River Nile. The seven fat cows grazed among the rushes, which is in the marshes, where grass was plentiful. But here in Hosea 13, God will now dry up these rushes and strike them with drought. The allusion to Genesis 41 is not accidental. Israel fled to Egypt to escape drought. After the Assyrian invasion, Israelite refugees would again flee to Egypt for refuge but this time would not encounter conditions that would help them to flourish.

As for the reference to the east wind, this was the wind that drove back the Red Sea. According to Exodus 14:21, it turned the sea into dry land that allowed Israel to flee from the Pharaoh. But because of their sin and rebellion, all of this would now be reversed. Instead of saving them from an enemy, God will open the way for the enemy to take their land, and instead of giving them water in a desert, He will parch their pastures.

STRIPPED OF TREASURE

As well as drought, they will be stripped of their treasures. This is a new strophe that goes through the first half of v. 16. They had stored up their wealth for safe keeping but they would lose it all. The storehouses would be plundered of everything of value.

THE SWORD

In the phrase, 'they shall fall by the sword', is the implication that Israel's soldiers would be defeated, that their rulers would flee and their priests would be slaughtered. However, only two groups are explicitly mentioned: children and pregnant women.

The mention of these two groups brings moral revulsion and pathos. Why end the warning section on this note and to this section of society? Because the final outcome of the fertility cult is the carnage of babies and pregnant mothers throughout the country. What Hosea has said metaphorically about mother and child, is now being brought home literally. Mother Israel has sought to obtain children through gods other than Yahweh and the results will be catastrophic. The path Israel has chosen has led to judgement. Gruesomely, the pregnant mothers in Israel will be ripped open by Assyrian soldiers (v. 16). Real slaughter.

However, the final judgement at the end of the world will be even worse. On that day, people will receive their wages for living for sin—consigned to the wrath of God in Hell forever and ever.

Still hope

Despite all of this, there is still hope. One of the outstanding features of the book of Hosea is its sudden changes of tone from the sternest of threats to the warmest of resolutions. Verse 14 says:

> Shall I ransom them from the power of Sheol? Shall I redeem them from Death? O Death, where are your thorns? O Sheol, where is your sting? Compassion will be hidden from my sight. (NASB 1995)

This verse poses a big question: Does God deal a death blow or does He extend life? Are these rhetorical questions that God will answer negatively? That is, is His answer that He will not ransom them from Sheol; that He will not redeem them from death, and therefore compassion will be hidden from his eyes? This is how some modern translations have interpreted the verse to provide consistency. Otherwise, verse 14 is the exception to the darkness of the rest of the chapter.

Yet, this verse is similar to 1 Corinthians 15:55–57. There the apostle Paul writes those famous, triumphant words:

> O death, where is your victory? O death, where is your sting?' The sting of death is sin, and the power of sin is

the law. But thanks be to God, who gives us the victory through our Lord Jesus Christ.

In these verses Paul is affirming that death will be defeated and sin will be destroyed. It would seem that this is what is in mind here in Hosea 13:14. In agreement with the older versions, and as far back as the Septuagint (the Greek translation of the Hebrew Old Testament), the NIV translates verse 14 as two statements, not two questions: 'I will ransom them from the power of the grave. I will redeem them from death.'

There is a deep reluctance of God to resort to judgement (11:8), and all the while His longing is that at last it may bring His people to their senses (5:13–15; Chapter 14). No matter what may come on the current generation, the Lord will not allow sin and death to have the final word. As we have seen, indulging in sin will sting you with death, and not just natural death but something worse—spiritual death; eternal separation from God and all that is good. But God will provide a Saviour who will conquer death and sin. He will deal with sin on behalf of all those who trust in Him. Death and hell will be destroyed (Revelation 20:14) and those who continue to live in sin and follow the path of death and hell will be destroyed with them. Yet, all those who have been victims of this but have turned to God in repentance and faith will never know its sting or be plagued by it. If you are in Christ, you can taunt sin and death and say, 'Where are your plagues?' 'Where is your sting?' (ESV). They are impotent!

However, it has to be stressed, the only way to escape the sting and plague of death is by trusting the Saviour.

According to verse 4, '... besides me there is no saviour'. While there is the offer of hope in this verse, it is not to be presumed upon. There are two responses to this Saviour which will result in two possible endings: verse 14 where there is hope for those who will come to God, or the destruction of verses 14b–16 for those who continue to rebel against and reject God. The abrupt conclusion, 'Compassion is hidden from my eyes,' brings down to earth any reader who may have seized upon 13:14 as meaning that calamity might not yet come after all. The only safety is in Jesus Christ.

> The only way to escape the sting and plague of death is by trusting the Saviour.

A fearful thing to fall into the hands of the living God

To reject God's offer to be saved is the most foolish, careless and frightening thing a person can do.

In Hosea 13:7–8, God describes himself in ferocious terms and reveals His divine fury. Yahweh compares Himself to the wild beasts of the wilderness, a predator. Nothing could be further from the common misconception of God as a tolerant spectator of world events.

It is noteworthy that the four beasts in this text—lion, leopard, bear and undefined wild beast—correspond to the four beasts of Daniel's vision (Daniel 7:1–8). The only difference being that in that text the bear proceeds the leopard. The number four can symbolise fury on the earth as in the four horsemen of Revelation 6:1–8. Taken together, it would seem that there is an apocalyptic breaking-out in the middle of this prophetic text. Hosea infers what Daniel makes explicit: Israel faces a whole series of onslaught from Gentile nations.

Lies in wait

Far from God not seeing or not going to do anything about Israel's sin, like a leopard, God lies in wait. He lurks besides the way. In the original Hebrew there is a play on words at the end of verse 7: with a slight change in pronunciation, it could be understood to mean, 'And Assyria shall be like a leopard by the way'. It was Assyria who, as an instrument of wrath in the hand of God, destroyed Samaria in 722 BC.

Bear robbed of her cubs

Not only does He lie in wait, He is also like a bear robbed of His cubs. God has been robbed of His children (the common people) by his wife (the royal and priestly leadership).

DESTROYED

Israel will be totally destroyed. God will 'devour them like a lion, as a wild beast would rip them open (v. 8). Israel's destruction would be brutal. This took place when the Assyrians invaded and conquered them. To conquer a country in the Near East, an invader had to overthrow its fortified cities one by one. We know this from descriptions in the conquest narrative of Joshua and in the war annals of Tiglath-Pileser III.

And God would not help them. In fact, the hand of God was behind it all. Verse 9 says, 'He destroys you, O Israel, for you are against me, against your helper.' 'He' should be 'it' as it is a metaphorical reference to God's wrath in the four beasts. If God, who is their helper, is against them, what hope have they got?

'It is a fearful thing to fall into the hands of the living God' (Hebrews 10:31) because 'the wages of sin is death' (Romans 6:23)—eternal death.

For further study ▶

FOR FURTHER STUDY

1. Is anything more important to me than my walk with God?

2. When things go well, do we forget God, or thank Him?

THINK ABOUT AND DISCUSS.

1. Is it a comfort to know we can never stray so far from God that He cannot reach us?

2. Does looking back and remembering God's guidance give you hope for the future?

15 Come home

Hosea 14

The message of Hosea is primarily the story of God's continuing love for His people. He wants us to turn to Him and avoid this awful prospect. It reveals the heart of God.

In summary, the message of Hosea is:

- All of us are unfaithful—not just Israel but the whole of humanity. We have all turned our back on God and turned to other 'lovers'.
- These 'lovers' use and abuse us. And yet we still will not repent and turn to God.
- God's judgement is not only against Israel but against all humanity. Whereas the Assyrian army defeated and destroyed Israel, God is coming against us in an even more terrible judgement. We will all one day stand before His judgement throne and give an account of ourselves. If we are unrepentant and not trusting Him, then we will spend a never-ending eternity in hell.

This is seen clearly in Hosea 14, which is a prayer of repentance and a song of promise; a song that God himself sings to win our hearts.

Return

Hosea 14:1 says, 'Return, O Israel, to the LORD your God, for you have stumbled because of your iniquity.'

The root word, 'return' or 'repent', occurs twenty-five times in Hosea (although not always with the connotation of repentance). Hosea's message is clear. Israel urgently needs to turn back to God. Repentance and turning to God is essential to Hosea's theology (3:5; 6:1; 12:6; 5:4; 7:10). This is the different emphasis between Amos and Hosea. The prophet Amos cries out to the people, 'Turn from destruction'. Whereas Hosea pleads, 'Turn back to God'.

As a result of their immoral behaviour, they have stumbled and fallen into disgrace and defeat. Iniquity has brought the nation into ruin. The Israelites stumble because of iniquity (5:5) and the debauchery of the priests causes them to stumble (4:5).

They must repent, but up until now they have not. However, God will not give up. Like Hosea's marriage to Gomer, against all deserving, the marriage between God and Israel holds; He is still hers. God still loves Israel and wants her to return to Him.

Repentance is at the heart of Christianity. Easy

believism and a glib understanding of justification by faith, that has no place for repentance, is alien to Hosea—and for that matter Paul (Acts 20:21; Romans 2:4) and the Lord Jesus (Matthew 4:17).

You cannot love and indulge in sin and have Christ. That is not to say you will never sin but your attitude towards it has changed. You turn your back on it and run away from it. You never want to sin and when you do you hate it. William Gurnall said, 'To forsake sin is to leave it without any thought reserved of returning to it again.'[1]

But how?

But how can they return? What do they need to do? Hosea 14:2 says, 'Take with you words and return to the LORD; say to him, "Take away all iniquity; accept what is good, and we will pay with bulls the vows of our lips'

They need to go to God with words. They need to say something to Him. They need to pray to Him and ask Him for forgiveness; they need to say sorry to God. He wants us to come to Him with a broken and contrite heart (Psalm 51:15–17). We can tell God everything, come with our tale of sin confessing; He is the one person we can be totally honest with.

Our words will be like sacrificial bulls, like sacrifices offered on the altar before God—something God has said already: 'I desire steadfast love and not sacrifice, the knowledge of God rather than burnt offerings' (6:6). God wants us to be genuine. He does not want us to pretend or to try to sort ourselves out before we come to Him.

> We must not put our trust in anything, including ourselves, and put all our faith in God.

We must reject false faith and 'accept what is good'. That is, for the Israelites they must be purged from the evil influence of Baalism; do not trust in that. For us, we must not put our trust in anything, including ourselves, and put all our faith in God.

Martin Luther was determined to find peace with God. He became a monk and, in the monastery, Luther was driven to find acceptance with God through works. He wrote:

> I tortured myself with prayer, fasting, vigils and freezing; the frost alone might have killed me ... What else did I seek by doing this but God, who was supposed to note my strict observance of the monastic order and my austere life? I constantly walked in a dream and lived in real idolatry, for I did not believe in Christ: I regarded Him only as a severe and terrible Judge portrayed as seated on a rainbow.

He climbed the *Scala Sancta* (The Holy Stairs), supposedly the same stairs Jesus ascended when He appeared before Pilate. According to fables, the steps had been moved from Jerusalem to Rome, and the priests claimed that God forgave the sins of those who climbed the stairs on their knees. Luther did so, repeating the

Lord's Prayer, kissing each step, and seeking peace with God. But when he reached the top step, he looked back and thought, 'Who knows whether this is true?' He felt no closer to God.

However, Luther realized nothing is able to bring a person peace with God apart from what Staupitz urged him to do:

Look at the wounds of Jesus Christ, to the blood He has shed for you. Instead of torturing yourself on account of your sins, throw yourself into the Redeemer's arms. Trust in him—in the righteousness of his life—in the atonement of his death.[2]

Perhaps you are desperate to find peace with God and have been trying to do it in your own strength and relying on your own efforts. Bring your words to God and 'throw yourself into the Redeemer's arms'.

When we come to God like this, our praise will be acceptable to Him.

What they will find

A MERCIFUL FATHER

Verse 3 says, '... In you the orphan finds mercy.' Hosea encourages the people to return to God because in him orphans find mercy.

The people of Israel have become orphans. Their mother, which is the institution of Israel, will be dead very soon. Baal, the one they have treated like their father, will have given them no help. But Hosea encourages the people to return to God because He is kind, and in Him the fatherless will find mercy. 'Not-my-people' will become sons and daughters of the living God (Hosea 1:10).

God's compassionate nature is such that He cares for the weak and especially for orphans and widows (Psalm 68:5). God will be a father to all who come to Him in repentance. He will love them like a father.

By trusting the Lord Jesus Christ, God is your father. In John 20:17, the Lord Jesus tells Mary Magdalene to tell his disciples, 'I am ascending to my father and your father'. For all who trust Him, He says not to think first of all that God is your creator or your judge, but your Father. The Lord Jesus Christ did not say, 'When you pray say "Our creator who art in Heaven" or "Our judge who art in Heaven"' but 'Our Father which art in heaven' (Matthew 6:9). God says, 'Think of me as your father.' Some of you might have bad experiences of your father, but God is the perfect Father—what a father should be like.

Perhaps the best picture of God as our Father is in the parable of the Prodigal Son in Luke 15:11–32. The son had moved far away from home, as far away from his father as possible, but not before getting his share of the inheritance. He spent all the money on partying, prostitutes and generally living riotously, and then a famine came. No money, no friends, just a pigsty and the left-over food from the pigs. He is in want and decides to go back to his father, say how sorry he is and see if his father will take him on as one of his workers, living in the village near-by and just coming onto his father's estate to do some menial work. But the story says that while he was still a long way off, a dot in the distance, the father spots him (no doubt he had been looking out for him every day he was away) and runs to meet him. In that culture, distinguished Middle Eastern patriarchs just did not run. Children did, women were known to, young men might, but not dignified pillars of the community. But in this parable, the father is pictured picking up his robe, baring his legs like some young boy, and sprinting. He then pounces on his son in love, not only before he has a chance to clean up his life and evidence a change in heart, but even before he can recite his repentance speech. And the same God right now in heaven will tuck up His robe and run to all His children who call out to Him, however much of a mess they are in. He will also come to anyone who calls out to Him for the first time.

In Isaiah 9:6, one of the names given to the Lord Jesus is 'Everlasting Father'. This is not a reference to the eternal nature of His person but the never-ending care of His fatherhood. He is a father forever. This father will not leave home!

The God of the Bible is a big hearted, merciful Father who will abundantly pardon (Isaiah 55:7).

LOVE

If Israel returned to God, as well as mercy they would find love. God's anger would be turned away and He would love them freely (v. 4). No ifs and buts. No caveats. He will love them forever. Sin will no longer come between them and God because God will remove the offence.

This was accomplished by the Lord Jesus Christ on Calvary. My sins have put me in debt with God, a debt that I would spend eternity in hell paying off. But when Jesus cried out, 'It is finished' (John 19:30), He made full atonement for these sins. *Atonement* means 'a making at one' and points to a process of bringing into unity those who are estranged. In theology, it denotes the work of Christ in dealing with the problem of our sin and in bringing sinners into a right relationship with God.

The atonement He made was vicarious; that is, He made atonement in the place of others. On the cross He was putting right, making up, paying a debt on behalf of all those who trust Him—those who lived before he came (like ancient Israel who trusted in the coming Messiah) and all who have lived since. All our sins were laid on Christ (Isaiah 53:6, 12; John 1:29; 2 Cor. 5:21; Gal. 3:13; Heb. 9:28; 1 Peter 2:24). He took upon himself all my sin and paid for them all. He paid off every last one of them: the secret ones, the 'little' ones, the shameful ones, the ones I commit time and time and time again, the ones I have forgotten, the wilful ones. All paid for. He 'bore our sins in his body on the tree' (1 Peter 2:24). God thought of our sins as belonging to Christ (2 Cor. 5:21; Isaiah 53:6).

There was once a chief of a tribe who was just and good. Someone in the tribe had been stealing and the chief said that whoever it was must be beaten. The thief turned out to be his elderly, frail mother, but justice had to be done. They tied her to the pole and were just about to beat her when the chief cried out, 'Stop!' He got up and walked towards the pole and took off his shirt. He wrapped himself around her and said, 'Proceed'. On Calvary, justice had to be done. A price had to be paid. A debt had to be settled. Someone had to take a beating. But for every man and woman, boy and girl who trusts in Jesus Christ, He wrapped himself around you on Calvary and said to God, 'Proceed'. The beating is over. The debt we owe has been fully paid. The wrath has been expended.

> God thought of our sins as belonging to Christ.

Yet, it is not just clearing my guilt. By trusting in the Lord Jesus Christ, I am declared righteous before God. Jesus lived a perfect life. This is called His active obedience. By trusting Him, the life He lived becomes mine; His righteousness becomes mine. I take off the sinful life I have lived and put it on Jesus and He clothes me with His righteousness. When you stand before God, whose lifelong record would you rather rely on, yours or Christ's?

I am accepted by God in Christ (Ephesians 1.6).

Through Christ's death we can be friends with God, get close to Him and have direct access to Him. On the cross, when Christ cried out 'It is finished,' all the wrong and grievance was put right and we can be accepted by God and be loved by Him freely.

Acceptance is the thing that worries young people the most. They worry that their friend request will not be accepted on social media. Well, can I tell you that if you sent God a friend request, He would accept you. In fact, He is waiting for you to send it. This sounds amazing, yet so many of us who are Christians still feel condemned. We live with this horrible sense of shame and guilt. We feel there is still unfinished business between us and God. We still worry that we will be found out; something will come to light and it is only a matter of time. So, we do this or that to ease the guilt. We never feel totally safe with God. But there is no more condemnation for those who are in Christ Jesus (Romans 8:1). Everything that we should be afraid of has been dealt with by Jesus (Rom. 8:15; 2 Tim. 1:7).

It is not that your sin has not been dealt with, or that it has been swept under the carpet and may crop up again at any time. God, the Son, took the condemnation instead of you. He suffered in your place. Tertullian used the startling expression, 'a crucified God'. Our sin has caused suffering; it does deserve to be punished eternally: but incomprehensibly, God suffered for you! Barth said, 'God's own heart suffered on the cross.'[3]

Having such a God as this, 'who passes over the rebellious act' (Micah 7:18, NASB 1995), should bring goose bumps to our souls!

HEALING

As well as love and mercy there is healing. Throughout the prophecy of Hosea, the fact that Israel is apostate is repeatedly stressed (4:15–19; 5:3; 6:10–11; 9:10–17; 10:5–8; 11:2, 7, 12). But, here in Chapter 14 verse 4, Yahweh promises to heal their apostasy.

Apostasy was like a spiritual blindness to Israel that only God could cure and heal. Israel would continue to turn away and be unfaithful to God, without a saving act from Yahweh.

When Israel come to God in repentance and faith, He will heal them of all their apostasy. He will make them well, cure them. He does the same for all who come to Him—complete healing of the soul.

He has blotted our sins out of His memory as Hebrews 8:12 reminds us, 'I will remember their sins no more.' Do you grasp the full meaning of that? It means that when we come to the God of our salvation with a broken heart, mourning over a past sin, He asks, 'What sin was that? And when was it? I don't remember it.'

What you will become

When we return to God, not only are there things we will find, but there will also be things we will grow into and become. We will flourish and become healthy. To show this, Hosea 14:5–6 uses rich horticultural imagery.

DEW

'I will be like the dew to Israel' (v. 5). Imagine living in a place where it did not rain for months on end. Without dew, agriculture cannot survive, but unlike a downpour that can become a flood, dew is gentle. This dew signifies a return of God's favour. It is refreshing.

BLOSSOM

As well as being refreshed, God's people will blossom: '... he shall blossom like the lily' (v. 5). While it is translated 'lily', the same term is used for a variety of flowers. Maybe here the yellow iris that is also the *fleur-de-lis* of France is in mind.

DEEP ROOTS

God's people will also have deep roots. They will endure and be resilient. It calls to mind the righteous person in Psalm 1:3. In the Amplified version (Classic Edition), it says:

> He shall be like a tree firmly planted [and tended] by streams of water, ready to bring forth its fruit in its season; its leaf also shall not fade or wither; and everything he does shall prosper [and come to maturity].

The new nation, the true Israel, will thrive and increase. As in springtime, there will be renewal of life.

We were once spiritually dead (Ephesians 2:1–3); 'dead

in the trespasses and sins' (Ephesians 2.1) but God breathed life into us and made us alive. This is called regeneration. According to Packer, regeneration is 'God renovating the heart, the core of a person's being, by implanting a new principle of desire, purpose and action.'[4] It is a work which only God the Holy Spirit can do. Without the Holy Spirit, we would have no interest in God. We would never put our faith in Jesus Christ or believe the gospel unless the Holy Spirit enabled us. Neither would we be able to persevere and endure as a Christian. After we become Christians, the Holy Spirit lives within us and makes Jesus Christ more and more real to us, and He will give us a greater assurance of our faith. He produces within us the fruit of the Spirit, which is love, joy, peace, patience, kindness, goodness, faithfulness, gentleness and self-control (Galatians 5:22–23a). As we read our Bibles, pray and seek to live lives which please God, this fruit will cultivate and grow (John 15:1–7).

BEAUTY

As well as having deep roots, we will be beautiful. Hosea compares us to the splendour of the olive tree. Olive oil served as food, fuel, medicine and hairdressing. It was necessary but relatively expensive. It speaks of wealth and wellbeing.

FRAGRANCE

The renewed Israel will bring sensory pleasure. No longer a diseased or dying creature, loathsome in its decay (Hosea 5:11–13), the nation would give off the scent of life.

LEBANON

Verse 7 says, 'Their fame shall be like the wine of Lebanon.'

Up until now Hosea does not include a single reference to Lebanon but now there are a burst of Lebanon references at the end of the book. Israel would strike roots like Lebanon (v. 5), would have the fragrance of Lebanon (v. 6), and memory of it would be like the wine of Lebanon (v. 7). It is striking—almost forced. Why does Hosea suddenly draw our attention to Lebanon?

Lebanon, specifically, was a mountain range in Syria north of the Litani River, but in the Bible, it more generally describes the territory north of the Galilee region. For Hosea's first readers, Lebanon meant the region to the north of Israel. In Israelite minds, Baal was the god who came out of the mountains of the North, whereas Yahweh was regarded as the God of Sinai of the South, so they associated Baal with Lebanon. It was the Sidonian princess Jezebel, daughter of the priest-king Ethbaal, who brought into Israel the priests of Baal and who established shrines to him (1 Kings 16:31–33). Lebanon was famous for its trees (1 Kings 5:1–12) and Hosea describes Lebanon as a place of almost supernatural bounty. It would seem that the Israelites may very well have concluded that all the good things came from Baal.

In making references to Lebanon, Hosea is saying that all the earth is Yahweh's and every good thing comes from Him. He will make Israel into a fragrant paradise.

'Fame' here in verse 7 means 'remembrance'. Yahweh is saying that the remembrance of Israel brings Him pleasure. For the most part in this prophecy, memories of Israel are not pleasurable and Yahweh is quite condemning of the nation of Hosea's generation (6:4–8; 7:15; 8:4–6; 9:1, 10, 15; 10:9–10, 11; 11:1–4; 12:2–4, 9–10, 12–13; 13:1–2, 4–6). However, the prophecy also contains Yahweh's tender memory of Israel's childhood (11:1–4), which led to the outburst of divine compassion in 11:8, where He says, *'How can I give you up, O Ephraim?'*

When Yahweh thinks about what Israel was and what she will one day become, she is like the wine of Lebanon, something to be savoured and enjoyed.

To God the church is precious and one day will be glorious. Ted Donnelly once told a story of when he visited an old lady in hospital who had been a member of his church. She was about to die. She lay in bed unconscious; the cancer had ravaged her body and she looked in a terrible state. Her husband was also there by her bedside. He turned to Mr Donnelly and said, 'Isn't she beautiful!' Today the church may look in a terrible state: ravaged by trials, temptations, persecution, splits and sin. But God sees what we will one day be and says, 'Isn't she beautiful!'[5]

The influence on others

In verse 7, the botanical metaphors continue. 'They shall return and dwell beneath my shadow; they shall flourish like the grain; they shall blossom like the vine; their fame shall be like the wine of Lebanon'.

Some maintain that in this verse Hosea is describing Yahweh. However, to place Israel in Yahweh's shadow is to make Yahweh the metaphorical tree and Israel into something else. To maintain the unity of the text and for Hosea to continue the image of Israel as a plant giving joy to others, it would seem to be Israel not Yahweh in mind.

The metaphor of the vineyard was to become a fixture among the prophets (see Isaiah 5:1–7; Jeremiah 12:10; Matthew 20:1–16). The plant is the vine, and the wine and the grapes are the joy that it brings. The text implies that Israel is the agency by which God extends mercy to the world. The grain and the vine indicate that Israel will sustain itself and others with food and drink. The verse could be translated, 'they like grain shall sustain people'. Israel will be a source of life to the world; the world needs the new Israel.

The shade denotes that Israel will be a shelter for others. This is echoed in the parable of the mustard seed, where the kingdom of God will grow from small beginnings into a great tree that would offer its branches to the birds of the air (Luke 13:18–19).

Going into exile, Israel would appear like a dead tree, but new growth would appear after a long winter and young shoots would grow. The nations will remember Israel with fondness.

Christianity throughout the centuries has been a source of light and shade to the nations. The church is the means by which God extends mercy to the world. Christianity led to the end of the murder of slaves in the coliseums of the Roman world, the beginning of healthcare for the masses and education for the common man. It ended the slave trade and slavery itself through the work of William Wilberforce and others. It brought workers' rights through Lord Shaftesbury, and child protection agencies, like the RSPCC. Christian leaders like Elizabeth Fry fought for prison reform, and the first Workers' Union was set up by a Christian preacher and his friends, fighting for fair pay, better working conditions and a day of rest. Modern democracy is in huge debt to non-conformist Christianity. Christianity in addition shaped politics, which gave us laws that protected the common man, as the Bible's teaching on the equality of all people shaped our civilisation. Without Christianity, the story of Europe, the United States, Canada, Australia and New Zealand and other nations would be totally different. In Africa, it was Dr David Livingstone, the missionary, who worked to end slavery and introduce Christian values to much of the continent. In the field of science, many of the founding fathers of numerous areas were Christians, with a devout belief in the God of the Bible. And the same is true for the leaders of the Industrial Revolution, which shaped the world we live in. We take all this social enterprise for granted today and forget that Christianity was the source of this civilisation; worse still, we are increasingly turning our back on it.

As well as the way Christianity has benefitted the world socially and morally, far more important is the way the church has been a source of light to the nations through the preaching of the cross of Jesus Christ. Throughout history God has raised up preachers and missionaries who have pointed the nations to the only Saviour of sinners. There is a multitude of people, more than any man can number, who are in heaven not hell today because of the preaching and witness of the faithful church.

So, stop playing about

If all of this was on offer, surely the only response was to stop playing about.

Israel must abandon faith in political power and alliances. Verse 2 says, 'Assyria shall not save us; we will not ride on horses; and we will say no more, "Our God," to the work of our hands.'

Assyria was the superpower of the day. Horses were

a symbol of military strength. Israel must stop looking to these and turn to God. They must turn from their old ways and forsake everything else they depended upon, including their own strength. There can be no compromise on the issue of loyalty to God.

Today we need to realize that nothing can protect us, only God. I wonder what you are trusting in. What is your security? Your career, possessions, knowledge, family, friends, world view, your own wits and self? But all of these are false securities. None of them will help you on the day of judgement or when the storms of life roar. Nothing can protect us except God.

> Today we need to realize that nothing can protect us, only God.

IDOLS

In Hosea 14:8, God says, 'O Ephraim, what have I to do with idols? ... I am like an evergreen cypress; from me comes your fruit.'

The 'O' is a plea. Please give up your idols! He has already spoken so much about idols; He now has nothing more to say. It is as though He is fed up with talking about idols, done with them, and so should Ephraim. He wants to leave behind the whole subject, never to come up again.

Yahweh then applies the botanical metaphors of the proceeding verse to Himself—coniferous tree with edible fruit, possibly the stone pine. In ancient Near East, the tree was a common symbol of kingship, divinity and fertility. These were the qualities Israel attributed to Baal. The final appeal of the book is that all the good things that Israel has sought in the fertility gods can be found only in Yahweh.

Stop wasting time with idols that will never fulfil you. Stop thinking that satisfaction is found in the world and the gods of this world. Augustine said, 'Our hearts are restless until they find their rest in you.'[6] While according to Piper:

> If you don't feel strong desires for the manifestation of the glory of God, it is not because you have drunk deeply and are satisfied. It is because you have nibbled so long at the table of the world. Your soul is stuffed with small things, and there is no room for the great.[7]

There are so many idols we worship today instead of God. Yet what good can the god of football be to a person when they are diagnosed with terminal cancer? How will your bank-account god help you at the judgement?

Put your idols away and say with Joshua, 'As for me and my house, we will serve the Lord' (Joshua 24:15).

Be wise

In keeping with Hosea's style, the last verse of the prophecy is difficult to understand. Chapter 14 verse 9 says, 'Whoever is wise, let him understand these things;

whoever is discerning, let him know them; for the ways of the LORD are right, and the upright walk in them, but transgressors stumble in them.'

The first readers would have found this hard to interpret. They would need wisdom. As with the parables of Jesus, we need to think what it is actually saying. The prophecy is open ended. We need to think about what we have read. We need to really contemplate our unfaithfulness, God's righteous judgement and His love. The wise thing is to acknowledge the truth of Hosea's message; not just to know it but to walk in it—to put God's word into practice (James 1:22–25; Matthew 7:24–27).

Importantly and relevantly for us is the word, 'Whoever'. While in the first instance the prophecy of Hosea spoke to and was directed at ancient Israel, the Word of God goes on speaking, and so through the words of this prophecy God speaks directly to us today.

How will you respond? The prophecy of Hosea has revealed to us the heart of God. What we do with it reveals the condition of our heart.

Verse 8 says, 'It is I who answer and look after you.' This is better translated: 'I have answered him and I am watching him'. Yahweh has said all that He needs to say. He now watches to see what your response will be.

For further study ▶

FOR FURTHER STUDY

1. What challenges have you faced while reading the book of Hosea?

2. Does this book encourage you in your Christian walk?

THINK ABOUT AND DISCUSS.

1. Is our worship acceptable to God?

2. As God is our heavenly Father, do we approach His throne with confidence?

Endnotes

Background and summary

1 Noted while listening to a sermon, source unknown.

2 Source unknown

Chapter 1: Go and marry a whore

1 Calvin, J., *Calvin's Commentaries Volume XIII Daniel 7–12 Hosea*, (Grand Rapids, MI: Baker Book House, 1979), p. 43

2 Mackay, J.L., *Hosea: A Mentor Commentary* (Ross-shire: Christian Focus Publications, 2002), p. 50

3 Calvin, J., *Calvin's Commentaries Volume XIII Daniel 7–12 Hosea*, (1979), pp. 43–46

4 Augustine of Hippo, quoted in a sermon by Andrew Davies

5 Guthrie, Thomas, https://gracequotes.org/author-quote/thomas-guthrie/. Sourced: 7/7/22

6 Lewis, C.S., *Mere Christianity*, Chapter 7, (1952) https://www.pbs.org/wgbh/questionofgod/ownwords/mere2.html Sourced: 13/7/22

7 Source unknown

8 Davis, D.R., *Judges* (Fearn, Ross-shire: Christian Focus, 2003), p. 38

Chapter 2: What's in a name?

1 'When a man screams to God then he will answer their prayer', *The Times*, 18 October 2010, p.28

2 Edwards, B.H., *Revival: A People Saturated with God*, (Darlington, England: Evangelical Press, 2004), p. 191

3 Noted while listening to a sermon, source unknown.

Chapter 3: Talk some sense to your mother

1 Davis, D.R., *2 Kings*, (Fearn, Ross-shire: Christian Focus, 2005)

2 Liddle, Rob, 'The Kid's aren't all right: we think we are protecting them but we are harming them', *The Spectator*, 28 October 2017.

3 Lloyd Jones, Martyn, https://www.goodreads.com/quotes/894185-when-the-church-is-absolutely-different-from-the-world-she. Sourced: 8/7/22

4 Gurnell, William, *The Christian in Complete Armour: ... Vol 3*, (London: L.B.Seeley, 1821), p. 120

5 Beeke, Joel R., *Fighting Satan: Knowing His Weaknesses, Strategies, and Defeat*, (Grand Rapids, MI: Reformation Heritage Books, 2015)

6 Welles, Orson, *Michael Parkinson:*

the Orson Welles Interview, 1974. https://www.youtube.com/watch?v=6dAGcorF1Vo Sourced 8/7/22

7 Tozer, A.W., *The Pursuit of God*, (Carlisle: OM Publishing, 1993)

8 Boller, P.F.Jr., *Congressional Anecdotes*, (New York: Oxford University, 1991), p. 261

Chapter 4: God so loved

1 Boice, J.M., *The Minor Prophets*, (Grand Rapids, MI: Kregel, 1996), p. 28

2 Dunlap, David W., https://www.nytimes.com/2016/04/06/insider/1964-how-many-witnessed-the-murder-of-kitty-genovese.html Sourced: 8/7/22

3 Newton, John, www.gospelweb.net/JohnNewton/newtontombstone.htm Sourced: 8/7/22

4 Woolsey, A., *Duncan Campbell* (London: Hodder, 1974), p. 98

Chapter 5: In court

1 Chesterton, C.K., https://www.goodreads.com/quotes/469053-for-when-we-cease-to-worship-god-we-do-not Sourced: From a sermon

Chapter 6: On the battlefield

1 Baxter, Richard, cited in: Stanton, Allen, 'Preach as a Dying Man to Dying Men', https://gospelreformation.net/preach-as-a-dying-man-to-dying-men/ 31 March 20. Sourced: 8/7/22

2 Lewis, C.S., https://existenceofgod.org/gods-megaphone-to-rouse-a-deaf-world/ 30 March 20. Sourced: 8/7/22

3 Bunyan, John, *The Pilgrim's Progress*, (Edinburgh: Banner of Truth Trust, 1997), p. 189

4 Davis, Dale Ralph, *Judges*, (2003), p.127

Chapter 7: Come to God

1 Davis, D.R., *Judges*, (Fearn, Ross-shire: Christian Focus, 2003), p. 63

2 Gurnell, William, *A Puritan Golden Treasury*, compiled by I.D.E. Thomas, (Carlisle: Banner of Truth, 2000), p. 281. https://gracequotes.org/quote/to-forsake-sin-is-to-leave-it-without-any-thought-reserved-of-returning-to-it-again/ Sourced: 9/7/22

3 Godwin, Thomas, Quote from a sermon by Ted Donnelly.

4 Campbell, Duncan, cited in: Edwards, B.H., *Revival: A People Saturated with God*, (2004), p. 26

5 Ritchie, *Yarmouth and Gorleston Times*, (10 November 1921) (1980), p. 106

6 https://www.christianity.com/church/church-history/timeline/1801-1900/jeremy-

lanphier-led-prayer-
revival-11630507.html
Sourced: 9/7/22

7 Packer, J.I., *Concise Theology*,
(Leicester, England: IVP, 1993),
p. 81

8 Hansen, Alan, 'Even after this
latest incident, Liverpool will
do everything they can to
hold onto Luis Suarez', *The
Telegraph*, 27 June 2014,
Sport p. 3 https://www.
telegraph.co.uk/sport/
football/players/luis-
suarez/10929347/Even-
after-this-latest-incident-
Liverpool-will-do-
everything-they-can-to-hold-
onto-Luis-Suarez.html
Sourced: 9/7/22

9 Laing, Sir John William, Quote
noted while listening to a
sermon, source unknown.

Chapter 8: What are you like?

1 Quote and story from sermon
by Gerard Hemmings preaching
at Amyand Park Chapel.

2 Shaw, George Bernard, cited
in: Sauls, Scott, 'Why we need
not fear the future', 17
September 2020, https://
scottsauls.com/
blog/2020/09/17/why-we-
need-not-fear-the-future/
Sourced: 11/7/22.

3 Bonar, Andrew, (1810–1892).

Quote noted from sermon,
source unknown.

Chapter 9: Israel has forgotten her Maker

1 Morgan, G.C., *Hosea: The Heart
and Holiness of God*, (Eugene,
Oregan: WIPF and Stock
Publishers, 1998), p. 71

2 Gurnall, William, 1616–1679,
https://gracequotes.org/quote/
say-not-that-thou-hast-royal-
blood-in-thy-veins-and-art-
born-of-god-unless-thou-canst-
prove-thy-pedigree-by-daring-
to-be-holy/ Sourced: 11/7/22

3 Rogers, John, 1570–1636,
cited in: Mills, Brad, 'Come,
Lord Jesus', 27 December
2020, https://gracefresno.
com/sermons/come-
lord-jesus/ Sourced: 11/7/22

4 Rabelais, Francois, c. 1494–1553,
https://minimalistquotes.com/
francois-rabelais-quote-228247/
Sourced: 11/7/22

5 Parris, Matthew, *Chance
Witness*, (London: Penguin
Books, 2003), p. 481

6 Davis, D.R., *1 Samuel*, (Fearn,
Ross-shire: Christian Focus,
2003), p. 99

7 Carrey, Jim, https://
quotesberry.
com/i-wish-everyone-could-
be-rich-and-famous-jim-
carrey/ Sourced: 11/7/22

Chapter 10: Do not spoil the party

1   Davis, D.R., *1 Samuel*, (Fearn, Ross-shire: Christian Focus, 2003), p. 85
2   Hendriksen, *More Than Conquerors*, (Grand Rapids: MI, Baker Books, 2006), p. 178
3   Edwards, J., *Select Works of Jonathan Edwards, Volume 2 Sermons*, (London: Banner of Truth Trust, 1959), pp. 191, 192, 197
4   Bridges, Jerry, *God Took me by the Hand*, (London: Banner of Truth, 2014)

Chapter 11: Time to seek the Lord

1   Ryle, J.C., *Holiness*, (Darlington, England: Evangelical Press, 2001), p. 9
2   Ryle, J.C., *Holiness*, p. 12
3   Campbell, Duncan, *Revival in the Hebrides*, (CreateSpace Independent Publishing Platform, 2016), p. 29
4   Blair, Tony, *A Journey*, (London: Arrow Books, 2010)
5   Dallimore, A., *George Whitfield: The life and times of the great evangelist of the 18th century revival, volume 1*, (Edinburgh: Banner of Truth, 1970)
6   Lewis, C. S., https://www.goodreads.com/quotes/7288468-humility-is-not-thinking-less-of-yourself-it-s-thinking-of Sourced: 12/7/22

Chapter 12: The heart of God

1   Elliot, Elisabeth, https://quotessayings.net/topics/spurgeon-sovereignty/ Sourced: 12/7/22
2   Owen, J., *Communion with God*, (Edinburgh: Banner of Truth, 1991), pp. 32–33
3   D'Aubigne, J. H. Merle, *History of the Reformation, Martin Luther*, (17 March 2003) p. 51.9 https://believersweb.org/the-history-of-the-reformation-martin-luther/ Sourced: 12/7/22
4   https://en.wikipedia.org/wiki/Port_Arthur_massacre_(Australia) Sourced: 12/7/22

Chapter 13: A history and geography lesson

1   Olyott, S., *Something Must be Known and Felt*, (Wales: Bryntirion Press, 2014), p. 135

Chapter 14: The wages of sin

1   Chesterton, C. K., *Orthodoxy*, p. 7 https://www.pagebypagebooks.com/Gilbert_K_Chesterton/Orthodoxy/The_Flag_of_the_World_p7.html

Chapter 15: Come home

1   Gurnall, William, 'Christian Quote

of the Day', 29 November 2016, https://christianquote.com/forsaking-sin/ Sourced: 12/7/22

2 Leahy, F., *Great Conversions*, (Belfast, Northern Ireland: Ambassador, 1999), p. 15

3 Barth, K., *Church Dogmatics* ed. G.W. Bromiley and T.F. Torrance, tr. G.W. Bromiley. (T & T Clark, 1956–57), p. 446

4 Packer, J.I., *Concise Theology*, (1993), p. 157

5 Donnelly, Ted, Story and quote from sermon, date unknown.

6 St Augustine of Hippo, https://piercedhearts.org/theology_heart/teaching_saints/hearts_restless_st_augustine.htm Sourced: 7/12/22

7 Piper, J., *A Hunger for God*, (Wheaton, IL: Crossway, 1997)

Bibliography

Books

Barth, K. (1956-57) *Church Dogmatics* ed. G.W. Bromiley and T.F.Torrance, tr. G.W. Bromiley. T. & T. Clark

Blanchard, J (2012) *Major Points from the Minor Prophets*. Evangelical Press. Darlington, England

Blair, T. (2010). *A Journey*. Arrow Books. London

Boice, J.M. (1996) *The Minor Prophets*. Kregel. Grand Rapids.

Boller, P.F. Jr. (1991) *Congressional Anecdotes* Oxford University. New York

Bunyan, J. (1997) *Pilgrims Progress*. Banner of Truth Trust. Edinburgh.

Calvin, J. (1979) *Calvin's Commentaries Volume XIII Daniel 7-12 Hosea*. Baker Book House. Grand Rapids, Michigan

Campbell, D. (2016) *Revival in the Hebrides*.

Chester, T. (2014). *Hosea The Passion of God*. Christian Focus. Glasgow, Scotland

Dallimore, A. *George Whitfield: The life and times of the great evangelist of the 18th century revival, volume 1*. Banner of Truth. Edinburgh.

Davis, D.R, (2003) *1 Samuel*. Christian Focus. Fearn, Ross-shire, Scotland

Davis, D.R, (2003) *Judges*. Christian Focus. Fearn, Ross-shire, Scotland

Davis, D.R (2005) *2 Kings*. Christian Focus, Fearn, Ross-shire, Scotland

Edwards, B.H (2004) *Revival a people saturated with God.* Evangelical Press. Darlington, England

Edwards, J. (1959) *Select works of Jonathan Edwards, Volume 2 Sermons.* Banner of Truth Trust. London

Garrett, D.A. (1997) *The New American Commentary Hosea, Joel 19A.* B&H Publishing Group. Nashville, Tennessee

Hendriksen, W. (2006) *More Than Conquerors.* Baker Books. Grand Rapids

Henry, M. (1995) *Matthew Henry's Commentary on the Whole Bible Complete and Unabridged.* Hendrickson Publishers. USA

Kidner, D. (2010) *The Message of Hosea.* IVP. Nottingham, England

Leahy, F, (1999) *Great Conversions.* Ambassador. Belfast, Northern Ireland.

Mackay, J.L. (2012) *Hosea A Mentor Commentary.* Christian Focus Publications. Ross-shire, Great Britain

Morgan, G.C (1998) *Hosea: The Heart and Holiness of God,* WIPF and Stock Publishers. Eugene, Oregon

Olyott, S. (2014) *Something Must be Known and Felt.* Bryntyrion Press.

Owen, J. (1991) *Communion with God.* Banner of Truth. Edinburgh

Packer, J.I. (1993) *Concise Theology.* IVP. Leicester, England

Parris, M. (2003) *Chance Witness.* Penguin. London

Piper, J (1997) *A Hunger for God.* Crossway

Ritchie, (1980) *Floods Upon The Dry Ground.*

Ryle, J.C. (2001) *Holiness.* Evangelical Press. Darlington, England

Stuart, D. (1987) *Word Biblical Commentary Hosea-Jonah.* Thomas Nelson.

Tatford, F.A. (1974) *Prophet of a Broken Home Exposition of Hosea.* Prophetic Witness Publishing House. Eastbourne

Tozer, A.W. (1993) *The Pursuit of God.* OM Publishing. Carlisle

Wenham, A.E. (1915) *Ruminations on The Book of the Prophet Hosea.*

Woolsey, A (1974) *Duncan Campbell,* Hodder

Articles

Thomas, G. (May 25th, 2017), 'God Took me by the hand', *Banner of Truth*

Newspapers/Magazines

The Spectator, 28 October 2017

The Telegraph, 27 June 2014

The Times, 21 November 2009